Medical Curiosities

Medical Curiosities

A miscellany of medical oddities, horrors and humours

Compiled and edited
by
Robert M. Youngson

Robinson
LONDON

Robinson Publishing Ltd
7 Kensington Church Court
London W8 4SP

First published in the UK by Robinson Publishing 1997

Collection and editorial content copyright © Robert M. Youngson 1997

A copy of the British Library Cataloguing in Publication data
is available from the British Library

ISBN 1–85487–902–2

Printed and bound in the EC

10 9 8 7 6 5 4 3 2 1

Contents

Contents

To cut or not to cut – that is the question • A surfeit of Caesars • Improving the palate? • A toe for a thumb • Suing for life

Contents

Introduction

In general, anecdotes, even medical ones, are notoriously unreliable. Doctors use the phrase 'anecdotal evidence' when they really mean 'quite interesting, but probably a pack of lies'. Doctors are, of course, concerned about the accuracy of evidence on which to base medical treatment; and for such purposes, anecdotal evidence isn't really good enough. At the same time, doctors are as interested in a good story as anyone else. Medical 'shop', in hospital messes, changing rooms and even, dare I say it, in operating theatres, is often notable for the quality of its tales.

I must emphasize, however, that this is not a book of anecdotes in that sense. All the modern tales, even those that for reasons of medical ethics and confidentiality have had to be substantially disguised, are based strictly on fact. The stories culled from my own long clinical experience I can vouch for; I have made them as close to the facts as my memory allows. For consistency with the rest of the book, however, these have been put into the third person and fleshed out. The remainder have a solid basis in medical fact, and this is always the central point of the story. In each case, the object is to put across a surprising, interesting, horrifying or amusing circumstance or incident that actually occurred or existed somewhere.

Many of the tales were reported by respectable authorities, mainly in the *Lancet*, the *British Medical Journal*, the *Journal of the Royal Society of Medicine*, the *New England Journal of Medicine* and the *Journal of the American Medical Association*. Since most of these concern living people, many of them patients and doctors who would not wish to be identified, I have had to take considerable liberties – inventing names, expanding and adjusting the known facts and sometimes introducing dialogue – engaging, in short, in the process known in publishing circles as writing 'faction'. The stories that concern well-known historical figures are in a different category. Information about such people is in the public domain and one need conceal nothing.

Medical anecdotes, old or new, can enlighten as well as entertain. They can be a painless way of assimilating a great deal of important medical information, so you will find that whenever I have introduced a medical concept likely to be unfamiliar, I have provided a simple explanation.

Here's hoping you enjoy reading them as much as I have enjoyed collecting and writing them.

Dr Robert M. Youngson

Medical Horrors

Maggots

Some time in the mid 1950s a young and inexperienced Scottish doctor called Murdoch was working as a locum junior surgeon in a hospital on a Shell oil field in Sarawak, Borneo. There were four doctors on the staff of the hospital looking after a workforce of 10,000 people, and they also offered a free service to the local people in the surrounding jungle.

One afternoon a young man was brought in looking very sorry for himself. There were runnels of dried blood all over his face and his hand was firmly pressed to the top of his head as if he were holding on a hat. Murdoch on duty in Casualty, so he sat the injured man down on a chair and asked him, in halting Malay, to put his hand down. This he refused to do until a more vocal male orderly shouted at him. When he complied, about half of his scalp fell forward over his face covering his eyes and nose. The inner surface of the scalp and the exposed part of his cranium were covered with a seething mass of maggots.

Murdoch had never seen a maggoty wound before and was

somewhat taken aback. But something had to be done, so he got the patient over to a sink, put a length of rubber tubing on the tap, and started to wash the wrigglers out. This was more difficult than he had anticipated as many of them were enthusiastically chewing their way deeply underneath both the front and rear edges of the scalp. The young doctor consoled myself, however, with the recollection that maggots were supposed to be excellent cleaning agents with a taste for bacteria, and persevered with the water jet. About two hours later, he reckoned that he had cleared the lot. The tiled floor was swimming with water and maggots.

Murdoch now folded the flap back on to the polished, ivory-coloured bare bone – the maggots had removed every scrap of the normal bone-covering membrane – and found he had a problem. There was a deficit of about two inches between the free margins. Scalp has a thick fibrous layer under the skin and is far too thick and unyielding to stretch. So, in desperation, he just put in a single nylon stitch, centrally, to hold the flap in place and give himself time to think. The patient was pretty groggy so the orderlies put him to bed under a mosquito net, to keep out the flies.

The wound had obviously been heavily infected and, as it is a principle of surgery that one does not close up infected wounds, Murdoch decided that he had sufficient justification for a bit of masterly inactivity. This decision was something of a relief, as the plain truth was that he didn't really know what on earth to do. So he just dredged on plenty of antibiotic powder and said he would see the patient the next day.

When he did, his surprise was equalled only by his satisfaction. During the night, plasma had leaked into the deficit, covering the bone in a thick layer. This plasma had then clotted and was beginning to form the basis of an excellent medium for the development of strong scar tissue. In three or four days the wound was well on its way to healing and skin surface was beginning to grow across from the free edges. Soon Murdoch was able to remove the single stitch and discharge the patient from hospital.

He had been unable to account for the man's injury, but as he was leaving hospital, fully recovered, a friend turned up who was able to resolve the mystery. It seems that the friend had been giving him a ride on the cross bar of his bicycle along a jungle path when they had hit a bump. The patient had fallen off and struck his head on a large stone. The friend, assuming he had been killed, and aware that the fine for riding two to a bicycle was $5, had left him where he lay and had said nothing. The large, bleeding scalp wound had, of course, attracted flies and he had lain there, unconscious, for three or four days, during which time the eggs had hatched.

To most people, maggots seem, at best unpleasant, at worst a cause of gagging horror and nausea. Young Dr Murdoch did not quite see it this way. He was also pleasingly modest about this little therapeutic triumph. As he was accustomed to say when recounting the incident, years later, 'Never before or since, have I seen such remarkable wound healing. One thing is sure – I can certainly take no credit for the outcome. That, clearly, must go to the maggots.'

The body builder

Norman was born stocky and nature had provided him with more than his fair share of anabolic sex hormones. By the time he was sixteen he was a young Hercules and had begun to attract the admiration of those who value such things. Someone suggested that he should join a body-building club and he did not take much persuasion. By his late teens he was winning competitions and had a string of adoring girls at his beck and call, all of whom were proud to be seen out with him.

In 1981 he turned professional and now that the bug had really bitten, there was no holding Norman. The work he put into muscle-building was frightening. Every day, for many hours he pumped and strained, using his Bullworker and six-strand chest expander, going through his sequence of isometric exercises, doing his 100 push-ups, working on each muscle group in turn. Norman took his profession seriously. When he was not working out he was studying the science of body-building. What he did not know about the physiology of muscle formation wasn't worth knowing.

Unfortunately, all this book knowledge led Norman astray. One of the things he learned was that anabolic steroids could save him a great deal of hard work and that, by taking these injections, the effects of his labours would be greatly enhanced. The temptation proved too great. It was easy to get supplies and soon his physique was more magnificent than ever. Norman was well aware that he was cheating but body-building was his ruling passion and nothing could override this. As is often the case, one lapse of this kind led, more easily, to another. He had heard that human growth hormone was even more effective than anabolic steroids in promoting muscle growth. So he made enquiries and discovered that growth hormone, from human pituitary glands, was available from a Hungarian source.

Norman was not squeamish. He didn't really care where the stuff came from so long as it worked. By now he was an incredible figure of a man, immensely strong and with astonishingly prominent muscles everywhere. He loved posing and couldn't get enough admiration. But he believed that the secret of real success was that one should never be satisfied. So, at great expense, he obtained a supply of growth hormone and gave himself the injections.

Norman's career was spectacular and for more than ten years he remained near the top of the tree. He never made it to National Championship level, but in his own little pond he was a very big fish indeed. Then things started to go wrong. He began to suffer severe headaches, so severe, indeed, that sometimes he even had to cancel a professional engagement. Then, in addition to the headaches he developed aching pains in his limbs and in his joints. For a month or so he was convinced that he had some kind of virus and he kept dosing himself with codeine tablets. But when he began to suffer uncontrollable double vision he decided that it was time to see a doctor.

The doctor could draw no conclusion from his symptoms and, impressed by his obvious superb fitness, was inclined to make little of them. He gave Norman a prescription for ibuprofen and suggested he should see an optician. Within days, however, Norman had developed an even more alarming symptom. Something seemed to have gone wrong with the muscles of his trunk so that keeping upright became increasingly difficult. At the same time, walking became almost impossible.

When he realized, after two days in bed, that this extraordinary and alarming state of affairs wasn't getting better, he called an ambulance and was taken to hospital. The doctors were puzzled. The clinical signs were unlike anything they had ever seen, and it was not until a particularly knowledgeable consultant neurologist was called in that the diagnosis became apparent. By now Norman was having difficulty in speaking and in swallowing and was beginning to find it increasingly hard to understand anything. So when the specialist told him, as kindly as he could, that he was suffering from Creutzfeldt-Jakob disease, this didn't mean anything to Norman. Soon he was mute, unresponsive and apparently unaware of where he was or what was happening to him.

Only three weeks after being admitted to hospital, Norman died. Two of his friends gave evidence at the coroner's inquest and it was then that the story of the growth hormone came to light. A medical expert testified that cases of this dreadful disease were known to have occurred as a result of injections of growth hormone derived from cadavers.

It is good to be able to report that the use of cadaveric growth hormone, even for legitimate purposes, has been entirely abandoned. The substance can now be produced, by genetic engineering, free from any infective contaminant.

Cold cure

Adolphus had been on skid row for a number of years and was well known to the local police. He was a quarrelsome character. Alcohol, which was his staple source of calories, usually just sent him to sleep, but sometimes drew him into fights.

During a particularly cold spell one December, he had a win on the dogs and went on a bender that ended up with his trying to wreck the hostel where he lived. The police were called but he ran off and found a corner under a railway bridge where he settled down to sleep it off. There he remained for almost two days until, late in the evening, he was noticed by a passing bobby. When roused, Adolphus immediately reverted to aggressive mode and punched the policeman between the eyes. He was arrested and taken to the local lock-up where he was accommodated in a familiar cell. Someone checked him through the flap a couple of hours later, thought he looked odd, went in, and found him blue and apparently dead.

A police surgeon was called. He confirmed that there was no breathing and no pulse, and sent for an ambulance. This came in about 15 minutes. The crew were trained in cardiac resuscitation and immediately got to work. The electrocardiogram showed that Adolphus had suffered a cardiac arrest of the kind in which the heart was fluttering rapidly but gently but was not pumping any blood – a condition known as ventricular fibrillation. The three paramedics immediately got to work. They passed a tube into the windpipe and began to inflate Adolphus's chest with air. At the same time they applied effective external heart compression and began to get his blood moving around the circulation.

When they got him to the hospital casualty department, and the doctors removed his wet clothes and examined him, the reason for the cardiac arrest became clear. Adolphus's core temperature, taken rectally, was only 28° C – nearly 10° below normal. This was a severe case of hypothermia and the outlook was very poor. After nearly an hour of external heart compression and repeated attempts at electric shock defibrillation, there was no indication that his heart was going to start beating spontaneously.

It happened that next to the Casualty department was the hospital Heart Surgery Unit. It also happened that one of the junior doctors on duty that night was an expert in the use of the heart bypass machine, normally used to allow patients' hearts to be stopped for heart surgery. So Adolphus was quickly moved next door, and in about 30 minutes was connected to a bypass machine via a large artery and vein in his groin. The blood being circulated by the machine was warmed to 30° C and after about 10 minutes Adolphus's core temperature had reached this level. At this point, a single shock from the defibrillator started his heart beating normally and spontaneously.

Soon afterwards Adolphus regained consciousness and, after a feeble attempt to fight the nurses in intensive care, contented himself with threatening legal action for the pain he was having in his chest. This was due to the prolonged attempts at external cardiac compression which had strained the joints between his ribs and his breastbone. He was assured that the pain would soon settle.

The doctors themselves were more interested in the effect that the long period of cardiac arrest might have had on his brain. Normally, 4–8 minutes without a proper circulation is enough to damage the brain so severely that consciousness is not regained. A full examination of Adolphus's nervous system, however, showed no abnormality. The explanation was that the severe drop in body temperature had greatly reduced the oxygen and glucose requirements of his brain.

Two days later Adolphus got out of bed, insisting that he was off to see his lawyer and was discharging himself from hospital. He made it only to the foyer, though, where he collapsed with a high fever from pneumonia in both lungs. Intensive antibiotic treatment brought this under control and two weeks later Adolphus finally took his leave muttering threats of revenge against the National Health Service.

Michèle's first death

Michèle had her first death only two weeks after she started work as a trainee assistant family doctor. Of course, there had been deaths in the wards when she was doing her hospital jobs, but there had always been a registrar or a consultant to cope and she never felt that she was exclusively in charge. So this was traumatic. Jimmie McGregor, the patient, was only about forty-five, a local solicitor, and she had been called urgently to his office just down the street. Rex Bucksburn, her principal, was away at the Cottage Hospital doing a well-woman clinic and she was the nearest doctor.

The worst of it was that Michèle had been consulted by Mr McGregor for an insurance examination two days before his death. Rex had brought him in, introduced him, and told him she was his 'clever new assistant' and would be doing routine examinations. She didn't skimp the examination. She took quite a detailed history and spent fully half an hour on the physical. He was a squash player and, so far as she could see, was in very good shape. His heart sounds and blood pressure were normal. She could have done an electrocardiogram (ECG) but the history suggested he had an excellent exercise tolerance and there was nothing to indicate any kind of heart problem, so she left it.

That was on the Tuesday. When his secretary called her on Thursday afternoon she was reviewing the lists for cervical smear screening on the computer. She just grabbed her visit bag and ran down the road.

It was hellish. She hardly recognized Jimmie lying back in an armchair, his face dead white and his mouth open. There was no sign of breathing, no pulse at the neck and his pupils

9

were widely dilated. She felt her own heart beating hard as she dragged him down on to the floor, turned him on his back and gave him a bash in the middle of his chest. At that stage she had no idea what had happened, but the presumption was a coronary. Trying to restart someone's heart on your own is no joke and very hard work. You have to squeeze the heart against the backbone fifteen times, then give two or three mouth-to-mouth blows to inflate the chest, then back to the cardiac compression and so on until you are in almost as bad shape as the victim.

She could have done with some help but McGregor's secretary was useless, so she got her to call an ambulance. By now, it looked as if she had an effective circulation going – Jimmie's pupils constricted a little. She desperately wanted an ECG to tell her what was happening and hoped the ambulance would have one, and a defibrillator. She had a bicarb drip in her bag, but there was no way she could take the time to put in a needle. But she never felt a spontaneous pulse. Every time she stopped the compressions everything else stopped.

It was over half an hour before the ambulance men came and by then she was pretty well exhausted. They brought in a portable ECG and it just showed a straight line with great humps every time she compressed the heart. Asystole. The ambulance men also had a tracheal tube and she got this down. After that, ventilation was easier. One of them did this, with a manual pump, while the other did the cardiac massage. She put up the drip and ran in a bottle of bicarb solution as fast as it would go. After another hour, the ambulance people began to look at her significantly, and eventually she said, 'OK. Pack it up' and they took the body away.

The next day Rex called a colleague in the hospital pathology department and in the late afternoon they drove to the hospital to see Jimmie's post-mortem. Michèle had never liked PMs and as she walked into the cold mortuary she had the familiar sinking feeling. And when they went into the PM theatre and she saw Jimmie's naked body lying on the slab she was painfully moved by the pity of it and the sense of waste.

When the heart was removed and the coronary arteries cut open the cause of Jimmie's death was immediately apparent. The pathologist held the organ in his gloved hands, slippery with blood, and spread open one of the two coronary arteries. She could see that, near its origin, it was completely obstructed by a blood clot which had formed on top of a lump of yellowish material protruding from the inner wall.

'Atherosclerosis,' said the pathologist. 'Man of his age – makes you think, doesn't it?'

Jimmie's coronary arteries were not the only vessels affected by atherosclerosis. She was shocked when she saw the state of the inside of his aorta – the largest artery of the body. When this was cut open, and the clotted blood washed out, one could see that it, too, was severely affected. Great plaques of irregularly surfaced fatty-looking material were scattered over the inner lining and some of these were so large that they reduced the cross-section of the artery by about one third. Down at the point where the artery branched to supply the legs, the atherosclerosis was especially severe.

'He would have had trouble from that if he had lived,' said the pathologist.

'What do you mean?' she asked.

'Well, look. Suppose he got a laminar clot on top of that one. Wouldn't take much to close off the iliac altogether and shut down the whole leg supply.'

'Gangrene?'

'Of course.'

'Pretty rare at his age – that sort of thing – isn't it?' asked Rex.

'Oh yes. This is the typical picture of the sixty or seventy-year-old atherosclerotic. But the worrying thing is that it is becoming commoner in younger people.'

On the way back she said, 'I'm really depressed about the fact that I examined Jimmie McGregor only two days before he died. Surely there must have been some indications.'

'You took a good history, presumably.'

'I think so.'

'Family history?'

'Well . . . no.'

'Obviously I should have told you that Jimmie's father and both uncles died of coronary thrombosis.'

She felt herself go red.

Rex went on neutrally, 'Did you enquire specifically about exercise tolerance?'

'Thank God,' she thought. 'Oh yes,' she said,' and I asked him about chest pain. He told me that he played squash every week and was not unduly breathless on effort.'

'Well, I suppose it's a lesson for us all on the importance of scepticism when we're doing insurance examinations.'

She was astonished. 'You mean you don't believe he was telling the truth?'

'You saw the state of his arteries. Do you really think he could have been free of symptoms on exertion?'

'If Jimmie had had an exercise ECG . . . do you think it might have shown up the problem?' she asked.

'You have to be careful, here. Exercise ECGs in young men

give up to 20 per cent of false positives. But if Jimmie had admitted to some anginal pain on exertion and there were signs of heart muscle damage on the ECG, I think coronary angiography would have been called for.'

'And something might have been done – maybe angioplasty?'

'Come on! You're not responsible for Jimmie McGregor's atherosclerosis. You can't afford not to be detached. I've had scores of patients who might have done better if only I'd done this or that, or known more.'

'Thank you,' she said, and meant it.

Drug body packers

Mohammed was a bright young Malaysian hopeful who, after trying a dozen reasonably honest jobs, got into bad company in the Bras Basah Road area of Singapore. One evening when he was leaving the Cathay cinema he was picked up by a gang of young Chinese men who invited him to come and have a few bottles of Tiger Beer. This was unusual, but the men spoke fluent bazaar Malay and Mohammed was impressed by the rolls of red hundred-dollar notes they were flashing, and went along with them.

Later that evening, when they were all good friends, one of the men addressed Mohammed in halting English. Mohammed had learned English at school and flattered himself that he spoke it well. The man asked him if he had a passport.

'No.'

'You want passport?'

'What for?'

'Travel. See world. Make plenty money.'

Mohammed was intrigued. 'How come?' he asked.

'We need messengers. We get you passport. Very good job. Easy work. Big money. OK?'

Mohammed had been hard up for months and the temptation was irresistible. 'You give me job international courier?'

'Sure. International courier. One trip – two thousand dollars. All expenses paid.'

'Where to?'

'All over. London, New York, San Francisco, Rome, Paris. Good time.'

Mohammed had never heard of some of these places but the idea of air travel appealed to him and the pay was fabulous. 'How many trips you want?' he asked.

'One or two trips a month. Maybe more.'

Mohammed's eyes gleamed as he did a rough mental calculation. 'OK,' he said, 'when do I start?'

A couple of weeks later Mohammed was taken to Orchard Road to see an older Chinese man and, after a lengthy interrogation, his duties were explained. He was then escorted to a tailor's shop and fitted out with a smart new suit and some shirts, and after that to a photographer. A few days later was given a passport and air ticket. Mohammed was delighted with himself and felt that he had suddenly risen in the world. He was well dressed, had money in his wallet, and was soon to become a jet-setter. His friends were astonished and impressed and endlessly curious. Mohammed had his cover story pat and showed them the expensive-looking leather folder with a chain and a wrist-strap in which he was to carry the 'business documents'. 'Very important papers. Multi-million business deals. Too risky to send in post. Need reliable messenger.'

Swallowing the filled condoms was more difficult than he had expected, but after the first two or three, he got the hang of it. Cutting down on food was no problem. He was accustomed to going hungry, and he consoled himself with visions of the blow-outs he would have after the delivery. He had had to memorize the address.

The flight to London was rather boring, but he had a supply of comic papers and he watched the movie and the time passed. At Heathrow he had some problems understanding the Customs officer and had a cursory body search, but was soon allowed through. He changed some money and took a taxi to the small hotel in Earl's Court where a room had been booked for him. After registering he went out to look for a chemist's shop. He had been well rehearsed.

'Terrible constipation,' he said, 'I need strongest opening medicine you got.'

The chemist showed him a bottle of a dark brown liquid. 'One tablespoonful only, OK?' he said.

Mohammed then hunted around for a household goods shop and bought a plastic bucket. 'You wrap it up good.' he said.

Back in the hotel, Mohammed took a spoonful of the mixture and waited for an hour. Nothing happened, so he took another. By late afternoon he had drunk the whole bottle. During the evening he settled down to watch TV but was soon disturbed by severe colicky pains in his belly. He decided that the laxative was finally working. After a time, however, the pains settled. There had still been no result. Mohammed wasn't worried. Indeed he felt remarkably pleased with himself. Positively euphoric in fact. Towards midnight, the euphoria gave way to an intense sleepiness and he decided to go to bed. He never made it.

About noon next day, the chambermaid summoned the

manager who, getting no response to his knocking, opened the door with his passkey. Mohammed was dead. His new suit was extensively soiled. Later, at the post-mortem examination, twenty-nine heroin-filled condoms and one ruptured condom were found in his intestines.

International drug smuggling is very lucrative, and criminal ingenuity in the concealment of drugs in transit has reached unprecedented heights – or depths. One of the most popular methods currently employed is 'body-packing' – the swallowing of packaged drugs or the concealment of them in the rectum or vagina. People who engage in this unique form of transportation are referred to by the staff of HM Customs and Excise as 'stuffers and swallowers'. Condoms, aluminium foil and latex material are used for packaging.

Heroin, cannabis and cocaine are the chief drugs smuggled in this way. As many as 180 packages have been retrieved from a single person. Swallowed packages can also cause problems of intestinal obstruction, and surgery may be necessary. X-ray examination readily reveals packages in the bowels. The size of the problem is unknown and it is certain that thousands are engaged in body packing. In a recent Customs and Excise exercise in Madrid, 800 suspicious passengers were X-rayed; 160 had packets of cocaine in their intestines.

Many of the pioneers of this method of smuggling were, like Mohammed, recruited from poor backgrounds and were unaware of the dangers. Of those detected up to 1981, over half died from poisoning and were doubtless considered expendable. Most contemporary drug couriers have now learned from others' bitter experience and are more careful with their packaging methods.

Nightmare

George Skinner was a thin, cantankerous Scotsman. He arrived exactly on time at the eye outpatient department and reported in. Ten minutes later, he was back at the desk complaining that he was being kept waiting. At intervals of about five minutes thereafter, and in spite of the disapproving stares of the other patients, he walked up to the nurses' station to remind them, with increasing bitterness, that he had not yet been seen.

Mr Skinner was shown in five minutes later.

'Well, sir,' said Miles Mariner, the ophthalmic consultant, politely, 'what's your problem?'

'It's ma eye. This one. It doesna' see.'

'Not at all?'

'Well, there's a wee bit vision to the side and down below. But in the centre, nothing. Jist blackness.'

'And how long has it been like that?'

'Well, ah don't know. Ah jist noticed it, by accident like, about a month ago.'

'And was it the same as now when you first noticed it?'

'Not quite as bad, then. There was a bigger area of vision, round about, at that time – '

'Did you have vision all round the black area, at first?'

'Aye, all round.'

'And the black area – was it circular?'

'Aye, it was round.'

'But now there's very little vision to the sides?'

'Yes, that's right. What is it? Is it serious?'

'Well,' said Mariner, 'there's a lot to be done before I can answer that question.'

Mariner now took a detailed history of previous eye troubles and those of Skinner's family. Then he went into the general medical history, asking questions about all the main systems of the body. He checked the visual acuity in the good eye – which was normal – and then asked Skinner to sit behind the slit-lamp microscope where he carefully examined the front parts of both eyes under high magnification and then put in anaesthetic eye-drops and a little fluorescein dye. This done, he measured the pressure in each eye and then put on a special kind of contact lens so that he could inspect the angle between the back of the cornea and the iris.

'Right, Mr Skinner,' he said, 'the next step is to widen your pupils so that we can get a really good view of the insides of the backs of your eyes and see what's causing this problem.'

'And how will you do that?'

'Just some more drops.'

He put in the mydriatic drops and said, 'These will take about fifteen minutes to work properly, so would you mind just sitting outside again, so that we can attend to another patient while the drops are working?'

Skinner went out like a lamb.

Mariner saw another patient and then Skinner was asked to come in again and to lie down on an examination couch. Miles checked the pupils then reached up to the wall above the couch and took down a binocular indirect ophthalmoscope which he fitted over his head so that he could see through it with both his hands free. He then picked up a Nikon condensing lens and turned out all the lights. As soon as Miles brought in the condensing lens he saw that his worst fears were confirmed. It was only by an effort of will that he prevented himself from drawing in a sharp breath. There, occupying most of the back pole of the eye was a large, hemispherical, darkly pigmented mass, covered with orange flecks.

In silence, Mariner completed his examination of the periphery of the retina and then did a careful survey of the other eye. When he had finished, he took off the ophthalmoscope and hung it on the hook on the wall.

'Can I just have a feel of your tummy, while you're lying down?' he said.

Reluctantly, Skinner unfastened his belt, pulled up his shirt and exposed a skinny abdomen. Mariner palpated the right side, just under the rib margin, asking him to take a few deep breaths as he did so. Then he felt all over the belly, using the flat of his hand and pressing in with straight fingers.

'All right,' he said, 'you can get up now.'

'Well, doctor?' asked Skinner, now anxious, 'what is it?'

'I'm very sorry to have to say that you have a malignant tumour at the back of your eye, inside, which has grown forward and detached the retina.'

There was a moment's silence, then Skinner said, 'Aye. Ah thought it must be something like that.' His voice was steady. 'Well, how long have ah got?'

'No, no!' said Mariner, quickly. 'There's no immediate indication that the tumour has spread, so no suggestion, at this stage, of danger to life. The appearances are very typical of a primary tumour of the choroid – that's one of the coats of the eye – and these tumours often don't spread to remote parts of the body until a late stage. Of course, we have to do a number of checks of this – CT scans, and so on – '.

'But ye'll be wanting to take ma eye out, won't ye?'

Mariner took hold of his hand. 'Yes,' he said, 'it would be very dangerous to leave it. You do realize, don't you, that the eye is already blinded and that we can't do anything about that? I mean, you'd not be losing any function, just the melanoma.'

'Well, it's a thought, havin' yer eye out,' said Skinner, 'I suppose ye'd give me a glass eye, would you?'

'Certainly.'

'All right, then. When do ye want to do it?'

'I think you should come into hospital today, for the tests, and we'll operate . . . the day after tomorrow. Do you agree?'

'Ah dinna hae much choice, do ah?'

'No,' said Mariner, 'you don't have much choice, if we're to save your life.'

Mariner visited Mr Skinner in the ward on the evening of the next day. All tests were negative. It seemed almost certain that the tumour had originated in the eye, rather than elsewhere, and likely that there was no secondary spread to other parts of the body. Skinner had just had this news from the houseman and was taking it well.

'Ah wanted t' say that ah ken ah was jist a wee bit impatient when ah first come in,' he said, getting as near to an apology as he was capable of, 'but ah was verra anxious, ye know.'

'Well, of course!' said Mariner, 'I appreciate that. And I must say I think you're taking the whole thing very courageously.'

Thursday was a busy day, with a long eye list in the morning and a very full clinic in the afternoon, but it was, in any case, almost six o'clock before the theatre was free. Mariner went straight up to theatre from the out-patients. He had an appointment that evening and was in rather a hurry, so he was annoyed to find that the theatre was still in use. An ENT surgeon was sitting by the head of a patient, with a forehead lamp shining into his mouth, cracking bits of bone out of the anaesthetized patient's maxillary antrum with heavy steel forceps.

Mariner went in and the surgeon looked at him. 'Hello Mariner,' he said, 'sorry to keep you waiting.'

'How long will you be?'

The ENT specialist shrugged. 'Can't say quite yet,' he said, 'this one turned out to be a bit different from what I expected.'

Mariner repressed an exclamation of annoyance and went out to see the sister in charge.

'I'm in a hurry,' he said, 'aren't any of the other theatres free?'

'Sorry. We've had a hell of a day and two of the others are still in use and the fourth one is dirty. I'm afraid you'll just have to wait. We have to wait too, you know.'

Mariner went through to the coffee room.

Half an hour later, the ENT surgeon came in for coffee. 'Through now,' he said. 'It's all yours.'

'About time,' said Mariner. He got up and went through to Sister's office. 'Send for the patient,' he said.

Mariner and the theatre sister scrubbed, gowned and gloved and went in Mr Skinner was on the table and the anaesthetist was busy with his ventilator and the nitrous oxide dose-rate meter.

'OK to go?' asked Mariner.

'Carry on.'

Mariner swabbed Mr Skinner's face and put in a speculum to keep the lids apart. Sister passed him a pair of fine forceps and spring scissors. With deft, controlled strokes he cut the conjunctiva all round the edge of the cornea. Then he hooked up four of the tiny eye-moving muscles in turn and cut them free of the globe. 'Now for the horrid bit.' he said.

'Quite.' said Sister.

Mariner slackened the tightening screw of the speculum so that the blades could come together a little, and pressed it backwards. At once the globe of the eye shot upwards between the blades so that its whole circumference was in front of the lids. The effect was, as always, grotesque.

Sister gave him a stout pair of curved scissors and a strong pair of toothed forceps. With the latter, he took a firm grip of the globe by the muscle stump on the outer side and pulled it forward as far as he could. Then he slipped the blades of the scissors round behind the globe and felt for the optic nerve. Giving Sister a significant look, he opened the blades and, with some difficulty, cut through the tough nerve.

At once the eyeball jerked forward and blood welled up behind it and ran over the towels. Quickly, he cut through the remaining two muscles and dropped the eye into a stainless steel kidney dish. Sister gave him a large gauze swab wrung out in warm water and he pressed this into the bloody cavity. Soon the bleeding stopped and, in a few minutes, he had stitched the four main eye-moving muscles together with catgut and then neatly closed the conjunctival opening with a horizontal, continuous suture. As he did so he caught up the muscles, so as to ensure movement in the artificial eye which would be fitted later. He then packed the socket with Vaseline gauze, put on an eye-pad and fixed it tightly in place with two strips of tape.

'All finished!' he said, and snapped off his gloves. He then went across to the table in the corner to write up the notes. He picked up a ball-point pen and opened the folder. He turned to the end of the out-patient clinical findings and wrote the date. Then he automatically read the last entry:

'List for enucleation of RIGHT eye under general anaesthesia.' He began to write, 'Operation under gen – ' Then the pen fell from his hand. His face turned deathly white. His heart started to race and there was an agonizing pounding in his chest. Slowly he turned his head and looked at the patient, just as the anaesthetist pulled out his tracheal tube. Mr Skinner's right eye was clearly visible. The left side was covered with the pad.

Mariner staggered to his feet and went out by the nearest door. He was gagging uncontrollably and only just made it to the changing room before vomiting violently into the wash-basin. It was the worst moment of his life.

Early the next morning Miles Mariner, accompanied by the ward sister, went through the main ward, with its curtained annexes, to the row of small single rooms where patients were put immediately after surgery. Sister opened the door of Mr Skinner's room and stood back to allow Mariner to enter.

'All right, sister. Thank you,' he said, 'I'll not trouble you any further.' He looked at her, meaningfully, and, after a moment's hesitation, she nodded and went away.

Skinner's right eye was open. Mariner moved nearer the bed and the eye turned towards him.

Mariner spoke. His voice was a little hoarse. 'Mr Skinner. How are you feeling?'

'Who's that?'

'It's Mr Mariner, the eye consultant. I saw you in the clinic two days ago.'

'Oh, aye. I mind. An the operation was all right, was it?'

There was a long silence, then Mariner spoke. 'Mr Skinner,' he said, 'I'm . . . I'm dreadfully sorry to have to tell you . . .'

'What, man? What are ye trying to say? I canna see you. What for have you covered up ma good eye?' He touched the eye pad with his fingers. 'Can ah no take the patch off?'

His fingers moved across to touch the closed lids of his right eye and he felt the globe with his finger-tips. 'Ah thought ye were going to – ' He remained perfectly still for a moment and then tore off the eye-pad. The lids were sunken and a trickle of dried blood showed between them. He pressed the lids with his fingers, then sat upright in bed and stretched his arms out in front of him. Frantically, he waved his hands in front of his face. Then he held his right hand to the side of his right eye and wiggled the fingers. 'What's this?' he cried, and again, on a rising note, 'what's this?'

'Mr Skinner,' he said, 'there's been a terrible mistake – '

'Mistake!' shouted Skinner, white foam appearing at the corners of his mouth, 'mistake! Whit in God's name are ye talking about?'

'I'm sorry . . . It's true. There was a mistake and – '

'Ye took out ma good eye! Is that it? Did ye?' His voice rose almost to a shriek and his trembling hands were stretched out in front of him.

'Yes,' said Mariner, 'I did. It was a . . .'

There was a moment's silence then Skinner, roaring in grief and outrage, threw the covers off the bed, swung his skinny legs over the side and managed to get to his feet. Staggering across the floor, his arms swinging wildly in his efforts to strike out at Mariner, he crashed into a bed table which tipped over so that he fell right across it.

Mariner could take no more and hurried from the room. Sister was waiting outside. 'See to him,' he said and hurried past her.

He went straight to the deserted out-patient department and let himself into his consulting room. His hands were shaking as he unlocked the dangerous drugs cabinet.

The cleaners found his body next morning. He was sitting back in his chair and seemed to be staring at all his framed degree diplomas on the opposite wall.

Aspirin

When Dr Meredith was a final year student he used often to go up to the hospital in the evenings to see what was going on in the receiving surgical wards. This he found greatly preferable to studying and there was always a chance that he might be able to assist at an operation. Failing that, he could always get into a gown and watch what was happening over the surgeon's shoulder.

One night a vagrant man was brought into the ward. He had been found wrapped in rags and lying in an empty wooden crate near the harbour. He was desperately ill and in severe pain, and a quick examination showed that his abdomen was as rigid as a board of wood. 'Peritonitis,' said the surgical registrar. 'We'd better get him into theatre right away. Do you want to assist, Meredith?'

'Certainly.'

The patient was in surgical shock – his blood volume was barely adequate to maintain his circulation – so they started by putting up a drip and running in some saline solution. They had no information on whether or not he had eaten recently and he seemed unable to tell them, so the anaesthetist put down a soft rubber tube and sucked out the contents of his stomach. It was empty, so they proceeded.

The surgeon knew that infected bowel contents had somehow got into the sterile peritoneal cavity of the abdomen through a leak in the intestine. His job was to find the leak and close it. The common sites were in the stomach or duodenum, where internal ulcers can penetrate, and at the appendix. There was really nothing to indicate which of these was most likely, so the surgeon made a long vertical incision, just to one side of the midline, running from the angle of the ribs down well below the navel. There was very little fat under the skin.

When the peritoneal membrane was picked up and opened, a gush of yellowish fluid emerged from the incision and the theatre Sister got busy with the sucker. After a bit, the surgeon took it from her and, while Meredith retracted the edges of the wound, the surgeon went into every nook and cranny, removing, so far as was possible, every scrap of foreign material. He then washed out the cavity thoroughly with saline. After that he turned his attention to the stomach which was now exposed in the upper part of the abdominal cavity, towards the left.

As he folded it back he exclaimed, 'Here we are! Here's the cause of the trouble!' There, on the rear surface, was a neat, round hole with inflamed edges. He inspected this closely. 'Perforated gastric ulcer on the greater curvature,' he said.

Something white caught Meredith's eye. 'What's that?' he asked, moving one of the retractors so that he could see better. There, lying free in the peritoneal cavity, on the outer surface of a loop of small intestine, was a perfect, unaltered aspirin tablet. Unthinkingly, he said, 'Well, that one didn't do him much good.'

The surgeon looked at him over his mask. 'You never spoke a truer word,' he said.

Meredith was confused. 'What do you mean?' he asked.

'Look at this hole,' said the surgeon, 'does that look like a typical penetrating gastric ulcer?'

Having never seen one before, Meredith had no idea what a typical penetrating gastric ulcer looked like. 'Hm . . .' he said.

'Look at the edges. See how white they are?'

'Yes. I see.'

'Now which more commonly perforates – a stomach ulcer or a duodenal ulcer?'

Hastily Meredith, who had no idea, tried to estimate which he had heard of more often. He guessed. 'Duodenal.'

'Right. There are at least ten DU perforations to every stomach ulcer perforation. Stomach ulcers rarely perforate.'

Greatly daring, Meredith said, 'Are you trying to tell me something?'

'My God,' said the surgeon, 'hasn't the penny dropped yet? It was the aspirin that caused the perforation.' He was too busy to look up as he was now quickly stitching up the hole with catgut.

'You're joking!' said Meredith.

'Certainly not. Try sticking an aspirin between your gum and your cheek for five minutes and see what happens. Aspirin is an acid. Acetyl salicylic acid. Mucous membranes turn white and cells die. If a hard unbroken aspirin sticks in a fold of the mucosal lining of the stomach, it could easily cause an ulcer.'

'I see.'

'So what's the moral?'

'Chew tablets before swallowing?'

'OK. But better than that?'

'Use only soluble aspirin.'

'Right.' He held up the ends of the catgut sutures. 'Cut these short, would you?'

After that, the surgeon shook a quantity of antibiotic powder into the peritoneum and then they closed the incision in layers.

Next day Meredith learned that the aspirin had done more harm than he had expected. The patient never made it out of the recovery room. The interval between the time of perforation and the time of surgery had been too long, his general condition had been too poor and the toxaemia from the peritonitis too severe. Irreversible shock had supervened and, in spite of every effort at resuscitation, he had died around daybreak.

In those days, hard, insoluble aspirin tablets were common. Happily, because of changes in formulation, such a tragedy could not happen today.

Treating hydrophobia

The history of medicine is full of tales of horror most of them resulting from ignorance of the real nature of disease and of how to manage it. A single example will suffice to show how greatly humanity has benefited from medical advances. This account is drawn from the correspondence of Henry Baker, Fellow of the Royal Society. It is given in a letter from a Dr Wolf of Warsaw, dated 26 September 1767.

In April 1767 in Warsaw, a rabid wolf attacked and bit seventeen people and many cows. One of the people bitten was an Army officer and we can infer that he was bitten on the lower part of the body because he developed symptoms in the seventh week and died in hydrophobia within days. In this disease, the interval between biting and the onset of symptoms (the incubation period) depends on the distance of the bite from the brain. This is because the viruses of rabies must travel along nerves to reach the brain before the disease manifests itself. Until very recent times, the mortality rate from established rabies has always been 100 per cent.

The officer remained well until he developed a low fever, loss of appetite, headache and tingling and then recurrence of pain at the site of the bite. He became increasingly anxious, jumpy and disoriented and soon developed the characteristic fear of swallowing. Although consumed with thirst, any attempt to drink at once induced violent spasms of the diaphragm, throat and larynx, with gagging, choking and a growing sense of panic. This is why the condition is called hydrophobia. As the disease worsened, even the sight or sound of water prompted these reactions and he exhibited periods of maniacal behaviour with thrashing, spitting, biting and raving. Delusions and hallucinations and seizures resembling epileptic fits developed. These attacks alternated with periods of lucidity in which he suffered acute anxiety and mental distress. The nerves controlling his eye movement and facial expression became paralysed, and coma supervened. He died within four days of the onset of symptoms.

Eleven of the other people bitten reported to Dr Wolf and he decided, with remarkable detachment, that this was an excellent opportunity to try out a variety of suggested treatments. All had their wounds deeply scarified with a knife and washed and fomented with vinegar, salt and theriaca (cummin, bay, germander, snake-root, cloves and honey in a treacle). The wounds were also deliberately kept open for so long as the patients lived. Every two weeks they were copiously bled and they were purged every week with salts and jalap. They were given various herbs reputed to be good for hydrophobia.

One of the patients developed symptoms, as described above, on the twenty-second day, so we can infer that he was bitten on the head or neck. The symptoms started immediately after he had been well purged with calomel. He was then 'blooded copiously, plunged abundantly in cold water and had several clysters (enemas) administered without effect'. Two pounds of oil, and as much of drink, were poured down by force, but he died on the third day.

Another fell sick on the thirty-third day. He was bled and made to vomit with ipecacuanha. This man 'was too strong to make experiments on by force; he refused every thing and died the third day'. Another, who developed symptoms at about the same time, was thrice bled and was 'plunged forcibly into the coldest water for the space of two hours so that he was almost drowned'. He was clystered 'with effect'. He, himself 'forced down, with incredible aversion and labour, a great deal of drink; by which he vomited more than fifty times abundance of frothy slime. He took several ounces of oil and several boluses of opium, and castor oil and died on the fourth day'.

In the words of the report, all the affected patients retained their senses and were all talking without intermission, praying, lamenting, despairing, cursing, fighting, spitting, screaming, belching and retching. Every one was convulsed by fits which came on every quarter of an hour or so, and in the course of which their faces became almost black and their lips livid. Towards the end, the fits became less violent and then ceased. The pulse became weak and intermittent, the victims composed themselves quietly as for sleep and so died.

It is unnecessary to multiply this catalogue of horrors by

describing the fate of all the other victims, as detailed in the letter. One, however, deserves mention. This was a woman who was 'seized with the hydrophoby on the fortieth day'. She suffered terribly in the night but less in the day time. Besides the usual symptoms she had great pain and swelling in her belly. In the space of two days she drank about two bottles of brandy, but nothing else. Dr Wolf ordered her to mix the brandy with equal volumes of oil and to take two boluses of opium and castor oil each day, and also two doses of turpentine. Unexpectedly these remedies 'vomited and purged her, and she recovered'.

In view of the known mortality rate from rabies, it is most unlikely that this woman was suffering from rabies and was cured by brandy, opium and turpentine. A bite from a rabid animal, although horribly dangerous, need not necessarily imply infection. In the circumstances of what was going on around her, it would hardly be surprising if this patient developed hysterical or psychosomatic symptoms.

Today, rabies can always be prevented from developing if proper treatment is started within a day or two of receiving the bite. Immune serum (human anti-rabies globulin) and rabies vaccine are used so as to provide both passive and active protection. The serum is injected around the bite and also intramuscularly elsewhere. The vaccine is given 3, 7, 14, 30, and 90 days after biting.

A small number of patients with *established* rabies have actually been successfully treated, using heavy sedation and intensive care facilities to maintain the action of the heart and the respiratory system until the disease has passed.

Bottlebahadur

In 1954, as a Captain in the Royal Army Medical Corps (RAMC), Johnson was posted to take charge of the Medical Reception Station in Majeedee Barracks, Johore Bahru in south Malaya. The MRS Johore Bahru was a small hospital with a staff of a dozen or so and Johnson's principal responsibility was to act as medical officer to the 1st and 2nd Battalions of the Tenth Gurkha Rifles who were accommodated in Majeedee Barracks. To perform this function he had to learn a smattering of Gurhkali but was, fortunately, provided with interpreters. There was also a Gurkha Families Hospital in the barracks where Gurkha midwives delivered the numerous progeny of the soldiers. Occasionally he would be called to the Families Hospital to deal with particularly difficult obstetric cases, but for most of the time the very capable midwives coped on their own – which was just as well, for they knew far more about delivering babies than he did.

Many of the Gurkha soldiers had names ending in '-bahadur'. This is the Gurkha word for 'brave' and hence was popular among people whose chief interest in life was jungle fighting. There were Bimbahadurs, Manbahadurs, Lalbahadurs, and so on.

Most of the general administrative work of the MRS was conducted under the capable eye of an RAMC senior NCO, a Warrant Officer, Class II, or 'wobbly-oh-two' as he would sometimes call himself in moments of uncharacteristic levity. One day, soon after Johnson had taken up the appointment, the WO II asked if he could speak to him privately, so the doctor invited him to come into the consulting room. As the WO II came in his eyes became fixed on the bottom section of a glass-fronted bookshelf behind the doctor's desk. Johnson asked him to stand easy and then to sit down.

'I'll tell you what it is, sir,' said the NCO hesitantly. 'In Captain Cunningham's time, two before you, one of the little black nippers in the Families Hospital had this headless monster. I don't suppose it worried her – they drop them like kittens, you know – but it certainly worried me.'

'Oh? Why was that?' asked Johnson.

'Well, you see, sir,' he paused and seemed genuinely distressed, 'my wife . . .'

'I see,' responded Johnson.

'It wouldn't have been so bad, but Captain Cunningham asked for it – said it was of great medical interest – and he put it in a bottle in that there cupboard.' The WO II tried to summon a smile. 'I call it Bottlebahadur,' he said, 'and it's no joke to me. Every time I think of it I'm reminded of . . .'

'I understand. So what have you in mind?' asked Johnson.

'Well, I just wondered, sir, if you could possibly . . . somehow . . . just get rid of it.'

Johnson could see he was serious and thought for a moment. 'OK,' he said, 'Leave it to me. I'll sort it out at 1800 hours today.'

With many expressions of gratitude, the WO II departed.

At 1755 that day Johnson realized to his astonishment that the MRS was deserted. As it happened, they had no patients in the ward and everyone – orderlies, cleaners, nurses, clerks, even the gardener – had disappeared. He was alone in the building. The Warrant Officer must have been gossiping, and there is no grapevine like the grapevine in a hospital.

Johnson got out the large glass jar and took it through to the kitchen. There he put it in a deep sink and broke the wax seal round the enormous cork. Immediately he was assailed by the pungent, eye-watering odour of formaldehyde. Captain Cunningham had obviously been determined to preserve the baby. Quickly he poured out the fluid, put the bottle under the tap and ran in fresh water. He then went to the large heating stove, opened the damper and gave it a good poke. After a few minutes he decided that most of the formalin solution would have gone, so he upended the jar.

Unfortunately, the formalin had done its work only too well and the body was now so hard that it would not come out. So he put his hand in and tried to pull. No luck. This was a difficulty. Gurkhas are Hindu and he had resolved that, at all costs, this baby would be disposed of respectfully and in a proper manner, by burning. So there was nothing for it but to turn away his face and drop the bottle from a height on to the stone floor.

By now, the stove was pulling beautifully and the obsequies were quickly completed. Johnson decided that it would be inappropriate for the Commanding Officer, even if quite alone, to clean up the mess, so he left it and went out. The WO II was pacing up and down outside, waiting to lock up. He approached, came to attention and saluted.

'All right, sir?' he asked anxiously.

'Ramro chha,' said Johnson.

There were tears in the NCO's eyes. And the salute he gave Johnson as he wished him good night would have done credit to the drill sergeant at the RAMC Depot and Training Establishment.

Johnson retired to the Officers' Mess, fell into an armchair, and called for a large pink gin.

Cautionary Tales

Check the container

Lead-glazed pottery is safe so long as the kiln temperatures are high enough to thoroughly melt and 'cure' lead-containing ceramic glazes. Unfortunately, this is not always the case. Wood-burning kilns used by many Mexican potters, for instance, can fail to reach the required temperatures. As a result such pottery can be a serious hazard to health. Tests have shown that blood levels of toxic lead can rise 20 per cent after a single exposure to fruit punch kept in traditional Mexican pottery.

In the case of one seven-year-old American child blood levels of lead rose by 400 per cent in less than four weeks after drinking punch from one of these vessels at a picnic. This child was treated with a drug to remove lead from the body and suffered no ill effects. Lead is, of course, a dangerous poison that can damage brain function and reduce intelligence. Decorative pottery of this kind is, on the other hand, entirely harmless if used for purposes other than the storage of liquid beverages.

Another health hazard from containers was discovered when a mysterious disease was being investigated in South Africa. Abnormally high levels of iron were found in the bodies of hundreds of people and the disease was eventually traced to a native beer that was being brewed in iron vessels.

Absinthe makes the heart grow fonder?

Once the favourite tipple of the French Foreign Legion, if PC Wren, author of *Beau Geste* is to be believed, this potent spirit has been scientifically proved to have all the evil properties attributed to it in this splendid adventure yarn.

Absinthe contained a number of flavoursome essential oils including anise and oil of wormwood and we now know that it is in the wormwood, derived from the plant *Artemisia absinthium*, that the real toxic principle is to be found – a drug called thujone.

This is very nasty stuff. It really does rot the brain, causing severe intellectual deterioration, hallucinations and convulsions. The effects were so severe that they came to be called 'absinthism' and eventually led to the drink being banned early in the twentieth century. Absinthe had been rotting brains by the million for at least 2000 years. It is mentioned in Pliny's *Historia naturalis*, published in the first century AD.

To some extent it was the thujone that made the drink popular. When a little water is added to absinthe, the dilution of the alcohol causes the precipitation of a colloidal suspension of terpenes including thujone. This made the drink turn white – always an impressive sight. You can do the same, today, with Pernod, which contains plenty of anise but no wormwood, and which is no more liable to rot your brain than any other strong spirit.

Botulism

The poison or toxin produced by the germ *Clostridium botulinum* is one of the most powerful poisons known to human-kind. It is occasionally found in home-prepared preserved, bottled or canned meats, raw fish, vegetables and non-acid fruits that have been inadequately sterilized. Contamination of commercial preparations is rare but has occurred.

Contaminated food usually tastes or looks abnormal. When it is eaten there is a delay of twelve to thirty-six hours and then the eyelids begin to droop. This is not because of sleepiness but because of a specific paralytic action of the poison. Conscious-ness and mental function are unaffected. The alignment of the eyes is also affected and there is double vision, but this is soon concealed by the drooping lids. Next, speech becomes slurred and the victim finds that he or she is unable to swallow. Soon the breathing becomes difficult and speech impossible. Sometimes there is cramping pain in the abdomen and, for a time, vomiting and diarrhoea. Urination may become paralysed. Death may occur within twelve hours of onset, but usually takes longer.

Botulinum toxin operates at the junction of nerves and muscles, causing a blockage of nerve transmission so that the muscles, although perfectly normal, are effectively paralysed. In recent years, the toxin has been increasingly used, in a very highly diluted form, to treat certain conditions, such as squinting eyes, spasmodic closure of the eyelids, or other conditions of muscular overaction.

There is a tale, well known in medical circles, of a fisherman's punt found floating on a Scottish loch. There were four well-dressed fishermen aboard, surrounded by their expensive equipment. All four were dead and all four had their eyelids propped open with broken match-sticks. On the floor of the punt was a jar of home-made meat paste.

Irony of ecstasy

In 1993 a seventeen-year-old girl tried ecstasy for the first time. She took one and a half tablets. Four hours later she had three convulsions resembling epilepsy after which she remained unrousable. She was left to 'sleep it off'. After nine hours, however, she was obviously not right and was taken to hospital. She seemed drowsy and, although she opened her eyes from time to time, she made no response to questions and seemed unable to recognize anyone. She was incontinent. It was not until more than two days after taking the drug that she began to respond and to recover. Eventually she returned fully to normal. This case is not unique. It is easy to imagine the feelings of this girl's relatives and friends as she remained completely inaccessible. None of them could have known that she would recover. They were, sadly, among the fortunate ones.

Ecstasy (methoxy-methylene-dioxyamphetamine) is an amphetamine-like drug similar in chemical structure to the natural hallucinogenic drug mescaline. In low doses it acts like amphetamine and in higher doses it acts like LSD. It is more poisonous than mescaline in increasing doses and may cause death. Because there is no official standardization either of dosage or purity, no one can be sure what, or how much, they are taking. Ecstasy is an illegal 'designer' drug, produced for profit by people who care nothing for the safety or well-being of the young. Many tragic deaths have resulted from the use of this drug at 'rave' parties. Some of these deaths result from dehydration, some from drinking excess water in an attempt to avoid dehydration, and some from causes that have not been established. To the friends and relatives of the victims, the name 'ecstasy' must seem a singular and bitter irony.

Dangerous ice-cream

Probably the most popular foodstuff in the USA today is ice-cream. The quantity consumed is one of the reasons why half the American population is overweight. In the mind of the public, ice-cream is almost universally regarded as safe; in fact it is highly dangerous. Obesity is one of the important risk factors for the development of the dangerous arterial blocking disease atherosclerosis – the number one killer of the Western world that causes heart attacks, strokes, limb gangrene, and kidney failure. Obesity is also responsible for many other serious disadvantages.

But this is not the only danger. Very few people are aware that there are germs that can easily resist the low temperature of ice-cream. One of the principal causes of food poisoning, the salmonella range of organisms, is very comfortable at temperatures well below that of the coldest ice-cream. These germs may not grow much, but they will survive happily. In 1994 there was a national outbreak of salmonella food poisoning in the USA, affecting an estimated 224,000 people.

All the cases arose from eating a single brand of ice-cream that was widely distributed from door to door. The firm that made this product was, of course, scrupulous about its preparations and the ice-cream premix they used was always carefully pasteurized. But there was a loophole. Some of the ice-cream premix was transported to the plant in tanker trailers that had, immediately before, carried non-pasteurized liquid eggs!

Happily, although the affected people had gastroenteritis, fever and diarrhoea, often with blood in the stools, none of them died. Fortunately the salmonella species involved was *S. enteritides*. Had it been *S. typhi*, the organism responsible for causing typhoid fever, this might have been a disaster of the first magnitude. There are about 1500 different species of salmonella organisms.

Drugged drivers

The ever-increasing use of cocaine and marijuana as 'recreational drugs' has led to much concern in medical circles over the effects of these drugs on the performance of drivers. American research has shown that alcohol is not the only drug to affect drivers adversely, and that driving under the influence of cocaine or marijuana is a growing cause of car accidents, injuries and death.

Whereas it is easy to observe and test for the effects of alcohol in drivers, the effects of these other drugs are more subtle and easily concealed. The standard tests for alcohol intoxication may well fail to detect intoxication with cocaine or marijuana. A research study conducted in 1993 on drivers in Memphis, Tennessee, arrested for reckless driving but who did not test positive for alcohol, produced some interesting and significant results. One hundred and fifty people in this category stopped by the police for reckless driving were persuaded to provide urine samples. Just under 60 per cent of these tested positive for one or other of the two drugs. Thirty-three per cent tested positive for marijuana, 13 per cent for cocaine and 12 per cent tested positive for both drugs.

These are horrifying figures but there is worse to come. Ninety-four of the 150 drivers were considered by the doctors to be clinically intoxicated, although almost half of those intoxicated with cocaine were easily able to pass the normal tests for alcoholic intoxication. The effects of these drugs was to induce slowness, sleepiness, aggression, combativeness, loss of concentration, swaying, staggering, loss of balance and a reduction in the sense of responsibility. All the drivers who refused to provide a urine sample for testing were deemed to be 'extremely intoxicated'.

It is hardly necessary to add that nearly all the subjects studied in this research project were men.

Cholesterol is good for you

There is no longer any argument about the dangers of high levels of cholesterol in the blood. High blood cholesterol is associated with a higher risk of heart attacks and other unpleasant and dangerous conditions. Lowering the blood cholesterol in a population reduces the incidence of heart attacks; and heart attacks are one of the principal causes of death in any Western population. It has, however, been conclusively shown that lowering the blood cholesterol does *not* reduce the overall mortality in the population. Several clinical trials have shown that lowering blood cholesterol levels is associated with an increase in deaths from other causes including suicide, violence and accidents. There is good evidence that lowering cholesterol causes depression and some experts maintain that there may be a general link between low cholesterol concentrations and psychiatric illness.

Statistics have to be regarded with suspicion. A report of a major study in the *British Medical Journal* in August 1994, involving 10,898 men and 11,534 women found that there was no connection between the blood level of cholesterol and the likelihood of death from suicide, violence or accidents. There were 193 deaths from these causes among the men and 43 among the women. The only common factors were smoking and high alcohol intake. The authors of the research concluded that lowering blood levels of cholesterol in a population does not increase accident or violence.

Is this a valid conclusion? The population studied in this research was not a population that had had its cholesterol levels lowered. It was a random population containing the usual spread of blood cholesterol levels. Some were high; some were low. These were the levels natural to these people whether induced by an unhealthy life-style or not. All the apparently conflicting results from the many trials could be consistent with the suggestion that there is a basic difference between having naturally low levels of cholesterol and having your levels artificially lowered by drugs.

A hearty handshake

A fifty-year-old man struck his hand painfully and, convinced that he had suffered a broken bone, went straight to a hospital casualty department. X-ray showed that he had, indeed, sustained a fracture of one of the metacarpal bones of the hand. Unusually, the fracture was in perfect alignment with no displacement. For this reason it was decided to treat it conservatively by 'protected active mobilization'. The man was advised to use the hand but to be careful to avoid any action that might displace the bone ends.

This worked very well and he was allowed to go home. Two weeks later he visited his GP. Unfortunately, the GP had not yet had the report from the hospital and greeted his patient with a hearty handshake. There was an audible click and a sudden exacerbation of the patient's pain. There was now a visible lump on the back of the patient's hand and a second X-ray showed that the fracture was now widely displaced. Attempts at external realignment failed and an open operation and internal fixation were required to stabilize the fracture.

Chocolate can damage your eyesight

Angelica, better known as Angie, was a jolly, convivial woman in her late sixties whose main interest in life was organizing outings for her friends. Nothing pleased her more than being able to persuade a gang of like-minded acquaintances to go up the West End for an evening's entertainment. She was a dab hand at talking people into subscribing so that she could get a row of tickets for a good show.

One Christmas Angie decided on a pantomime and, in due course, she and five of her friends found themselves sitting near the front being thoroughly entertained. The star of the show was a comedian of international reputation and a very good time was had by all. That is until, as part of his act, the star began to throw small chocolate bars into the audience. This seemed quite a good idea at first and the ladies, entering into the spirit of the performance, tried to catch the chocolates. Unfortunately, Angie was rather more successful than the others and one of the bars struck her painfully in the right eye.

Angie was a lady of spirit, however, and was not going to let a minor matter of that sort spoil her evening. The eye was acutely painful at first and watered profusely but she just held a hankie to it and told the others she was all right. Her friends were quite concerned and kept asking her if the eye was hurting but Angie bravely reassured them.

By the time she got home her eye felt a little better and she just took some aspirin and went to bed. The next morning the watering had stopped but the eye was rather red and she noticed that the vision in it was blurred. She felt sure that this would soon clear up and tried to ignore it. Two days later, however, it had become obvious that her vision was seriously affected. She could see fine with her left eye but when she covered it up all she could see was a milky glow with the right. Angie decided it was time she saw an eye specialist, and her GP referred her urgently to the eye department in the local hospital.

The ophthalmologist listened to her story and asked a few questions. He then checked her vision and found that with her right eye she could not even make out for sure where the eye chart was. The vision in her left eye was normal. The doctor turned down the lights, then examined her eyes with a microscope and a bright light. What he saw made him frown. There was a tiny ragged tear in the margin of her iris and the internal lens, lying just behind the pupil, had turned a dense white. This was why she couldn't see.

'I'm afraid you have a traumatic cataract, my dear,' he said.

Angie was not much the wiser for this comment and asked him what that meant.

'It's the internal lens of your eye,' he said, 'the one you focus with – or used to, when you were younger.'

'What about it?'

'Well, this lens doesn't take too kindly to being thumped. A smart bang can damage its delicate capsule and allow water to get in. This disrupts the lens fibres and so instead of being clear it goes white. That's what we call a cataract. Usually this just happens gradually, as a natural thing, to old people, but a bang on the eye can bring it on very quickly.'

Angie digested this information. 'Will it clear?' she asked.

'I'm really sorry. There's very little chance of that. Once it has got to this stage it isn't going to get better.'

'So it's permanent, is it?'

'No, no,' said the specialist, 'I didn't say that.'

'But . . .'

'Your eye is still inflamed and I'm going to prescribe some drops to help it to settle down. And when it's completely quiet we'll just take out the opaque lens and pop in a new clear one.'

'You mean . . . an operation.' Angie shuddered.

'Now, don't start worrying. This is a routine matter. As far as you are concerned it will just be a needle in your hand to send you off to sleep and that's that.'

It was exactly as the doctor said. Three months later Angie was admitted for an intracapsular extraction of cataract and an intraocular lens implant. A week after the operation she read the bottom line of the chart with her right eye perfectly.

Speak or eat

Here is a report from the Philosophical Transactions of the Royal Society for the year 1765. The account, by William Martin, Esq., of Shadwell, was sent to the Librarian of the Royal Society.

'On Tuesday the 23rd of October 1764, about six in the evening, as one of my maidservants was eating toast and butter, and while attempting to speak hastily in the very action of swallowing, unfortunately forced a piece of the crusty part under the epiglottis, which made its way into the larynx or upper part of the windpipe; which notwithstanding the many vigorous efforts nature made (by a violent and incessant cough) to discharge it, yet it fixed like a wedge. In a few hours she was deprived of her senses and her speech and lay in great agonies, with violent agitation of body resembling strong convulsions, fetched her breath very short, and it was expected she would expire that night.

As I was in the house when the accident happened, every method that I could possibly think of was made use of for her relief, but without effect; and as respiration was attended with the greatest difficulty, I ordered about ten ounces of blood to be taken from her arm, which seemed in some measure to relieve her breath; this was two hours after the accident. The cough continued about three hours, till her strength was in a manner quite exhausted, and she seemed to be entirely senseless, except at intervals, pointing to her breast; and whenever I examined her pulse, forcibly and in great agonies, she pressed my hand to the scrobiculus cordis or heart-pit as the seat of her disorder.

I left her about twelve o'clock that night; and desired my servants, who attended her, to call me if they observed any sudden alteration; which they accordingly did about two in the morning, when I was informed she was expiring (as they thought), and indeed as I soon hastened to her assistance, I was of the same opinion. However, as I found her somewhat more sensible, but in great agonies, and making motions to be blooded again, as she had a full pulse, and the greatest difficulty in respiration; I took away about the same quantity as before, which seemed to give her some relief, and she continued much more quiet.

At this time her cough had left her; and I was convinced by her complaints, the extraneous body had made its way into one of the lobes of the lungs. In this languid state she continued for several days, begging God to release her by death; and desiring me to open her body, which I promised.

But what was very remarkable in this case, notwithstanding the great agonies she was in whilst awake, yet, the second night after the accident happened, she fell asleep about twelve o'clock and slept sound for several hours. Whilst in that state of relaxation, fetched her breath quite easy, as she did every night after, when asleep, with a serene pulse, but always waked in exquisite pain, and in great agitations.

In a few days I observed her breath to smell very strong, and I made a prognostic, that nature (in order to expel the enemy) would form an abscess or apostemation in the lungs (as the only chance for her life), and would bring it up, by the same channel it went down; though I was not without apprehensions (as there was a prominence, pointing outwards, and attended with great soreness), that an empyema, or collection of matter, would be formed, which, if it made its way outwards, would (in all probability) have proved fatal.

However, on the eleventh day from the accident, she was of a sudden seized in the morning, in bed, with a nausea, violent sickness, and a cough, when the impostume in her lungs broke, and discharged itself by the mouth, with a large quantity of bloody matter, in which the portion of the crust was happily intangled, about the bigness of a large hazel nut, with a great quantity of slimy substance, in which it was enveloped. After which, for an hour or more, she complained of violent pain and soreness, in the whole cavity of the breast, with great tremors; however they soon went off and her speech returned immediately, though languid. She is now in a fair way of recovery, though weak.

I would beg to observe that the late Baron Suaffo's lady died by an accident similar to this, only different as to the extraneous body, viz. a cherry stone, which was the cause of her death. And the famous Greek poet Anacreon died by the kernel of a grape in the same manner. Another instance happened lately to an acquaintance, who was killed by a piece of chestnut, which went the wrong way, as we commonly express it. And a gentleman, not long since, had the misfortune of swallowing a quarter of a guinea, in the same manner, which killed him. Nor did I ever hear of any person's recovering in a case of the like nature.'

Lockjaw

Here is a report by Mr Woolcombe, surgeon at Plymouth Dock, to Dr Huxham, FRS, that was read before the Royal Society on 7 March 1765.

'According to your desire, I have sent you the case of the locked jaw I lately had under my care.

On Saturday 2 June, in the afternoon, I was sent for to a poor woman, who an hour or two before had been taken with an oppression in her breast, attended with a slight pain in her side, and at the same time complained of a soreness in her jaws, and a little difficulty in swallowing; as I then took it to be only a common cold, she had fourteen ounces of blood drawn off, and some nitrous medicines sent her.

Upon visiting her the next morning, I found her relieved as to her breast and side, but her jaw was fixed, and almost closed, with a very great difficulty in swallowing. Upon a further inquiry, and short reflection, I was soon convinced that she had that terrible symptom a locked jaw.

As this disorder is more frequently the consequence of external injuries than from internal causes, I inquired whether she had any kind of wound or cut; and was told that, about eight days before, a rusty nail had run into the bottom of her foot; and though the wound was painful for two or three days, yet it had been well four days before she was taken with the above complaints.

I therefore examined the foot and found it quite whole, though upon pressing the tendons, she expressed a little uneasiness. I now endeavoured to relieve this terrible malady; as the blood drawn the preceding day was of a firm texture and her pulse firm and tense, I took away fourteen ounces, which proved fizzy; and having procured some stools, gave her an anodyne of *T. Thebaica*, in a very small vehicle, which she swallowed with great difficulty. I then applied a large blister to her back, but without any relief.

Soon after she was seized with frequent convulsions, which for the time deprived her of her senses; and though in the intervals they were quite perfect and her jaw not quite so shut, but a little might be put in her mouth by a teaspoon; yet so great were the spasms, that she never after could swallow any thing; and in this manner she continued, with short remission of the spasms, till two o'clock the next day, Monday, when death put an end to her misery. I have since been told, that an hour before she died, she could open her jaw, at which she seemed to be greatly rejoiced; but it was of short duration, the convulsions again returning, and an universal one carried her off.

We are certainly much in the dark, in regard to the nervous system; but I think it a strong presumption, that from the first impression of the nail, the nerves were so peculiarly affected, that though the irritation was not sufficient to hinder the external wound from healing, yet it might be sufficient to dispose them to suffer those violent agitations which ended so fatally.

If the above case is worthy of your mature reflections, it will be a great satisfaction to, Yours etc.'

Looking back at this case in the light of present-day medical knowledge, one can say that this is an classic account of a case of tetanus. Lockjaw, although the most obvious feature, is, of course, only one of the effects of this dreadful condition.

Tetanus is caused by the soil and bowel organism *Clostridium tetani*, which was discovered in 1884. If this germ gains access to an unprotected person by way of a small cut or prick, it produces a powerful poison that diffuses through the body and affects motor nerves, triggering off intense and sustained contractions of the muscles. Often the spine becomes arched backwards so that the heels approach the back of the head (opisthotonos).

Until quite recently, no one who developed tetanus spasms was ever known to have survived. The annual death rate from the disease, mainly in developing countries, still runs into hundreds of thousands. Babies are commonly infected by way of the cut end of the umbilical cord. Intravenous drug abusers using dirty needles account for a high proportion of the cases in the West.

And yet, tetanus is one of the most easily preventable of all diseases. The toxin can be modified to produce a harmless substance, tetanus toxoid, that acts as a vaccine and produces high levels of antibodies to the germ. These provide complete protection for years. Everyone should have it, ideally in infancy. You can have a course of toxoid at any time.

The accidental patch

An attractive, middle-aged woman turned up at a hospital casualty department complaining of severe faintness, dizziness on standing and a throbbing headache. The symptoms had started while she was still in bed that morning, and there was nothing in her history to suggest a cause. She was taking no medication of any kind and had suffered no head or other injury.

The symptoms were suggestive of a toxic effect of some kind but she assured the doctors that she had not been exposed to any substances that might have produced such an effect. The faintness and dizziness were so severe that it was decided to admit her for full investigation.

A full examination was performed and many tests were done, but none gave any clue to the cause of her problem. The full blood count, the blood sugar levels, blood electrolyte and protein levels, urinalysis and electrocardiogram all gave normal results. The doctors were severely puzzled. Nothing they could do seemed likely to help the unfortunate lady.

Where medical expertise had failed, however, the keen observation of a nurse succeeded. While changing the patient's sheets she noticed that there was a nitroglycerine medication patch firmly attached to one of the lady's buttocks. This was not quite in accordance with the lady's assurances that she was not on any form of medication. The embarrassed patient then explained that her history had indeed been honest, but that her husband, who suffered from angina, was in the habit of applying a nitroglycerine patch each morning. In the light of this development she now became aware of the significance of a particularly ardent bout of love-making in which they had engaged shortly before her symptoms had started.

The patch was at once removed and all the symptoms quickly disappeared.

Smoking

Tim started smoking when he was eleven and the habit persisted. By the time he was twenty he was a two-pack-a-day man and it was about then that he first noticed pain in his left leg. This always came on after he had walked a certain distance, and before long he realized that the distance was getting steadily shorter. He wasn't too keen on seeing a doctor about this as he was already fed up with being told that he should quit smoking.

In the end he had to go, and the GP sent him to hospital for tests that had something to do with the blood flow in the arteries of his legs. Finally, the consultant had him in.

'You have Buerger's disease,' he said. 'This is a fairly rare disease of arteries affecting young men in much the same way as commonly happens to quite old people. Your arteries are inflamed and are rapidly developing thickened linings and raised bumps that are making it harder for the blood to get through. When you walk, the arteries in your left leg are not able to supply as much blood as your muscles need. That's why you have pain.'

'So what causes it?'

'Smoking.'

'I thought you would say that. Don't ask me to stop.'

'I'm not asking you. Listen, if this disease goes on getting worse, you are going to lose your left leg.'

'What do you mean?'

'The main artery will close off, and when that happens your foot and lower leg will turn black and will shrivel up. This is called gangrene and it means your leg will have to be removed. Do you understand?'

'Yes.'

As soon as he was out of the consulting room Tim lit a fag. A month later his left leg was amputated, but they gave him a nice artificial leg and he was able to get along quite well to the newsagents on the corner every morning to buy his cigarettes. Soon, however, the pain started in his right leg and before the year was out, that, too, had to be amputated. This made it a bit harder to get to the newsagents, but a motorized wheelchair solved that problem.

At the age of twenty-three Tim began to have a pain in his right hand and within a month or two he had lost the use of it. First the fingertips and nails became black and narrowed, then, quite suddenly, he lost all feeling in his hand and forearm and the whole of his lower arm went black. A third amputation followed. By now, his parents were frantic with worry and tried everything to get him to stop smoking. The newsagent agreed not to supply him, but Tim had a good friend who got them for him in a supermarket. He justified this by saying to his mates in the pub, 'It's the only pleasure the poor bugger has left.'

Finally, Tim's left hand went, and managing the cigarettes became a bit of a problem. At this point, Tim decided that the people who made and sold cigarettes ought to have warned him properly about what could happen. So he got legal aid and persuaded a solicitor to take up his case against the tobacco manufacturers. This gave him a new interest in life.

Suicide frustrated

Finally, in the autumn of 1993, Paul decided that the game was no longer worth the candle. It was, he thought, a reasonable decision, calmly arrived at. There was no question of the balance of his mind being disturbed. It was simply that there was no possible point in continuing to live in utter hopelessness, loneliness and misery.

Carefully and neatly, he wrote all this down, smiling a little at the irony that he should care what others thought of him. His hands were barely trembling as he signed and dated the letter, glanced at his watch and meticulously added the exact time. He propped the envelope prominently against the telephone, turned out the room lights, and went through to the garage. He turned on the light, shut the communicating door and checked that the outer doors were closed. He felt a small pang of regret as he contemplated his new car, but he pushed the hosepipe into the exhaust, let down a rear window an inch, and shoved the other end of the pipe into the interior of the car. He then sat in the driving seat, started the engine and waited to die. The decision to act seemed to settle his mind. He became drowsy and soon fell asleep.

Paul did not die. About an hour later he was wakened by someone opening the car door, turning off the engine and crashing open the outer doors of the garage. Confused, he felt himself being dragged out into the cold night air and then being driven in another car. Soon he recognized that they were at the accident and emergency department of the local hospital. He was aware that a plastic mask was being put over his mouth and nose and that he was breathing deeply.

The doctors were puzzled. Paul ought to have been dead. He was able to talk; his blood pressure was normal and there were no signs of brain damage. He was perfectly clear as to the time when he had turned on the car engine and the time he was found was known. So they decided that he must be mistaken, or lying. Car exhaust kills because the carbon monoxide in it combines immediately with the haemoglobin in the blood to form a stable compound, carboxyhaemoglobin, that prevents the blood from taking up and transporting oxygen. In suicide attempts of this kind, a lethal concentration of carboxyhaemoglobin usually builds up in about ten minutes. By the end of that time, the brain and other organs, deprived of oxygen, are irreversibly damaged. Yet Paul remained alive and apparently well. Obviously, he could not have been in the car for an hour.

A test of the level of carboxyhaemoglobin in Paul's blood showed that it was only 6.6 per cent. This was far lower than would be expected in anyone exposed to car exhaust for so long. Indeed the levels in the blood of heavy smokers can often rise to about this figure. Paul was left on high flow-rate oxygen by mask all night. In the morning he was checked over and was found to be entirely normal in every respect.

Paul now felt differently about ending it all. There were several reasons for this. One was that he had actually enjoyed the argument with the doctors who were insisting that he could not have been in the car for an hour. He had almost forgotten what it was like to talk to people. Another reason was that he had had a long conversation with a very pretty nurse who did not seem to find him in the least boring. She was intelligent, too, and interested in cars, about which she knew a surprising amount. She knew, for instance, that all cars of the vintage of Paul's were fitted with a three-way catalytic converter that removed about 90 per cent of the carbon monoxide from the exhaust . . .

Joe Grouse and Mrs Bliss

Joe Grouse was a forty-seven-year-old systems analyst working for a major software house specializing in producing computer systems for hospital patient administration. He was good at his job, which involved making a detailed analysis of the requirements of hospitals using large computers, and progressively updating the systems. He spent a lot of time talking to hospital staff and studying their requirements.

One day when, by pure coincidence, he happened to be talking to a consultant physician about extending the disease indexing facility, he became aware that his thoughts had become confused and that he had lost the thread of what he was saying. At the same time a most extraordinary thing happened to his vision – the right half of everything he looked at seemed to have disappeared. Then he noticed that his right arm seemed to have lost almost all its power. Embarrassed and alarmed, and anxious to give himself time to think, he managed to fumble a cigarette out of its packet, using his left hand, lit it and took a deep drag.

The consultant was looking at him curiously. 'Are you all right?' he asked.

Grouse felt for a chair and sat down suddenly. With a trembling hand, he put the cigarette to his mouth and pulled the smoke down into his lungs. For a moment he wasn't sure whether he was going mad or was about to die. Then he noticed that his vision to the right was beginning to come back again and with a sense of unutterable relief he realised that his thoughts were becoming ordered once more. Almost afraid to try, he began to speak.

'I'm . . . sorry,' he said slowly, 'I don't know what came over me.' He held up his right hand and flexed his fingers. Then he covered one eye at a time and looked around.

The consultant held out both his hands. 'Grab my fingers,' he said, 'grip as hard as you can.'

Joe looked surprised but did as he was asked.

'Checking your muscle power,' explained the consultant, 'seeing if the strength is the same in both hands.'

'And is it?'

'Just about. Maybe a little weaker on the right.'

He unhooked the stethoscope from his neck, put the ear pieces in his ears, and, to Grouse's surprise, leaned forward and pressed the bell of the instrument firmly to the right side of his neck.

'What . . .?'

The consultant listened to the left side of Joe's neck. After a moment he sat back. 'How are you feeling now?' he asked.

'Scared . . . but better. How did you know my arm . . .?'

'Your speech was confused. That's called aphasia. And I noticed that you were checking the vision in both eyes – '

'So? What does that mean?' Joe looked around but there were no ashtrays.

'You've had a transient ischaemic attack – a TIA – and you're going to need a full check-up.'

'Is it serious – a TIA?'

'Not in itself. But it's a warning that you ignore at your peril.'

'Of what?'

'Of a stroke. Actually, you're quite lucky. Lots of people have a stroke without anything they can recognize as a warning at all. There nearly always *is* warning, but not usually as dramatic as that.'

'I know what "transient" means,' he said hoarsely, 'what's "ischaemic"?'

'Insufficiency of blood to any part of the body. In this case, a part of the brain. Your body tissues need oxygen and sugar if they're to work. The main function of the blood circulation is to transport these two vital supplies to all parts. The sugar is the fuel and the oxygen is needed to oxidize it so that energy can be released. The blood picks up oxygen from the lungs and sugar from the gut or liver and carries them to the tissues. The brain is acutely sensitive to oxygen and sugar lack and any reduction in the blood supply is a serious matter – '

'Well, how can that happen?'

'Various ways and we'll be checking, in your case, to find out the actual cause – whether narrowing of blood vessels, thrombosis, embolus or whatever. I think it would be best if you came in for a few days so that this can be done properly – and as quickly as possible. What do you say?'

'Absolutely!'

'Right, I'll fix it at once. But there are two things you can do to help yourself.'

'What's that? I'll do anything – '

'One is to stop smoking. Right now.'

Joe looked stricken. 'But I don't see how that can – '

'Listen,' said the consultant, 'smokers have much more atherosclerosis than non-smokers. This has been shown by thousands of post-mortem examinations. Smoking increases the heart rate and raises the blood pressure – both factors associated with atherosclerosis. High blood pressure is one of the main risk factors for stroke. Figures show that after the first TIA there is about one chance in twenty of a stroke occurring in the first year. I'm afraid that for most patients this risk continues – that is, about five per cent of them get a stroke each year.'

The medical work-up produced two important findings – angiography showed that Joe's left carotid artery was almost occluded by a large atherosclerotic plug, and repeated measurements showed that his blood pressure was much higher than it should have been.

'Does the pressure ever burst the arteries?' asked Joe.

'Sure. Sometimes, if the smaller arteries are very hardened one of them may be unable to resist the pressure and bursts. The bleeding that results may not matter very much in most parts of the body, but, inside the skull, and especially inside the brain, the damage caused may be devastating. Cerebral haemorrhage causes the most serious kinds of strokes and many patients who get it die from the first episode. Fortunately, most strokes are not caused in this way and, as I've said, by finding out that you have high blood pressure, and getting it treated, you can greatly reduce the risk of this happening. The worst combination of all is high blood pressure and smoking. This carries a particularly high risk of developing stroke and coronary thrombosis.'

About two weeks after entering hospital Joe was taken to theatre where a delicate operation was performed on his left carotid. The tests had shown that the other carotid and the two vertebrals were much less affected, so the surgeon felt that it would be safe to clamp off the affected artery and rely on the blood getting around the linking channels from the other vessels. This proved to be so. After the artery had been clamped above and below the position of the obstruction, it was carefully opened, by a longitudinal cut, and the atherosclerotic plaque shelled out. When this had been done, the artery was closed again with ultra-fine silk stitches and the clamps removed.

Joe never looked back. His recovery was uneventful, and angiography, done afterwards, showed that the blood flow in the artery which had been operated upon was now entirely normal.

'You've come through a pretty major operation with flying colours,' said the vascular surgeon. 'Do you propose to continue smoking, overeating and taking no exercise? Because, if you do, I'll just have been wasting my time and you'll be as bad as ever in a couple of years.'

'Do you think I'm crazy?' asked Joe. 'This is day one of my new life.'

'No smoking?'

'No smoking. Low fat diet. Weight control. Plenty of exercise.'

The surgeon smiled. 'Well, we'll see,' he said, 'maybe you've got more sense than all the others.'

Mrs Bliss was not so lucky.

People with threatened stroke may present to specialists in various disciplines. Most are seen by GPs or by physicians, but referral to neurologists, neuro-surgeons and to eye specialists is common. This is how Mrs Bliss finally reached an ophthalmologist. She was a delightful person, well-preserved, in her late fifties, lively and attractive and able to express herself clearly. She said she had only come because her GP had insisted.

The eye specialist asked her to sit down and tell him what had been worrying her.

'I didn't believe, at first, that my headaches had anything to do with my eyes, but in the past two or three weeks my vision has been quite severely blurred and I'm beginning to wonder.'

'Tell me about the headaches,' he said.

'They're quite different from ordinary headaches. For one thing I get them while I'm sleeping and they actually wake me up in the mornings.'

'Every morning?'

'Well, yes. Recently anyhow.'

'Where is the pain?'

'Everywhere. All over my head.'

'How would you describe it? What's it like?'

'It's a steady, pounding headache and my head feels as if it's going to burst.'

'Pounding? Like a pulse?'

'Yes. I wondered about that, so I felt my pulse and the headache beats at the same rate.'

'Are there any other symptoms?'

'Well, I've noticed that I get breathless much more easily than I used to and I often feel terribly giddy.'

'Are these new symptoms?'

'Oh yes. Only for the last month or so.'

'And you never had them before?'

'No, never.'

'Do you have to walk more slowly than you used to?'

'Yes,' she said, then smiled, 'but I just put that down to age.'

'Tell me about the blurring of vision.'

'Well, I naturally assumed that it was my glasses needing changing, but I was a bit upset, because I've never needed glasses for distance – only for reading.'

'And did you get new glasses?'

'Yes. But they didn't make a bit of difference. Very expensive they were, too.'

'Is the blurring all over your field of vision?'

'No. I can see all right straight ahead, but I don't seem to see nearly so well to the left side – '

'To the left side with each eye separately?'

'No. It's really my left eye that's affected. The right one seems quite normal.'

When he tested her vision the ophthalmologist found that on the left side it was only about one quarter of normal (6/18) and on the right, about half normal (6/12). Then he had a look inside her eyes with an ophthalmoscope and at once the cause of her trouble was clear. The optic nerve heads were swollen and surrounded by flame-shaped patches of free blood. Similar haemorrhages were scattered about on both her retinas and, in addition, he saw the ominous 'cotton-wool' spots, indicating that, already, parts of her retinas had been destroyed. The retinal blood vessels, emerging from the optic nerve in each eye, were irregular and twisted. The whole picture was unmistakable. Mrs Bliss was suffering from severe high blood pressure – a kind known as malignant hypertension – and was at considerable risk from stroke.

'Roll up your sleeve, please,' he said neutrally, reaching for the sphygmomanometer.

As he wrapped the cuff carefully round her upper arm, she said, 'I wondered if it might be blood pressure . . .'

Mrs Bliss's running pressure, between heart beats – the diastolic pressure – was 116 millimeters of mercury, and with each beat of her heart the peak, systolic pressure shot up to an alarming 210.

'Yes,' he said, 'I'm afraid that's the cause of the trouble.'

'Is it bad?'

'Pretty bad. I'll want to get you into hospital right away.'

'To tell you the truth,' she said, 'I'm quite relieved. I've been terribly worried. I'm so glad something is being done.'

Regrettably, there wasn't time to do anything. While the specialist was writing up her admission notes, Mrs Bliss suffered a massive stroke, with complete paralysis down the right side of her body and deep coma. She was taken at once to the intensive care ward, but the coma was rapidly deepening and, as she was being lifted on to the bed, she died.

When the ophthalmologist heard the news, he thought, bitterly, 'Why didn't she come earlier? She could easily have been saved, if she had come sooner.'

But Mrs Bliss was the sort of person who didn't like to trouble anyone, and, right to the end, she was very little trouble.

Airport trolley assaults

A doctor from Israel, writing in the *British Medical Journal*, reported a rise in the incidence of injuries to the Achilles tendon caused by airport trolleys used as weapons of offence. It is not clear from the short paper whether the evidence suggests that Israelis are more pushy than those of other nationalities, nor is it made apparent whether the victims were fellow Israelis or were of other nationalities.

Pincher Martin

Martin's illness was remarkable and it was not surprising that his GP had a problem diagnosing what was wrong. It started with headache, fainting, double vision, mental confusion, palpitations of the heart and a weird hunger that had him eating almost continuously to try to relieve it. These attacks occurred three or four times a year and the results, predictably, were an enormous increase in weight. In the course of a single year, Martin gained sixty pounds.

Gradually matters got worse until, after one particularly severe attack, Martin was admitted to hospital. His condition was extraordinary. The doctors found that even two-hourly high-calorie meals were insufficient to control his attacks and that it was necessary to keep up a continuous intravenous infusion of sugar solution. Investigation of this remarkable state of affairs went ahead but in the meantime another problem arose. Martin's nurses complained that he was always pinching and nudging them. This occurred especially while they were checking his blood pressure and became so annoying that the nurses were always trying to persuade each other to take on the chore.

Their complaint was, of course, taken seriously, and Martin was warned by the physician to behave himself. He was even seen by a psychiatrist. Martin strenuously denied ever having molested the nurses and insisted that he was innocent. He was a religious man, was deeply upset by the accusations, and became very depressed.

At last the explanation for everything was found. Martin had a rare tumour of the pancreas called an insulinoma. This was actually a tumour of the insulin-secreting cells and, during an attack, the levels of insulin in his blood were soaring to astronomical levels. This explained his hunger and appetite and it was also the reason for the uncontrollable and unconscious pinching hand movements.

Martin's insulinoma lay between the body and the tail of his pancreas and there was no particular problem in removing the whole tumour surgically. From that day on, Martin had no further attacks and there were no further complaints from the nurses.

Of pigs and appendicectomy

Some epidemiological research in Finland showed that there was an unaccountably high incidence of operations for appendicitis in people whose work brought them into contact with pigs. This seemingly improbably association was first postulated and then confirmed by Dr Markhu Seuri, a senior lecturer in occupational health at the University of Kuopio.

Dr Seuri knew that *Yersinia* bacteria (of the genus that causes plague) can both cause appendicitis and an inflammation of the intestine that closely simulates appendicitis. He also knew that at least 35 per cent of pigs slaughtered in some parts of Finland were infected with *Yersinia*. So he decided to look into the matter. He compared the surgical fate of a large number of abattoir pig workers and pig farmers with that of a large number of grain or berry farmers. The abattoir workers came off worst and were nearly four times as likely as the grain and berry farmers to have had the operation. The pig farmers were 2.3 times as likely.

Ironically, because of the way *Yersinia* produces symptoms indistinguishable from those of appendicitis, surgeons had no alternative but to operate. A great many of these operations revealed a normal appendix.

The killer – forty years on

The man who proved that smoking was a major killer as a result of causing lung cancer and other diseases was the medical statistician Richard Doll. The most important research conducted by Doll and his colleagues was a major study of 34,439 doctors in 1951 who agreed to take part in a prospective trial and give details of their smoking habits and their health.

About 10,000 of the doctors died during the first twenty years, and another 10,000 died in the second twenty year period. This study, the results of which were published in the *British Medical Journal* in October 1994, showed that smoking substantially increased the risk of developing cancer of the mouth, throat, larynx, gullet, lung, pancreas and bladder; it increased the risk of chronic lung disease, arterial disease, duodenal and gastric ulcer, cirrhosis of the liver and poisoning. Doctors who had stopped smoking before middle age later lost almost all the extra risk they would have incurred had they continued to smoke. Those who stopped in middle age were substantially less at risk than those who went on smoking.

Doll concluded that the published results of the first twenty years of the trial had considerably underestimated the risks of long-term smoking. The second part of the study showed that about half of all regular cigarette smokers would eventually be killed by smoking.

In 1996 the first successful legal action was brought against an American tobacco manufacturer with an award of substantial damages to one of the victims. At the same time public protests against smokers became so vigorous and common that governments – long dependent on tobacco revenues – began to realize that they, too, had a problem on their hands.

DES claim settled for $4 million

DES is diethylstilboestrol, a synthetic female sex hormone that was first produced in 1938 and promoted in the late 1940s. DES appeared under various trade names such as Estrobene, Cyren A, Domestrol, Stilboestroform, Sexocretin, Sebol, Bio-des, and so on. There were at least twenty-eight different trade names for the same preparation. DES was manufactured by many companies and was widely used for many years. It was given by mouth, by intravenous injection, and by vaginal pessaries and creams. It was even included in cosmetics and skin creams sold over the counter.

DES was prescribed for a variety of conditions including oestrogen deficiency, unwanted lactation and a tendency to spontaneous abortion. It was also extensively used in veterinary medicine and in livestock farming for the caponization of chickens and to increase weight gain in young cattle, sheep and pigs. It was used as a contraceptive in dogs.

In 1971 a paper appeared in the *New England Journal of Medicine* linking maternal treatment with stilboestrol and cancer of the vagina in the *daughters* of women who had taken the drug early. Intensive research followed and it was discovered that not only was DES of no value for preventing abortion but that exposure of the foetus at an early stage to this and other synthetic oestrogens could have a number of serious effects on the child after puberty, especially in females. These effects included adverse changes in personality and behaviour; depression and anxiety; menstrual irregularity and infertility; probably excessive pituitary gland secretion of the milk-promoting hormone prolactin; and, worst of all, abnormalities in the womb, cervix and upper vagina including vaginal and cervical cancer. Forty out of sixty women who had been exposed to the drug were found to have a T-shaped womb. These distressing complications occurred in the daughters of women who took DES while they were pregnant. Most of the women who developed cancer were twenty to twenty-five at the time it was detected, but some were younger. The incidence was somewhere between 1 in 1000 and 1 in 10,000. It was also found that DES could produce genital abnormalities, but not cancer, in male offspring of women who took the drug. DES is still used to help to treat certain cancers of the breast and cancers of the prostate gland in men.

In the United States the drug was prohibited for use in pregnancy in 1971. In Britain it was not until 1973 that the Committee on Safety of Medicines advised that it should not be used in pregnancy. By then an estimated two to three million American women had received the drug during pregnancy, and a survey in Britain indicated that about 7500 women had taken it, mainly during the 1950s. The women themselves suffered no significant ill effects but had to wait, sometimes for as long as thirty years, before discovering whether their children were affected. By then, of course, most of those who had had the drug were unable to find out which drug manufacturing firm had supplied it. This made claims for damages difficult, but US courts, sympathetic to the plight of these women, introduced various methods of circumventing this impediment to justice. In America, some women even tried to bring legal actions as the grand-daughters of women who had taken DES, but such actions were deemed inadmissible by the New York Court of Appeals.

Nevertheless legal actions began to succeed. In the case of one woman who made a successful claim against the American drug manufacturer Eli Lilly, the jury awarded $2 million to her and a large sum to her husband. The judge, however, proposed that she should have $200,000 a year for the next fifty-one years – a total of over $20 million. It seemed almost certain that the drug firm would appeal against this award and the case would have dragged on. On 17 October 1991 the woman settled for $4,250,000. This was by far the largest sum paid out for a DES damages claim.

In Holland, where many thousands of affected women had banded together in a society called DES Action to bring claims against eight drug firms, the courts initially insisted on strict proof and these mass claims failed. In 1992, however, the Supreme Court ruled that it was unfair that compensation should be denied because a drug company had ceased to exist or that appellants could not name the company concerned. Following this decision lawyers hoped that every affected woman would receive £37,000. The drug firms were horrified and pointed out that claims of this size would be ruinous and would, at best, seriously interfere with innovative research.

The DES story, like the thalidomide tragedy, underlines the dangers of taking drugs in pregnancy, especially during the early stages when the body organs are only developing and the tissues are most sensitive to damage.

Sargenti takes a belated pasting

Forty years ago a Swiss dentist called Angelo Sargenti developed what he believed was a greatly improved root canal filling. Instead of the generally used gutta percha filling that required three sessions of work to ensure canal sterility, Sargenti produced a paste that was cheaper and, he thought, better. This was a semi-liquid product containing paraformaldehyde that was easier to insert and had the advantage of continuously killing bacteria and rendering any residual tooth pulp inert. A Sargenti paste root filling could be done in one session.

Sargenti paste became very popular with dentists and was widely used. But around 1992 suspicion began to be aroused that all was not well with the Sargenti method. In that year two US state supreme courts ruled against two dentist defendants in lawsuits brought against them for pain and loss of sensation in the face believed to be caused by the Sargenti paste. Paraformaldehyde is a nerve poison and it is possible for the material to leach out of the tooth or to spread into the mandibular canal.

In three widely publicized cases, the dentist's choice of the paste for a root canal filling was deemed to fall below the required standard of care. In one of these the patient had repeatedly complained of numbness of the face and pain, but the dentist failed to remove the paste. In another case damages of £250,000 were awarded against the unfortunate dentist.

In view of the wide use of the material it seems strange that there were so few complaints. The symptoms could be attributable to a poor standard of dental work rather than to the real culprit, but even so it may not be such a bright idea to bury long-term poisons anywhere in the body – even in a hollowed-out tooth.

Trombonist's neck

Albrecht was something of a musical child prodigy with a taste for the more exotic instruments. He could play a Bach five-part fugue on the harpsichord at the age of six and could give a fair rendering of a Mozart horn concerto at seven. But his principal love turned out to be the trombone and before long he was working hard at the few solo concertos that had been written for the instrument, especially the Rimsky-Korsakov, and some of the chamber music.

At the age of thirteen Albrecht suddenly developed a sore throat after playing and this was followed by a painful swelling in his neck. He had difficulty in swallowing and pain when swallowing solids, noisy breathing on exertion and a fever. He was taken to hospital for investigation. A CT scan showed a large mass in the front of his neck that was pushing the windpipe to one side and displacing the large blood vessels of the neck.

At operation, Albrecht was found to have a massive neck abscess full of foul-smelling pus. This was drained and emptied and a course of antibiotics was prescribed. His recovery, which took three or four weeks, was complete. The doctors concluded that Albrecht had produced such high air pressures in his throat that he had caused multiple tiny perforations in the inner wall lining. These had allowed mouth germs to escape into the sterile regions of the neck and set up an infection. Albrecht was advised to give up playing wind instruments.

Video game epilepsy

About one in twenty of the people who suffer from epilepsy can have seizures induced by what are known as photic stimuli – regular, repetitive light flashes. It has been well known for many years that epileptic seizures have been induced by people driving past fence posts or railings through which the sun had been shining. A TV set with unstable vertical hold that produces a rolling image can have the same effect. Disco lights and various striped patterns such as those of venetian blinds or escalators have also been incriminated. Flicker frequencies between ten and thirty per second are most likely to have this effect.

The latest type of photic stimulus to come to medical attention is the video game. By 1994 at least fifty reports of precipitation of an epileptic fit by this means had appeared in medical literature. Subsequent research showed that many more cases were occurring. Most of the people concerned were children and three-quarters of them were boys. The peak incidence was at around age thirteen.

Indeed, there has been some concern that video games can actually *cause* epilepsy. There is little evidence to support this idea and nearly all the cases have occurred in children with a genetically determined sensitivity to flickering light. The suggestion has not, however, been completely ruled out and guidelines have been produced by broadcasting authorities to restrict the use of flashing images and repetitive patterns.

The breast implant affair

The breast is a symbol of female sexuality and desirability, and strong cultural pressures are imposed on women to conform to current notions of the optimum size and shape. These pressures sometimes induce dissatisfaction either in the woman concerned or in her partner or in both. Breasts may displease because they are too small, too pendulous, too large, too heavy or, perhaps most important for those severely affected, lacking in symmetry.

In most cases, the desire is for 'normal' breasts, but, as the normal range of breast configuration is so wide, and the concept arbitrary, plastic surgeons may have a problem. Attempts have actually been made to quantify the matter. An unconsciously hilarious, but quite serious, paper appeared in a surgical journal, in which the author described a breast measurer – a plastic gadget like an enormous, open-ended hypodermic syringe – into which the breast was sucked by pulling back on the piston, so that the volume could be read off on the scale.

There is an enormous demand for surgery to increase the size of the breast and the procedure which brings about this happy outcome is called 'augmentation mammoplasty'. Breast augmentation has a long and painful history. Many previous attempts have been made to amplify female contours and many of them ended in dismal failure. One partially successful attempt was made as early as 1895, when a surgeon transplanted a fatty growth from a woman's leg to fill up a gap left in her breast by the removal of a benign tumour. This prompted further experiments and all sorts of materials were tried, including chunks of normal skin and fat, paraffin oil, ivory shapes and even little glass balls. But the results were not good. Artificial implant material was either rejected, caused horrible abscesses from infection, or migrated embarrassingly. The best that could be said for it was that implanted natural tissue was usually simply absorbed, thereby deflating both the patients' expectations and their breasts.

With the dawn of the plastics era in the 1940s and early 1950s many new materials became available and were tried. Again, there was disappointment. Even spongy plastic implants proved unsatisfactory, often leading to progressive hardening of the breasts from ingrowth of fibrous scar tissue. The use of artificial plastics culminated in a vogue for the injection of liquid silicone. This was used in many patients, but the material could not be relied upon to stay in the right place and other complications occurred, including infection and the formation of cysts and nodules which could not be distinguished, by feel, from cancer. The injection itself was not entirely free from danger. In a few cases the material got into the bloodstream and was swept away to block vital arteries in the lungs. Some patients died. So liquid silicone injections were eventually abandoned.

Silicone rubber, however, is an outstanding material for surgical implants and has been successfully used for all sorts of supporting and structural purposes in many parts of the body. It is used as a standard material for the treatment of retinal detachment and has thoroughly proved itself as safe and stable. The real breakthrough in augmentation mammoplasty came in 1963 with the development of an implant consisting of a silicone rubber capsule loosely filled with a soft silicone jelly. Silicone rubber is very strong and leakage of the jelly is most unlikely. This method proved more satisfactory than any other and has been widely used. Some surgeons, still a little worried about the possibility of leakage of the silicone jelly, modified the implant, filling it with other liquids, such as saline or dextran. There were even implants with a sort of valve in them which allow saline to be injected so that the size of the breast could be adjusted after the operation.

Eventually, the silicone oil-containing silicone rubber bag became the norm, and many millions of women, mostly in the USA, were augmented. The principal manufacturer of these implants was Dow Corning. In the late 1980s and early 1990s reports began to appear that some women who had had breast implants were developing severe adverse reactions, either as a result of a possible leakage of silicone or even to the silicone rubber bag itself. This, of course, excited much media attention. It was alleged that these women were developing autoimmune diseases such as rheumatoid arthritis, systemic lupus erythematosus and scleroderma. These are all serious conditions and aroused great alarm among women who had had silicone implants. They also aroused alarm in the manufacturers of these products.

The American Food and Drug Administration (FDA), the Government agency responsible for maintaining the safety of all such things, were in a real quandary. On the one hand were large numbers of women who wanted to be augmented, large numbers of cosmetic surgeons who wanted their bank balances to be augmented and manufacturers who wanted to continue to enjoy the huge profits resulting from the sale of implants; on the other hand were worried women, worried doctors, the anti-implantation feminist lobby and many lawyers who saw in this situation a magnificent opportunity to augment their incomes.

So the FDA dithered for a time and then eventually decreed

that implantation should be stopped until they had enough real evidence on which to make a decision. Most of the medical experts were advising them that there was no real clinical evidence to prove that these diseases were caused by silicone. Dow Corning behaved very well. In early 1992 they offered to fund thirty laboratory and clinical trials and to set up a national registry of patients with implants. They even offered to pay for removal of the implants from patients who did not have medical insurance, if doctors advised it.

The risk seems to have been greatly exaggerated. By the end of 1992, of the more than a million women who had had implants, only about eighty-eight cases of these conditions had, according to a report in the *Lancet*, been reported. In such a large number of women, it would be natural for some instances of these diseases to occur. By February 1994, however, more than 25,000 women had brought lawsuits against the firms making the implants, especially the unfortunate Dow Corning. These firms were forced to pay over four billion dollars into compensation funds. Saline implants were still allowed.

As a consequence, many women have had their implants removed, probably unnecessarily.

Baby smothered by cat

The idea that a baby might be killed by a cat lying over its face is part of folklore but has been generally dismissed by doctors as nonsense. The *Lancet* of 11 March 1995 reports a case in which this tragic event actually happened.

The report was first published in the *New Zealand Medical Journal* the same year and concerns a three-week-old baby boy who was found in his cot with an adult long-haired cat lying across his face. The baby's skin had turned a bluish tinge, indicating that he had been severely short of oxygen and this had progressed to the stage at which breathing had stopped. Serious obstruction to the air passages is the most critical and urgent emergency of all – far more dangerous than severe bleeding or major injury. In spite of all efforts this baby could not be revived.

It was clear from the post-mortem examination of the body that in his struggle to breathe the baby had inhaled cat fur. Some of this had been drawn into the larynx and there was fur in the baby's mouth. There were other signs indicating suffocation. At the inquest, the coroner accepted, on the medical evidence, that overlying by the cat had been the cause of the baby's death.

Although this seems to have been a most exceptional case, the common tendency to reject all traditional tales as imaginary can have tragic consequences.

French folly over folic for *femmes*

It is now an established fact that the tragedy of spina bifida and other neural tube defects such as absent brain (anencephaly) can be prevented if women take 400 micrograms of folic acid each day before conception and during the first twelve weeks of pregnancy. The experts assure us that 50 to 70 per cent of cases of neural tube defect can be prevented by taking these tiny doses of the vitamin. A scientific explanation of how the folic acid works has recently been provided. It is perfectly harmless and is present in many foodstuffs.

Two to three British babies per 1000 are currently born

with spina bifida or other tube defects and the figure could be reduced by at least half if all women were to take the vitamin. About one American baby per 1000 is born with a neural tube effect. The figures are about the same in France. Britain's Health Education Authority has mounted a campaign to ensure that as many women as possible are aware of these facts and the Americans are sufficiently concerned to have passed laws requiring that folic acid be added to certain grain products including bread.

Unaccountably the French seem unimpressed with these findings. Of 733 women interviewed by midwives in maternity wards in Paris, only three had taken folic acid specifically to prevent neural tube defects. A spokeswoman for the French Ministry of Health said that the incidence of neural tube defects in France was low and that many people in France did not consider that folic acid supplements were necessary because women with a balanced diet were already getting enough.

Varied presentations

Here are two connected tales about a very common condition. They illustrate how the same disorder can manifest itself in quite different ways.

Young Douglas, only fourteen years old, felt terribly tired. For weeks he had been less energetic than normal and often just sat around doing nothing. He knew he should be working for his 'O' levels but he just didn't feel up to it. He had even lost interest in his computer. And his clothes seemed to be hanging loose on him. It was strange, too, how thirsty he seemed to be. One glass of orange was never enough and he was always making himself great mugs of coffee. As a result he was never out of the loo; he even had to get up at night. Once he splashed the leg of his blue pyjamas and the urine had dried leaving a white stain.

One day he returned early from school, feeling really rotten, and was promptly sick. His mother, alarmed, went through to help and noticed a peculiar, sweetish, fruity smell – rather-like nail varnish remover. 'Glue!' she thought. 'He's been sniffing glue.' Douglas was breathing very rapidly and deeply, and when he looked at her as if he didn't recognize her, his mother became seriously alarmed and ran for Douglas's father.

One look was enough for his father. 'I'm taking you to hospital,' he said grimly.

Douglas passed out completely on the way and was carried into the casualty department unconscious. The Casualty officer sniffed his breath.

'Glue?' asked Douglas's mother, anxiously.

The doctor didn't answer. 'Has he been drinking a lot?' he asked.

'Yes. Far more than usual.'

'And passing a lot of urine?'

'Well, he's always in the toilet. I've heard him get up in the night, too.'

The doctor was pushing a needle into a vein in Douglas's arm. 'Do you think he's been losing weight?' he asked.

'Yes, I think so.'

'What is it?' asked Douglas's father. 'Why are you putting up a drip?'

'Just a sec,' said the Casualty officer, adjusting the drip rate, in the chamber below the plastic bottle of saline. He took a narrow strip of paper from a jar and touched the end of it to a drop of blood near the needle in Douglas's arm, looking at his watch as he did so.

Douglas's father started to speak again, but the doctor silenced him with a glance and continued to look at his watch. After a minute, he picked up a wash bottle and carefully washed the blood off the end of the paper strip. Then he blotted it with a tissue and slipped it into a machine on the nearby bench. He stood looking at the read-out for a moment, then turned to Douglas's parents.

'It's diabetic coma,' he said, quietly. 'He's desperately in need of insulin . . . and fluid.' He turned the control on the drip set so that the saline ran more quickly, and began to inject soluble insulin into the plastic tube.

Roughly one young person in every thousand develops this kind of severe diabetes, requiring insulin for treatment. They don't all go into coma, of course, for in most cases it is clear, long before that stage, that something is seriously wrong. Incidentally, the white stain on the trousers of Douglas's pyjamas was caused by sugar. An untreated diabetic passes large quantities of sugar in the urine. Much of this comes from muscle protein that is converted into glucose. This is why diabetics can lose weight rapidly. In the absence of insulin, the body cells can't take up sugar so it accumulates in the blood and passes out in the urine. Body water is rapidly lost and there is a great thirst.

Untreated diabetes results in body fats being used as fuels. This leads to the production of acidic substances known as ketones. These smell like acetone and are very dangerous. It is the ketones that lead to coma. When this happens, insulin is urgently needed to allow the body cells to use the normal fuel – glucose. Once insulin is given, the ketones soon disappear.

Jennifer was forty-seven and had always had a problem with her weight. Her general health was pretty good, on the whole, but for several months she had been feeling exceptionally tired and had been annoyed, and dreadfully embarrassed, by a constant itching down below. The doctor called it 'pruritis' and said he suspected thrush. He had given her some pessaries, but they didn't seem to help. Her periods were irregular, too, and she was beginning to feel that she should ask for a referral to a gynaecologist, when something new came along to worry her.

She had been watching television and trying not to scratch when, to her amazement, the picture and everything else at that end of the room became so blurred that she could not make out any detail at all. Trying not to panic, she picked up the *TV Times* and was surprised, and rather relieved, to find that she could make out the print perfectly clearly, without her reading glasses. She could even make it out with the magazine held only a few inches from her eyes – thing she had not been able to do since she was an adolescent. To calm herself, she took a long swallow from her pint glass of Coca-Cola.

Over the next day or two, Jennifer's vision seemed to vary a little, but distance vision remained very blurred and it was not long before she paid a visit to an optician for an eye test. She thought the optician was very young, but he seemed confident. After shining some lights at her eyes, he put on a trial frame and slotted two lenses into place. 'How's that?' he asked, indicating the test chart at the far end of the room.

'Brilliant!' said Jennifer. 'I can read the bottom line.'

'You're short-sighted,' said the optician. 'You have myopia.'

'But it came on so suddenly. Is that usual?'

The young optician hesitated, then said uneasily, 'These things happen.'

Jennifer chose a nice pair of frames and was told that her glasses would be ready in ten days' time. But within a week her vision had returned to normal and she needed her reading glasses again for close work.

When she went back to the optician and told him that she could now see clearly in the distance, he looked embarrassed and an older man came across and said, 'Shall I see this lady, Peter?' The young man turned pink and went through to the office.

Jennifer's tests were repeated and they confirmed that her distance vision was normal. She felt a bit sorry for the young optician and said, 'I *was* short-sighted. When I came before, I couldn't read the chart – not without the lenses. But now it's quite clear.'

The older man looked closely at her. 'Have you been unusually thirsty recently?' he asked. 'I mean really thirsty?'

'Oh yes! For weeks!' said Jennifer, astonished. 'How on earth did you know?'

'I'm going to give you a note for your GP and I think you should see him as soon as possible. He'll explain it all to you.' He took a green form from a drawer and began to write on it.

'What about the glasses?' asked Jennifer.

'Forget it,' he said. 'You're not going to need them.'

When Jennifer's doctor read the optician's note, the probable connection between her tiredness, itchiness, thrush, visual disturbance and thirst at once became apparent and he sent her through to his nurse so that a sample of urine could be tested.

'Over two per cent of sugar,' reported the nurse.

You may be wondering how the same disease could affect two people so differently. Douglas was losing weight rapidly, while Jennifer remained her usual tubby self. Douglas went into a dangerous coma after only two or three weeks of illness, while Jennifer was able to carry on reasonably well for months. These two people, however, did have one thing in common. When samples of their urine were tested they both contained considerable quantities of the sugar glucose. Now this is quite abnormal. Glucose in the urine, except in very rare cases, must always be regarded as serious. High blood sugar is the hallmark of diabetes and it has a number of undesirable effects. In Jennifer's case, the sugar content of her vaginal area – derived, of course, from the urine – encouraged the growth of the thrush fungus, *Candida*, and this caused the itching.

But the high levels of sugar in her blood had another effect. Some of the sugar got into the lenses inside her eyes, causing water to be drawn into the lenses and making them swell so that they became more powerful. As a result, the only things she could see clearly were close to her, sending out diverging rays for which her stronger internal lenses were appropriate. Short-sighted people wear glasses that weaken the power of the eyes, but this was not what Jennifer needed. Once her diabetes was controlled, she would have no further episodes of 'pseudo-myopia'.

Where to tie the cord

Throughout the ages it has been standard obstetrical practice in the case of boy babies to tie off the umbilical cord some way from the abdominal wall. In the case of girl babies the cord was tied close to the body. By the sixteenth century the origins of this practice seemed to have been lost in the mists of antiquity but it was generally held that leaving the cord long would encourage the male member to grow long also by a sort of process of imitation.

The real reason goes back to ancient times. Anatomical studies show that there is in the baby a cord-like structure that extends from the top of the bladder to the navel. This structure is known as the urachus. The idea held by the ancient physicians was that if the cord was tied off too near the abdominal wall there would be an upward pull on the bladder and hence on the penis, which would grow short. Their advice, therefore was to tie off the cord well away from the body so as to leave the urachus slack and allow the fullest possible development of penile longitude.

On the face of it this seems a more sensible idea than the later superstition but, unfortunately, both ideas are nonsensical. The position of the tie in the cord has no bearing whatsoever on the length of the penis. Modern midwives and obstetricians clamp and cut the cord 1–2 cm from the wall in both sexes.

It may not be generally known outside medical circles that the cord should not be tied until the baby has begun to cry vigorously and pulsation in the cord has stopped. When the baby's lungs expand, about 20 ml of blood are drawn out of the placenta into the baby's circulation. This blood, which represents a significant proportion of the total blood volume, may be lost to the baby if the cord is tied too soon.

Medical letters

Doctors' letters, although usually concise and informative, are often dictated hurriedly, commonly on tape. To compound this, medical secretaries may not always understand the doctors' hasty diction. As a result, grotesqueries may sometimes be committed to paper.

The following extracts were taken from the Internet and illustrate that doctors are not always the most articulate bunch.

'This patient attended with a severe eczematoid rash which I sent over to the dermatologist. Despite treatment, I gather he improved. I could be wrong about this, however, as I can barely read his writing.'

'Mrs Jones had a significant family history: her mother, age fifty-two, is a diabetic. Her father, who is separated, lives with an irritable bowel. Soon after I had done the sigmoidoscopy Mrs Jones went to the toilet and produced a prolapse, which she brought back to the consulting room. I wasn't too pleased about this. However, I thought she could go home. She was followed by a most enterprising male district nurse.'

'This patient slipped on the ice and I gather her legs went in separate directions in early January. She said, however, that she felt too bad to be in the hospital and would come back when she felt better.'

'After comprehensive examination I concluded that this patient has no significant physical disease. For this reason I have advised her to return to you. She denied any exposure to coitus and became pregnant with an IUD.'

'This patient had a well-known surgical condition, the name of which I can never remember when I try to. During the operation, because of his age, I had to speed up considerably for fear of the patient going bad on the table. Happily I was through in time for the ~~golf~~ happily I was through before he actually – no take all that out – regrettably he passed peacefully away in the recovery ward. On a happier note, can you manage eighteen holes next Thursday afternoon?'

'This patient should be watched carefully. She took twelve ibuprofen tablets given her by her dentist with a bizarre suicide note. I understand that the principal marital problem is a teenage daughter. I am pleased to say that the barium enema on the phone was normal.'

'This lady is a thirty-three-year-old widow. It is my feeling at this point in time that she is in need of surgical intervention for the purpose of providing a more definitive diagnostic orientation, and hopefully solution, to the immediate problem that is at hand.'

'This charming lady of German extraction is suffering from the 'und hier' syndrome. Or, as we say in English, 'Here a pain, there a pain, everywhere a pain, pain.'

'I am pleased to say that there is no evidence of endocrinological abnormality. The child will probably be shorter than he wants to be, but if he wanted to be tall he should have picked different parents.'

'This gentleman was delightful to talk to until it came out that I was a psychiatrist. At that point, he became belligerent and markedly hostile and threatened me with grievous bodily harm if I did not immediately leave the ward. For this reason I was unable to form any useful opinion on his mental status.'

'This patient states that he is already too screwed up to try medication. I am not inclined to blame her. It appears that she took uppers and her partner took downers so the relationship did not work out too well.'

Compassion and Dr Cox

Lillian Boyes was a seventy-year-old patient, whose general condition was so desperate and whose pain so terrible that she screamed whenever she was touched. Her doctor, consultant rheumatologist, Nigel Cox, who had looked after her for thirteen years and whom she knew to be a caring and dedicated doctor, promised her that she would not be allowed to suffer terrible pain during the last days of her life. Mrs Boyes' condition had been deteriorating for many months: her arms and legs were ulcerated, her hands and feet were deformed with arthritis and she was suffering from gangrene. She had lost a great deal of weight.

As her condition worsened and her body became unable to

absorb the very large doses of diamorphine needed to control the pain, she pleaded for her life to be ended. Dr Cox was in a terrible quandary because the failure of the diamorphine made it impossible for him to keep his promise. Five days before her death she begged for release and Dr Cox refused. But a few days later, when she was not expected to survive for the rest of the day he gave her a lethal injection of potassium chloride. The lady died peacefully a few minutes after the injection. Dr Cox then made a clear entry in the case-notes, stating what he had done and why. His action was fully supported by Mrs Boyes' two sons.

Some time later, a Roman Catholic nurse saw this entry in the notes and reported the matter to the hospital authorities. The police were called and Dr Cox was arrested. He was indicted for attempted murder of a patient. By then, the body had been cremated and it was impossible for the prosecution to prove that it was the injection that caused her death. Because of this the charge, which would otherwise probably have been murder, was reduced to the lesser one.

At his trial at Winchester Crown Court, Dr Cox freely admitted what he had done. In accordance with the strict letter of the law, the jury was instructed to be guided by Dr Cox's intent rather than by his motives, and after painful deliberation for eight hours they felt they had no choice but to bring in a verdict of guilty. Dr Cox was then convicted and was sentenced to 12 months' imprisonment. The sentence was suspended.

This verdict caused great distress in the court room. Some of the jurors wept. The judge, Mr Justice Ognall, was not unmoved. He said to the jury, 'There are times when, speaking for myself and, I strongly suspect, speaking for all of you, a criminal trial is an almost overwhelming burden.'

The medical profession, too, has its strict rules, and Dr Cox was immediately suspended from duty as a hospital consultant and faced what amounted to a further trial by the General Medical Council. The usual penalty for a doctor following a conviction such as this is to have his name erased from the Medical Register and to be banned from medical practice. Two months later, at the end of November 1992, the General Medical Council found Dr Cox guilty of serious professional misconduct.

Happily, they too were able to exercise compassion. If Dr Cox would acknowledge this, he could, subject to certain conditions, return to work. The President of the GMC told Dr Cox that it was both unlawful and wholly outside a doctor's professional duty to a patient to give a lethal substance with no therapeutic value, whose only purpose was to shorten the patient's life. Dr Cox would have to accept a senior consultant as a 'mentor', and would have to attend a palliative care unit for a time to learn the full range of available techniques.

The Wessex Regional Health authority, who were Dr Cox's employers stated that they took an extremely serious view of the doctor's conduct and the effect it would have on the hospital. The authority wholly supported the action of the nursing sister in reporting the matter, as was her duty under her professional code of conduct.

This tragic case was fully reported in the *British Medical Journal* and the *Lancet* and had the effect of stimulating a great deal of public interest in, and debate over, the subject of euthanasia. It led to the setting up of a Select Committee of the House of Lords which produced a report on euthanasia in February 1994. The report concluded that there was no case for making euthanasia legal and no new legislation was needed. It recommended, however, that the medical colleges and faculties should develop a code of practice for doctors.

Most of the representatives of bodies such as the Home Office, The Department of Health, the British Medical Association, and the Royal College of Nursing, who gave evidence to the committee, were strongly against legalizing voluntary euthanasia. In May 1994 the Government endorsed the findings of the House of Lords' committee.

Superglue

Cyanoacrylate adhesive is remarkable stuff and anyone who has used it is likely to be familiar with the ease with which it will glue human tissue to itself or to anything else. This knowledge was not lost on surgeons and pharmaceutical firms who at once saw the potential of the adhesive as an alternative to more traditional needle-and-thread methods of closing wounds.

In 1989 a paper by David P. Watson, a Guy's Hospital surgeon, appeared in the *British Medical Journal* describing the use of Superglue to close wounds in children's faces and thus spare them the ordeal of stitching. The preparation used was a special medical formulation of cyanoacrylate tissue adhesive, trade name Histoacryl. This was spread as a thin film along one surface of the cleaned wound and the edges held together for thirty seconds. In this paper, Watson reported treating fifty children with excellent results, both surgically and cosmetically. Many other reports of the use of Superglue for surgical purposes have appeared. Ophthalmologists have even used it to keep eyelids closed to protect the cornea and to promote healing of corneal ulcers.

This has not, however, been one-way traffic, and surgeons have had their fair share of having to deal with the results of accidents with the adhesive. The Superglue ampoules have, occasionally, been mistaken for eyedrops or eardrops with distressing results. A seventy-year-old man, for instance, instilled some Superglue into both his ears, having mistaken the bottle for his eardrops. This did not do much to help his hearing. When he was seen in hospital three days later it was found that both external ear canals were filled with completely adherent dried glue. This gentleman had to be very patient; it was four weeks before the last of the glue could be removed using an operating microscope. A boy who used Superglue by mistake, thinking he was using his eyedrops, had his lids firmly glued together and had to be given a general anaesthetic before they could be prised apart.

Happily, nature has provided an answer to the Superglue problem. Skin has an outer dead layer, called the epidermis, which is progressively cast off as new epidermal cells grow and are pushed towards the surface. So if two layers of epidermis are glued together it is only a matter of time – a month at the most – before the glued epidermis detaches spontaneously from the underlying skin layers and all is well.

Stories of Sex and Such

Mr Swinburne's particular fancy

Algernon Charles Swinburne (1837–1909) is no longer so highly regarded as a poet and the excitement over his paganism and 'feverish carnality' has long since died down. He was, however, a talented and scholarly man much of whose literary work still deserves attention. His poetry is remarkable both for its inherent qualities and for its sadomasochistic implications, and it is a pity that much of today's interest in him centres on his special proclivities rather than on his writing.

He was the son of an admiral and the grandson of an Earl and was educated at Eton and Balliol College, Oxford from both of which institutions he was expelled. His removal from Oxford was for some unspecified but 'scandalous' activity. It is unfortunate that he was unable to take a degree; he was a brilliant scholar and later devoted his life to the study of literature and became a notable man of letters and dramatist. After being sent down from Oxford, he showed no inclination to take up a 'respectable' profession so his father provided him with the then substantial income of £400 a year, so enabling him to devote himself to literature.

The young Swinburne was the idol of the rebellious youth of the time for his rejection of normal mid-Victorian values. He was passionately antitheist and wrote strongly rhythmical verse, full of insistent alliteration, melody and pace. He was also an important critic of the English literature of his day and of Shakespeare, Victor Hugo and Ben Jonson.

Swinburne was an uncontrollable seeker after sensation, and from time to time suffered from a kind of manic state that would leave him exhausted. His constant heavy drinking – he is said to have been introduced to brandy by Richard Burton of *Arabian Nights* fame – also led to attacks variously described as 'epileptic' or 'fainting fits'. It was, in those days, more socially acceptable to be epileptic than to be alcoholic. At the age of forty-two he had a severe health crisis but at this point his good friend, a solicitor called Theodore Watts-Dunton, started to take care of him and became a kind of guardian until the end of his life. During his last thirty years Swinburne published thirty-three volumes of poetry, prose and drama.

But it was in his unpublished writings that the real man was revealed. Swinburne was a dedicated masochist, capable of achieving sexual arousal or gratification only by the experience of physical or mental pain or humiliation. Masochism, a term derived from the name of the Austrian novelist Leopold von Sacher-Masoch, (1835–95) is said to result from a partly repressed sense of guilt which inhibits orgasm but which can be assuaged by punishment so that orgasm becomes possible. Be that as it may, Swinburne was certainly impotent with women, but regularly visited a flagellation brothel where he paid prostitutes to flog him, thereby, presumably, achieving some kind of sexual release.

He was obsessively and continuously interested in, and preoccupied with, the infliction of pain. In the British Library there is an amusing but revealing manuscript poem of his called 'The Flogging Block – An Heroic Poem by Rufus Rodworthy Esq.', which starts:

> I sing the Flogging block. Thou red-cheek'd Muse,
> Whose Hand the Blood of smarting Boys imbues,
> Scholastic Dame, revered of State and Church,
> Whose Lords to be have writhed beneath the Birch,
> Thou that canst see, and smile, before they Frown
> A budding Bishop take his breeches down,
> And, tingling at the Terrors of thy Nod,
> A Judge that shall be, stripped to taste the Rod,
> And ere his Brow be ripe for Boys to come
> Birch, Birch entwine the beardless Poet's Bum.

The superficial ambiguity that the poem might be a condemnation of corporal punishment of schoolboys, might have led to its preservation; but much other evidence indicates that his attitude to this was actually one of unqualified approval. Swinburne's taste for flogging was formed at Eton where sadomasochism, conscious or otherwise, was then an important part of the culture. There is reason to suppose that the authorities began to recognize that he had become unnaturally fond of the birch because, in spite of the excellence of his academic performance, his parents were asked to take him away.

After he left, loaded with prizes, he wrote to a fellow pupil, George Powell, to say how much he missed the flogging block and to ask for news of that 'institution' and of those who were currently its *habitués*. This, he said, was always a 'most tenderly interesting topic' – an interest based on a 'common bottom of sympathy'. Powell sent him a used birching rod and a photograph of the flogging block and these were gratefully acknowledged.

All Swinburne's close friends, especially the Pre-Raphaelite Rossetti whom he met at Oxford, were well aware of his masochistic leanings. He was never reticent about these and there are countless references to flagellation in his correspondence. Another of his friends was a rather unsavoury character called Baron Houghton who had a large collection of pornography including all the works of the Marquis de Sade that were then available. These books were lent to Swinburne and, although he was intensely interested in them, his scholarship and judgement soon led him to recognize and clearly state that, as literature, the works of the Marquis were non-starters. Indeed, Swinburne's initial sensitive analysis of these books provides a damning criticism of, and a valuable commentary on, pornography in general.

Unfortunately, this realistic and useful evaluation did not last. Because de Sade's work contains a great deal of description of flagellation, and because of Swinburne's constant preoccupation with the subject, he became fascinated with these negligible works and gradually came to regard de Sade as one of the immortals, and books such as *Justine* as being of high literary value. This extraordinary perversion of judgement illustrates the fragility and arbitrariness of artistic taste and demonstrates how relative it may be to the particular values of the critic.

It is not clear whether Swinburne was homosexual. Two of his close friends were overt and practising homosexual men and there is evidence that he had some naked fun and games with one of them. But it must be remembered that, in those days, although masochism was barely recognized as a serious entity and could be openly joked about, homosexual practices were criminal offences carrying heavy custodial penalties. Men engaging in homosexual intercourse, therefore, had to be extremely guarded both in word and deed; so it may not be surprising that we have no real evidence on this point. Swinburne's letters to one of these men, called Solomon, have disappeared and this man was arrested, convicted and sentenced for indecent behaviour. Later, Solomon tried to blackmail Swinburne but the outcome is unknown. Guy de Maupassant met Swinburne and a friend in Normandy and concluded that they were both homosexual. At Putney, Swinburne became deeply and permanently devoted to a little boy called Bertie, the son of Theodore Watts-Dunton's sister.

It is natural to speculate on the nature of the relationship between Swinburne and Watts-Dunton. Despite all appearances, it is most unlikely that it was an actively homosexual one. Although Watts-Dunton gave up his career as a solicitor to look after Swinburne and attend to his business affairs with publishers, he was himself a literary man and greatly respected Swinburne's status as a man of letters. There is, however, some pretty strong evidence that Swinburne adopted the role of 'fag' in the boarding-school sense and that he was, from time to time, perhaps frequently, allowed the pleasure of being thoroughly beaten.

Throughout the whole of Swinburne's published dramatic and poetical oeuvre, the informed reader will, time and time again, find clear references to masochism. His unpublished work is full of it, as is his correpondence with his intimate friends. The principal medical interest in all this is the way in which, for Swinburne, flagellation became the substitute, physically, mentally, artistically and perhaps even spiritually, for more traditional sex.

The no-joke erection

The Greek god Priapus, the symbol of fertility and sexuality, is usually depicted as having an enormous erect penis. This fanciful notion has been adopted by the medical profession to provide a name for an embarrassing and potentially dangerous condition. Priapism means a prolonged and painful penile erection which, whatever the circumstances that provoked it, is no longer associated with any sexual interest. Priapism results from the failure of the blood to return to the circulation from the spongy columns of the penis. This, of course, normally occurs after the orgasm.

Noel was a very virile young man and on this particular occasion his partner was delighted and astonished with his performance. After a time though, what had been an exciting and pleasurable activity acquired a certain mechanical quality. Finally, Noel desisted and disengaged.

The lady was rather put out by this, especially as she observed that Noel was still apparently capable of further efforts. But Noel soon realized that something was seriously wrong. Excusing himself, he collected some ice cubes from the fridge and made for the bathroom. An hour later, the lady had departed in a pet and Noel was desperate. Fortunately, he was an intelligent young man who recognized that he might be in danger and, with his penis against his belly, made his way by car to the casualty department of the nearest general hospital.

Of course, the casualty department was crowded and he was asked to wait. After half an hour he decided to speak to the sister in charge. She was inclined to be impatient with him, assuming that he was trying to jump the queue. A doctor came out of an examination cubicle, however, while he was trying to explain and overheard something of what he was saying.

'I think this one needs priority, sister,' he said.

Noel was taken to a cubicle and examined. The casualty consultant was called. He was a man of few words.

'How long has the erection lasted?' he asked.

'Oh, it must be nearly three hours now.'

'Too long. We'll have to drain.'

Noel was asked to lie on a trolley. His penis was carefully cleaned with a brown antiseptic fluid and most of the rest of him was covered with sterile towels. The surgeon took an alarmingly wide-bored needle and stuck it into one side of the organ. He did the same on the other side. Blood ran out.

Noel gasped.

'That will take the pressure off the veins, and let the blood out,' said the consultant.

The penis wilted and shrank. The consultant asked his junior to take a history and to refer the case to a GUM specialist. By now Noel was feeling greatly relieved, if a little sore.

'You were lucky,' said the casualty houseman, 'another couple of hours and the blood would have had the consistency of thick oil. We might not have been able to get it out. You could have been in real trouble.'

'I see. Well thanks.'

'If the blood had been allowed to thrombose you would have had permanent loss of erectile function.'

Noel turned pale. 'Will it happen again?' he asked.

A couple of weeks later Noel was discussing his problem with a specialist in genito-urinary medicine.

'But what could cause this awful problem?' he asked.

'Priapism,' said the specialist, 'can happen for a variety of reasons. In some cases there is a disturbance of the nervous control of blood flow to and from the penis due to disease of the spinal cord or brain. In others, blood disorders, such as leukaemia or sickle cell disease may be causing partial clotting of the stagnant blood in the penis, or there may be other disease processes, such as inflammation of the prostate gland, stone in the bladder, or urethritis, which interfere with the normal outflow of blood from the penis.'

'But surely I don't have any of these,' protested Noel.

'No. That's what is especially interesting about your case. All the investigations are negative. You are, I'm happy to say, in perfect health.'

'Maybe I'm too interested in sex . . .' ventured Noel.

'Maybe you are,' said the specialist, 'but there's no way that could cause priapism.'

'Well, that's a relief,' said Noel.

'There is, however, one other possibility,' said the doctor. 'A case of drug-induced priapism was reported in the late 1960s in the *Israel Journal of Medical Science*. Since then, the literature on drug-induced priapism has grown steadily and there are now scores of papers. Most of these cases relate to psychotropic drugs like Largactil, Mesoridazine, Haloperidol and so on. I take it that you are not being treated for schizophrenia or . . .'

'Certainly not!'

'I didn't think so. What about depression?'

'No. There's nothing wrong with me.'

'High blood pressure?'

'No. I'm not having any drug treatment. But there is one thing . . .'

'Yes,' said the specialist, looking at him keenly. 'I recollect a paper in *Urology*, I think it was in 1984, in which a case was described a case of priapism caused by the use of . . .'

'Marijuana?' asked Noel.

'Exactly!' said the doctor. He then proceeded to take a detailed history of Noel's sexual-enhancement practices, making careful notes as he did. 'You will not mind, I trust, if I give the world the benefit of your interesting experience?' he asked, 'I would not, of course, mention your name.'

'Go ahead,' said Noel. 'I take it weed is out?'

'It's your penis,' said the specialist.

The therapy of masterly inactivity

Alfred was a personable young man with a problem. He was not entirely clear in his mind whether the problem arose from his supposed lack of physical attraction or whether he was actually impotent – whatever that meant – or both. But the fact was that, although now twenty-six, he had never had any sort of sexual experience.

The story starts in Dr Pettigrew's practice, towards the end of the afternoon surgery, late one Friday afternoon in summer. Pettigrew was the principal in a two-doctor practice and, at nearly seventy, was coming close to retiring. His second-last patient that afternoon was a very attractive young woman who had come in to have a life insurance medical examination. Pettigrew took her medical history and then said, 'Just pop into the next room, take off all your clothes and jump up on the examination couch. I'll be with you in a minute.'

The young lady went through to the examination room. At that point Pettigrew remembered that he had promised to leave a prescription for another patient with the chemist, a few doors down the High Street. So he quickly checked up on the dosage he had been unable to remember, scribbled the script, tore it off the pad, and went out, telling the receptionist he would be back in a minute.

However, Pettigrew and Carlton-Jones the chemist were old fishing buddies and, as usual, they got chatting. After a quarter of an hour Carlton-Jones said 'I think I'll shut up shop. What do you say to a pint?'

So the two old gentlemen strolled off to the Rose and Crown.

Half an hour later, the medical secretary stopped Dr Pettigrew's assistant, just as he was leaving. 'Oh, Dr Williams, I wonder if you would mind terribly finishing off Dr Pettigrew's list? I'm afraid he popped out . . .' She looked at him meaningfully.

'Oh, really! How many patients are left?'

'Only one. He's called Alfred.' She gave the young doctor her most charming smile. 'Do be a dear. It's so embarrassing.'

The young doctor glanced at his watch. 'Oh, all right,' he said. He looked into Dr Pettigrew's consulting room and saw that it was empty. 'Alfred,' he called.

Alfred took some time to explain his problem, to an increasingly impatient doctor, but eventually the gist of it became apparent.

'OK,' said the doctor, 'we'd better take a look at you. Just go through into the next room, take all your clothes off and jump up on the examination couch.'

Alfred went through.

Dr Williams went out to the receptionist's desk and was just about to pick up the telephone when it rang. The receptionist picked it up and listened.

'It's an emergency,' she said, 'can you get along to Jones the fish. They think he's had a heart attack.'

Dr Williams grabbed the emergency bag and ran out. Within minutes he was in the fishmonger's shop where Jones was lying on the floor, writhing in apparent pain and surrounded by a crowd of sympathetic customers. On the way, however, Dr Williams had remembered what Dr Pettigrew had told him about Jones and so was not particularly surprised to find that none of the fishmonger's symptoms or signs were in the least suggestive of a heart attack. Meanwhile, Dr Williams was acutely conscious of having left a patient unattended to, but supposed that the receptionist would explain to him what had happened.

Indeed, the receptionist had gone into the consulting room and, finding it empty and hearing some noises from the adjoining examination room, had rightly inferred that Alfred would be naked. So she hesitated, then shrugged and went back to her desk.

Eventually, Dr Williams returned, flustered and bad-tempered.

'Dammit,' he said to the receptionist, 'I've still got that chap to examine, and I'm going to miss my train to London for the Royal Society of Medicine meeting.'

Just then the door of the consulting room opened and Alfred came out, holding by the hand a radiant young lady.

'I'm so sorry,' said Dr Williams, looking a little confused, 'I'm afraid I've had to keep you waiting . . .'

'Not at all,' said Alfred. 'The time went like a flash. Oh . . . and, incidentally, my problem seems to have solved itself.'

'Oh good,' said the relieved doctor. 'Then everyone's happy?'

'Ecstatically!' said the young lady.

Menstrual misconceptions

Throughout the ages, menstruation seems to have exerted a peculiar, and usually pejorative, fascination for men. Women, of course, have more sense than to be bothered with superstitious ideas on this subject, but men simply have not been able to leave it alone.

We must, of course, remember that until comparatively recently, no one had the least idea of what menstruation was for. The Renaissance French physician Laurent Joubert (1529–82), whose principal aim in life seems to have been to dispel supersitious ideas about medicine and who was much better informed than most of his contemporaries, stated categorically that menstrual blood was necessary to nourish the sperm (by which he meant seminal fluid) and make it strong enough to form a child. This, he said, was why the menses are known as the 'flowers'. For the flower 'is the preparation for the seed and for the fruit'. Joubert went on to state that women produced more blood than was necessary for their bodies, and that when a woman reached her twelfth year and stopped growing, the superfluous blood accumulated around the womb in preparation for conception and that the excess of it was ejected each month.

Joubert's ideas were, of course, no more than fanciful imagination and illustrate the most advanced views of his time, but they were at least healthy and were in striking contrast to the much more generally held view that menstrual blood was evil. A far more widespread belief than this was that menstruation was the ejection of female *impurities*. Menstrual blood, mucus and shed mucous membrane are, of course, sterile and totally harmless, but primitive men were not to know this. So arose the belief among the ancients, and even among many people today, that a menstruating woman was 'unclean' and had to be shunned. The Roman scientific writer Gaius Secundus Pliny (23–79) a typical pundit who, like many of his kind, believed something was true for no better reason than because he said it, wrote: 'When a menstruating woman approaches, fermenting wine will be soured; seeds she touches become infertile; grass withers; garden plants shrivel; and fruit falls from the trees.' All this without a shred of evidence and in plain contradiction to experience.

Another ancient pundit, the Greek philosopher Aristotle (384–322 BC) asserted that if a menstruating woman looked in a mirror it would lose its polish. Moreover, the next person to look in it would be bewitched. Even Joubert advised strongly against sexual intercourse during menstruation, which he considered 'contrary to good manners' as well as being contrary to the specific prohibition of God as laid down in the book of Leviticus. Joubert dismissed the superstition that children born from intercourse during menstruation would become lepers, but stated that he was against this practice because it was used as a contraceptive measure. Even this remarkably enlightened man, however, could not restrain himself from stating that sex during a menstrual period was a 'foul, indecent and beastly act'.

The Scottish anthropologist, James Frazer (1854–1941), in *The Golden Bough*, relates that among the Australian aborigines, superstition about menstruation was immensely strong. He cites that case of a man who, when he found his wife lying on his blanket during her period, killed her and within two weeks died himself of terror. In this group, menstruating women were forbidden to touch anything that men use. In many cases, menstruating women have been required to segregate themselves during the days of their periods. Sometimes special houses were set aside for the purpose.

Ideas of this come about, and persist, because they produce in men a pleasant sense of superiority over women. Typical of the way in which logic can be perverted by such motives is the case of the man who reported that a tree in Goa withered because a menstrual knapkin had been hung to dry upon it. The cloth was hung; the tree withered; therefore the cloth must have been the cause of the withering. *Post hoc, ergo propter hoc* – one of the commonest of all logical fallacies. No weight at all is given to the evidence of all the trees that did not wither when they were used as sanitary towel wash-lines or all the trees that withered without having towels dried on them. Men will believe what they want to believe and will then manufacture reasons to support their beliefs.

In orthodox Jewish culture women are considered 'unclean' from just before menstruation to seven days after the end of the bleeding. Sexual intercourse is forbidden and a ritual cleansing bath is prescribed. The Muslims have a similar belief. A menstruating woman may not enter a mosque and be allowed to pray. Eastern European traditions are similar. Women who are menstruating and who make butter or bread or spin yarn can cause a wide variety of 'evil consequences'.

Even as late as the fourth decade of the twentieth century doctors were still trying to prove these ridiculous and damaging superstitions. Various trials were conducted and various papers published to show that menstrual blood contained substances called menotoxins. These trials were badly designed and conducted and served more to reveal the authors' prejudices than to contribute to scientific knowledge.

Menstrual superstition is just one more example of the abuse of male power in a male chauvinistic world.

In the light of the physiological facts it does seem rather silly to try to maintain the superstitious nonsense about women being 'unclean' at the time of menstruation. The amazing fact is that two of the great religions of the world appear to be quite unable to see this.

Fecundity

The sixteenth-century French scholar Laurent Joubert relates as a fact the story of Madame de Beauville. This lady had a beautiful servant girl, and Madame suspected that her husband was paying her unseemly attention. So the wife arranged for the girl to be married. Within a year the girl produced triplets. Now Madame de Beauville, in her jealousy, and convinced that her husband must have been implicated, went about slandering the girl and repeatedly stating that a woman could not have more than twin children by one man. Triplets necessarily implied that more than one man must have been involved. Her reason for this assertion was that a man had only two 'stones of generation'. This statement was widely believed and the innocent girl fell into serious disrepute.

But nemesis was at hand. Soon afterwards the lady herself became pregnant and quickly grew to an unprecedented size. Her husband was away hunting when she was delivered and when nine girls were born it was apparent to her that she was in danger of being accused, on the grounds of her own pronouncements, of grave fornication. Terrified, she kept the matter secret from her husband and determined that all but one of the babies should be drowned. This dreadful task she entrusted to a chambermaid.

Happily the husband, returning, came across the chambermaid preparing to drown the babies and rescued them. Saying nothing to their mother, he then arranged for them to be brought up secretly and had them all baptized with the same name – Bourgue – as the baby the mother had kept. A few years later he quietly brought the eight girls, all dressed identically, to his house and hid them in a room adjoining the main chamber. He then arranged for the one remaining daughter to join them.

His wife and all their relatives and friends being assembled, the husband referred to the disgraced girl and encouraged his wife to recount her reasons for believing her to be dishonest. The wife did so with great vehemence. The husband then asked her to call her daughter. All nine, on hearing their name, then came into the room . . .

This delightful story is so full of improbabilities that it has certainly been greatly embellished in the telling. Joubert, however, insists that when he visited Agen in 1577 he saw the remains of a sepulchre to the mother, 'raised on a portal among nine others made for her daughters'.

The vasectomy mystery

Joan and Colin, with three lovely children, had decided that their family was now complete. They had, in fact, planned on a limit of two, but little Colin had insisted on arriving, all the same. The family budget was now tight and they certainly could not afford any more kids.

Colin was a loving, fair-minded man and, in spite of his instinctive shrinking from the idea of surgery, proposed that he should have a vasectomy. Joan, who adored him, was not very keen on the idea either but, knowing that other methods of contraception had let them down, and aware that the last pregnancy had been due to her carelessness with the pill, finally agreed.

The operation was done under local anaesthesia and was much less alarming than Colin had expected. He was aware of a kind of grating sensation at various stages of the procedure, but felt no pain. There was a bit of an ache for a few days afterwards and then he felt fine. Tests done three months and five months after the operation showed that there were no sperms in Colin's seminal fluid. The operation proved a real boost to the couple's sex life. Freed from the worry about pregnancy they felt able to let themselves go and the results were spectacular. Unfortunately, two years after Colin's operation, Joan found she was pregnant.

A confused and worried Colin went to see his doctor and

asked him what actually happened at a vasectomy operation. The doctor explained that the two tubes that carried sperms up from the testicles to the base of the penis were cut right through, and the ends folded back and tied off. This made it impossible for any sperms to get to the penis. When Colin told him that his wife was pregnant there was an awkward silence.

Then the doctor said, 'I see. That's embarrassing ... But I'm not sure what you think I can do about it.'

'Are you suggesting,' asked Colin, 'that I can't be the father?'

The doctor hesitated. 'Well, no,' he said, 'I'm not suggesting that. But I think it would be a good idea for you to have another sperm count test.'

This was immediately arranged, and a week later Colin went back for the result. The doctor looked unhappy. 'Well,' he said, 'there are no moving sperms in the sample.'

'But there were some?' asked Colin.

'Yes. Just a few. But none of them were moving and there were not nearly enough to ...'

'To get Joan pregnant?'

'I'm afraid so. I'm really sorry.'

Colin was devastated. 'So what you're implying is that Joan ...?'

'So it would appear,' said the doctor.

When Colin told Joan what the doctor had said, she was outraged. For the first time since they were married they had a major row. Colin did not openly accuse Joan of infidelity, but insisted that he had to believe in that possibility. Joan was deeply hurt and appeared crushed that he could suppose such a thing. The marriage moved dangerously close to the rocks.

This time Joan went to see the doctor. 'Look here,' she said,

'I *know* that Colin must be the father. There is simply no other possibility. Unless,' she smiled wryly, 'this is an immaculate conception.'

The doctor remained sceptical.

'Isn't there some way,' asked Joan, 'of *proving* that it's Colin's child. What about DNA fingerprinting?'

The doctor was surprised. 'Do you mean that?' he asked, 'Would you really go through DNA tests of paternity?'

'Of course,' said Joan, 'gladly. It has to be Colin's child. And I want it proved.'

The doctor was in no possible doubt that DNA testing would show that someone else was the father, but he could not see how else to get out of his difficulty. 'OK,' he said, 'I'll see if I can arrange it.'

The people at the genetics laboratory were as sceptical as the doctor but agreed that the tests should be done as soon as the baby was born.

'No,' said Joan, 'I'm not waiting that long under suspicion. I want an amniocentesis.'

The doctor was impressed and called a gynaecological colleague. When he had explained the circumstances, the gynaecologist agreed to see Joan. She, too, was impressed by Joan's insistence. She was even more impressed when she met her and decided that the minor operation was justified.

Under ultrasound imaging control she passed a long needle through the front wall of Joan's tummy until it entered the womb. Then she carefully manoeuvred the point into the umbilical cord and drew out a small sample of fetal blood. In this way she was able to obtain white blood cells from the fetus. The nucleus of each white cell contains a complete specimen of the fetal genetic material. The gynaecologist then took some blood from a vein in Joan's arm. Colin provided a sample in the same way.

When they were waiting for the result, Colin was uncharacteristically tense and bad-tempered. But Joan was calm and confident. At no time did she show the smallest hesitation or doubt as to the outcome. Colin could not help being moved by her serenity. Either she was being utterly devious – a trait he had never suspected in her – or she was honest. At last, instead of the expected letter, there was a call from the genetics laboratory. Could they drop in to see the director?

The same day they were ushered into an office full of books and scientific journals, and were asked to sit by a table covered with papers. The director was affable but a little embarrassed.

'This is a very unusual situation,' he began.

'What's the result?' asked Joan.

'We have been at great pains to ensure that there is no mistake,' said the director.

'Good,' said Joan.

'So we have done DNA profile testing with ten single locus DNA probes and analysed seventeen protein polymorphisms. The conventional test results indicated a relative chance of paternity of 94 per cent. But this, combined with the results of the DNA profiling, increases the chance of paternity to over 99.999 per cent.'

'Do you think you could put in plain English?' asked Joan, with barely concealed impatience.

'Sorry,' said the director, and hesitated. 'In simple terms, then, provided there is no question that a . . . close male relative of your husband could be . . . er . . . involved . . .'

'My father died ten years ago,' said Colin, 'I have no brothers, uncles or cousins. My son is only four.'

The director smiled. 'Then I can say with complete certainty . . . you are the father. There can be no doubt about it.'

Two years after his fourth child was born, Colin had another sperm count. It showed no sperms whatsoever.

This case remains an enigma. Medical dogma has long held, with good reason, that men with a sperm count that shows only a few non-motile sperms are sterile. Never before, or since, has it been shown that such a man could father a child. As a result of this case, however, this dogma is no longer unshakeable. One expert in the field went so far as to state that if any sperms of any kind are present, there is a possibility that pregnancy can occur.

Sad fate of US Surgeon General

The second woman and the first African American ever to be appointed to the prestigious post of Surgeon General to the United States of America, Jocelyn Elders, was a lady of the highest qualifications, both academic and personal. Dr Elders joined the US Army at the age of eighteen and trained as a physiotherapist. She then studied medicine, qualified as a doctor, specialized in child care and, in 1976, became Professor of Paediatrics at the University of Arkansas Medical School. In 1987 the then Governor of Arkansas, Bill Clinton, appointed her chief of the Arkansas Department of Health. And when he became President of the USA he nominated her as Surgeon General.

When she took up the highest medical post in the US in September 1993 Surgeon General Elders was determined, unlike some of her predecessors, to be much more than a mere figurehead. Her principal responsibility was the health of the nation and from the outset she saw it as her duty to speak out fearlessly on any issue affecting public health. Fearless speaking can, however, damage your career health, as this lady discovered to her cost.

From the start of her term of office she was, of course, deeply concerned with the problem of AIDS and especially with the sexual behaviour of young people that was putting them at risk of HIV infection. She also took a strong stand on the question of the right of women to choose abortion, and on the attitude of the Roman Catholic Church to abortion and contraception. She was also deeply concerned at the clear evidence linking poor health to poverty and was greatly preoccupied with the problems of violence, guns, drugs and alcoholism.

Surgeon General Elders was, and probably still is, a pragmatist who could see clearly what was required to tackle some of these problems. She recognized that violence was a public health problem and a responsibility of the medical profession. She was seriously anxious about the quality of primary education so far as it related to social and sexual behaviour. She advocated strict control of handguns and the banning of automatic assault weapons. She advocated the issue of free condoms in schools. She pointed out that there was a lobby in America, which she called the 'very religious un-Christian right' who loved babies until they were born and were then against all the things that strengthen families and help children. She told the anti-abortionists to 'get over your love affair with the foetus'.

But, from the start, the forces of unreason were gathering against her and matters came to a head at a United Nations meeting on AIDS in December 1994. At this meeting she was asked whether masturbation should be encouraged so as to reduce promiscuous sex and lower the risks of sexually transmitted diseases such as AIDS. The Surgeon General's reply was measured and careful. She pointed out that masturbation was a part of human sexuality and that it was 'part of something that perhaps should be taught'.

This remark was enough to destroy her. It was relayed to the President and he is reported as having said: 'She must resign.' Allegedly, it was resign or be fired. And resign she did.

Abortion and after

Gelda decided to have an abortion because she felt she needed to maintain her independence and her career. She spoke of the advice her feminist friends had given her and of how they had emphasized her right to organize her life as she saw fit.

'The feminists think it's OK to have an abortion,' she said. 'They tell you that you shouldn't feel anything – that society, with its out-of-date attitudes, put this emotional thing on to you. So I was really surprised when I did start to feel. It came from inside of me. Now, looking back, the political analyses – the things they told me – seem amazingly simplistic. Now that all this has happened, I no longer accept that sort of thing. It's self-denying. I realize how deeply affected I am by my own biology – much more than I wanted to believe. Your biology makes you powerless. When I was pregnant I felt how positive it was to be part of something – I felt it in my guts. I felt less lonely – part of this bigger humanity.'

'After the first abortion I was appalled by the hysteria of the other women in the clinic. I was numb, calm, brave, remote. My man arrived when we were having tea, afterwards. There was a great rush of anger from the other women because *their* men hadn't come. There was a lot of hatred of men, but he busied himself handing round the sandwiches. I was proud of him for being there but we had a fight afterwards. I felt disoriented.'

Gelda had not been aware that she was mourning after her first abortion. But she was quite severely depressed and alienated for many months afterwards. She did not, at first, associate this feeling with the abortion and it was not until after a second abortion, when she was attacked by bouts of uncontrollable weeping, that she realized the connection. It seemed to her that to have an abortion, she must be unfeeling. She was confirmed in her worst fears about herself. She was very attracted towards the child of a friend and wanted one of her own. The second abortion brought so much distress that she realized she was experiencing grief.

'I tried to console myself by embracing a pillow. I wanted to hold a child. I was really surprised at this. I felt as if I had had an amputation. It was a physical need. My father was reading a sexy magazine and I was horrified. I wanted to talk about it but couldn't. Friends couldn't cope. I was crying all the time. I decided to go to the doctor and he sent me to a counselling group. I felt really emotional, withdrawn, unsure of myself, suspicious of people. I didn't want to know people. I rejected everyone. My illusions were all biting the dust. I wanted to go to London to escape back into the past and its illusions. I knew I couldn't do this. I kept making plans, forgetting that times had changed. I read psychology books trying to make sense of it all, trying to get in touch with the unconscious mind. I felt I was in a void, alone. I felt I couldn't create anything.

'For a time, I needed other people to reflect me. With no

reflected image I felt I was nothing. I was living through the image people had of me, but this wasn't really me. The recovery happened in stages. I got a flat and wanted to make a home. There was panic. I wanted to call people, stopped myself, calmed down and felt all right. At first I was completely detached from it all, but now I understand that life is real – I feel closer to the reality of life. I stopped crying. Sometimes, still, I feel very empty.

'A woman said how abortion is like a part of you that dies. Maybe that was what the grief was about. Life is more real now. I can't take it so lightly. You have to stop being a child yourself.'

Curiosities of coitus

Anomalies, oddities and rarities associated with copulation have always exerted a peculiar interest. A report in the *British Medical Journal* on the condition of benign coital headache led me to look into the literature on coital anomalies and curiosities.

Probably the commonest anomalies of coitus are coitus interruptus and coitus reservatus. The former is, of course, practised for contraceptive reasons and involves the complete withdrawal of the penis from the vagina before ejaculation. Havelock Ellis pointed out in 1900 that an early account of this is to be found in the Bible in the story of Onan. Onan's act was not, as is often thought, masturbation, but involved withdrawal before emission.

There is a substantial literature on coitus interruptus, mostly concerned with the alleged harm the practice is said to cause.

Freud's papers on hysteria in 1912 made it clear that he believed that anxiety neurosis in women was often the result of their husbands practising coitus interruptus or coitus reservatus. In 1922, the *International Journal of Psychoanalysis* proclaimed that these practices were particularly harmful to women.

Coitus reservatus, the *karezza* of the Sanskrit and Hindu erotic literature, is sexual intercourse in which, by a technique of deliberate control, ejaculation or complete orgasm is avoided and copulation thereby prolonged. This remarkably sophisticated activity is also sometimes regarded as a contraceptive measure, but to believe this is to carry optimism much too far. Coitus reservatus commonly features small and sometimes imperceptible spillage. It might, though, be regarded as a way of prolonging the orgasm.

Many different physical phenomena have been associated with copulation. There are recorded instances of hiccoughs or of vomiting occurring habitually with each act. More dramatically, severe trembling and even convulsions have been noted at the approach to, and at the moment of, the orgasm. Interestingly, what appear to be convulsions with orgasm have also been reported in birds. There is a report in the *St Louis Medical Journal* of a man who, whenever sexual intercourse was imminent, began to sneeze. It was not necessary for the act to have begun; even erotic thoughts were sometimes enough to bring on a paroxysm of sneezing. Some authors have gone so far as to claim that the lining of the nose is an erectile tissue. Certainly, there is a condition known as 'honeymoon rhinitis' that features constant or frequent running of the nose. This may reasonably be attributed to an increase in the blood supply in the nasal lining as a result of erotic stimuli. So there may be some substance in the view that this tissue can be erectile.

The records of the Boston Society for Medical Improvement contain an account of a remarkable case, reported by a recently married lady, of her husband who, just at the point of orgasm, would invariably lose all sensation in his penis, which became completely numb. Worse still, the numbness was succeeded by a pain, exacerbated so severely by the slightest movement, that it was impossible for him to withdraw. Sometime he had to remain *in situ* for more than an hour. On every occasion it was necessary for him to remain perfectly still until his member was completely flaccid. This case aroused much interest at the time among the local doctors and a number of suggestions were made as to its cause. Most seemed to think that it must be the result of some anomaly of the penile passage, prostate gland or ejaculatory ducts. Unfortunately, there is no record of whether the couple were ever relieved of this distressing misfortune.

The *New England Journal of Medicine* for 10 August 1995 reports a remarkable case of a man who went blind in one eye almost every time he had sexual intercourse. This had occurred on thirty recent occasions, the blindness coming on just before the orgasm. It affected his right eye which dimmed slowly to complete darkness over a period of about thirty seconds. The blindness lasted for three to five minutes and then slowly passed off until full vision was restored. The features of this strange phenomenon, which did not, apparently, discourage the victim from continuing to enjoy sex, strongly suggested that it was caused by a temporary shut-down of the blood supply to the eye. Attempts to provoke the loss of vision by other forms of exertion failed. The drug nifedipine (Adalat), normally used to treat angina pectoris, was, however, completely effective in preventing this extraordinary one-eyed orgasmic blindness.

There are many, usually apocryphal, stories of men getting

stuck while engaged in copulation. Talk of a downward slippage of the pubic bone reveals a lack of anatomical knowledge. This could happen only if there were a severe anomaly of the bony pelvis with failure of fusion of the component parts. Nevertheless, some of these stories are true. The female pelvic floor has two powerful muscles, one on each side, called the levatores ani. The edges of these twin muscles lie on either side of the vagina and, if they go into spasm, can constrict the latter very tightly. A case is reported in the *Archiv für Gynäkologie* in which this mechanism operated so strongly that a man became trapped. So long as the spasm continued it was not only impossible for him to withdraw but it was also impossible for his penis to detumesce. The pressure at the root of the organ blocked the venous return.

Another, very old and rather dubious report of disengagement difficulty was that of one Peter Borellus in a book in Latin entitled *Historiam et observationes medico-physicarum*, published in 1676. Borellus tells the story of a man who rubbed his penis with musk before making love to his wife. The result was that the couple stuck fast and could not separate. Medical attention was required and it was only after a large quantity of water had been injected into the vagina alongside the penis that adhesion gave way and the man was able to come out. Another early writer, Diemerbroeck, claimed that this really was a property of musk.

Spasm of the levatores ani muscles should be distinguished from vaginismus. This is a partly or wholly involuntary rejection of attempted sexual intercourse or gynaecological examination in a woman who may express or feel no emotional disinclination. The response to such an attempt includes straightening the legs, pressing the thighs together, and a tightening up of the muscles in the floor of the pelvis and surrounding the vagina. Such women often claim that their sexual inclinations are strong and all appears normal until actual penetration is tried. The condition thus prevents insertion rather than withdrawal.

Vaginismus tends to affect anxiety-prone women who have never been able to insert a tampon or even a finger into the vagina because of the anticipation of pain. Sometimes there are guilt feelings about sex induced by unimaginative and ignorant childhood teaching. Rarely, vaginismus stems from an earlier traumatic sexual experience or from a history of rape or sexual abuse during childhood. In a few cases, vaginismus is the result of actual disease of the vulva or vagina which causes pain on contact. A full explanation of the causes of vaginismus can be very helpful followed by training in the insertion of vaginal dilators of gradually increasing size. So long as this is tactfully done, the results are usually good.

It is, of course, common knowledge that copulation can be fatal. Like any other activity associated with a considerable rise in pulse rate and blood pressure, coitus can precipitate strokes, heart attacks or the fatal rupture of aneurysms. So far as heart attacks are concerned, though, it should be remembered that clotting of blood in the coronary arteries – coronary thrombosis – is, on the whole *less* rather than more likely during sexual intercourse, when the blood flow through these arteries is rapid. Even so, there are more instances of men dying while making love than is generally supposed. The reason for this is, of course, that the matter is seldom publicized. A number of cases are known in which the body of a prominent person who has died in this way in the company of a woman not officially recognized as his partner has been tactfully moved to a less compromising situation.

Many older writers have attributed death during coitus to excessive sexual activity. Naturally this makes a better story but there is no real reason to suppose that too much sex is dangerous, because nature has a way of preventing overactivity of this kind. Deguise, writing in the *Recueil periodique d'observations de médecine et de chirurgerie*, Paris, 1754, reports a case of a man who, allegedly, killed himself by having sex eighteen times in ten hours. An even less credible case is that recorded by a Dr Cabrolius. This account describes how a man who took an aphrodisiac potion containing a very large dose of cantharides, copulated with his wife eighty-seven times during one night, spilling a great deal of seminal fluid all over the bed. Cabrolius was called to see the man the next day when, he claimed, he was still ejaculating at regular intervals but was in a state of extreme exhaustion and died soon afterwards. Practically speaking it is more likely that the man died from cantharides poisoning than sexual exhaustion. Cantharides is a very dangerous poison, even in small doses, and a large dose would be invariably fatal.

New depths of depravity

A major ethical debate was prompted in medical and legal circles in the United States in 1996 when it was found that a young woman who had been in a persistent vegetative state for ten years was pregnant. She had been seriously injured in a car accident in 1985 at the age of nineteen and had never recovered consciousness. She remained in a coma and required constant close attention. The girl had been moved to a nursing home in February 1995 and in December of that year, it was noted that her abdomen was enlarging. Tests confirmed the pregnancy.

Rape is defined broadly as sexual intercourse without the consent of the woman. Many men have been convicted of rape after taking advantage of a woman asleep or otherwise unable to give consent and this, by any standards, was a case of rape. The ethical argument concerned the continuance of the pregnancy. The girl was a devout Roman Catholic and her parents immediately objected to the proposal by the doctors that the pregnancy should be terminated. They said that their daughter would certainly have refused an abortion. No one was indicted for this rape, but the reports of the case showed that the nursing home concerned had already been criticized by inspectors for numerous other shortcomings. One member of the staff had been charged with sexual abuse of a patient.

The stand taken by the parents in this horrifying case was regarded by many people as admirable and positive. Those who supported them found it hard to see why they should be criticized because they believed it good that some life should come from their daughter. Against that was the opinion that the continuation of the pregnancy offended the natural order and that the child would have to be told how it had come to be born.

Nature fights back

Female sterilization used to be done by removing the womb. Hysterectomy was certainly effective and could be regarded as 100 per cent reliable. Since then, gynaecologists have discovered that it is possible to do all kinds of operations through narrow tubes and optical devices passed into the abdomen and pelvis through tiny 'keyhole' incisions. Laparoscopic surgery has become very popular among both surgeons and patients largely because of the much greater post-operative comfort, shorter convalescence and speed of returning to normal life. Conventional surgery involves a large incision through the abdominal wall, creating a major wound from which the recovery is necessarily slow and painful. One of the most popular applications of laparoscopic methods of surgery was female sterilization by closing off the Fallopian tubes.

But recent evidence suggests that there has been a price to pay for the advantages of the newer methods, at least so far as sterilization is concerned. The Centers for Disease Control in Atlanta, Georgia, are the principal US body concerned with health statistics. They have found, in a large study involving over 10,000 women who were sterilized by Fallopian tube blockage, that about 1 in 50 (2 per cent) subsequently became pregnant. In some cases this occurred as long as ten years after the operation.

It is natural to suppose that certain types of laparoscopic operation were responsible for these failures. There are several different possible procedures. Tubes can be simply tied off with ligatures, or tied and cut through; they can have a segment cut out of each; they can be sealed with electric coagulation; folded up and clipped with a plastic ring, and so on. It was found that some methods were better than others – electric coagulation had the highest failure rate (3.6 per cent) – but the fact is that *all* methods were capable of failing.

Keeping abreast of one's hormones

The development of female breasts in a male is much commoner than is generally supposed. This unfortunate condition is called gynaecomastia – a word derived from the Greek roots *gynaeco* (a woman) and *mastos* (a breast). If one defines gynaecomastia as the presence of breast tissue that can be felt, the condition is almost universal. Up to 90 per cent of all newborn boys have it. This is because of the passage of oestrogens into the fetal blood by way of the placenta. Infantile gynaecomastia soon passes off. There is a second peak incidence around puberty when the hormones are getting busy. This is most marked about the age of thirteen or fourteen. A third peak of incidence occurs between the ages of fifty and eighty.

Many studies have been done to discover just how common this condition really is. Unfortunately the researchers have not agreed on criteria of how big the breast has to be to qualify. As a result, the figures for gynaecomastia occurring around puberty range from 4 per cent to 69 per cent. The lower figure was derived from a study of 3,522 American schoolboys and the criterion was that a disc of breast tissue of 1 cm or more in diameter must be present. Another figure, of 7 per cent, was reported in a study on Turkish schoolboys, the criterion being the presence of firm breast tissue under the ring round the nipple (the areola). The figure of 69 per cent can probably be discounted as this was derived from examination of only 29 boys, 20 of whom were found to have a firm disc of tissue under the areola.

The commonest condition causing the appearance, but not the substance of gynaecomastia is, of course plain obesity. This need not be severe to produce a handsome pair of breasts. Fat is selectively deposited in overweight people and one of the favourite sites is over the pectoral muscles. This appearance is sometimes dignified with the title pseudogynaecomastia. You can tell the difference between this and the real thing by carefully feeling inwards towards the nipple with a gentle pinching action. Real breast tissue has a firm, rubbery consistency and forms a mobile disc centred on the nipple.

Real breast enlargement, of a degree to cause embarrassment and distress, is much less common. There are many well-known causes. Men treated for prostate cancer by castration or by being given oestrogens, while very effective, will inevitably develop gynaecomastia. Certain prescription drugs commonly cause it, including both female and male sex hormone drugs; anabolic steroids; antiandrogen (anti-male hormone) drugs; certain antibiotics especially metronidazole (Flagyl) and ketoconazole; various drugs for heart failure and high blood pressure; some of the sedative drugs, such as diazepam (Valium); phenytoin, used to control epilepsy; tricyclic antidepressant drugs; and some of the anti-ulcer drugs such as cimetidine (Tagamet). Drugs of abuse, such as amphetamines and heroin, can also cause gynaecomastia, as can alcohol.

The most marked cases are those caused by serious hormonal upsets. The adrenal glands can secrete too much oestrogen or there may be a severe drop in the production of male sex hormones.

It is not a good idea to neglect gynaecomastia, unless it is an inevitable result of other medical treatment. Treatment is most likely to be effective during the growth phase of the breast tissue. And if the condition has been present for more than a year, changes occur that make it much less likely to respond to medical, as distinct from surgical, treatment. Various anti-oestrogen drugs can be used to treat gynaecomastia. If all else fails, unwanted male breasts can be removed by a fairly simple surgical operation.

Erection by prescription

Sydney remained remarkably cheerful in spite of his partial paraplegia. He was one of those admirable people who always tried to make the best of things; and the effort he made to make the best of being paralysed in both legs prompted the admiration of all who knew him. Arm-wise he was quite athletic and had a considerable-turn of speed in his special wheelchair. The para-olympics were his goal and he trained hard and regularly.

Sydney's secret sadness was his impotence. This was due to damage to the nerves that controlled the arteries that supplied his penis with blood. His girlfriend kept trying to assure him that she did not mind but Sydney knew better. Finally he decided to see a doctor.

The GP was well up in the management of this kind of impotence and suggested they do a trial of a drug called papaverine. This was a highly effective relaxant of the smooth muscle in the artery walls. The only snag was that it had to be injected directly into the penis. Sydney winced but agreed. The results were spectacular – a full, splendid erection. Sydney immediately decided that the needle prick was a negligible disadvantage compared with his new-found benefit and begged the doctor to let him do the job himself on an as-required basis. The doctor smilingly indicated that this was the usual practice.

So Sydney took his prescription to the pharmacist and went home happy. He thought it best, however, to have a dress rehearsal before the first night, so that evening he gave himself an injection. Unaccountably, he quickly felt very sleepy and before he knew what was happening he was deeply unconscious. Sydney was a man who deserved a bit of luck, and on this occasion he got it. His regular district nurse happened to be passing and, because she rather liked him, thought she would just pop in to see how he was. So she got down the key from its regular place and let herself in.

Half an hour later Sydney was in hospital having treatment with a morphine antagonist drug called naloxone. This soon had the desired effect and Sydney came to life again. When he was once more *compos mentis* his principal concern was to know what had gone wrong. Fortunately the nurse had brought his ampoules and syringes to the hospital and a brief investigation revealed that, although Sydney had been prescribed papaverine, the dispenser had given him a drug with a similar name – papaveretum. This is a natural opium extract containing a concentrated mix of the various alkaloids of opium, including a small percentage of papaverine, and is equivalent to about 50 per cent pure morphine.

This single dose, fortunately, did Sydney little harm and he was not one to get addicted on such a brief acquaintance. The pharmacist had his knuckles duly rapped, the correct stuff was dispensed and everyone, especially Sydney's girlfriend, was very happy.

Lightning strike

A doctor, writing in the *Journal of the Royal Society of Medicine*, recalled that as a young houseman he had been called to the casualty department one stormy evening. A young couple had been brought in after having been struck by lightning which, they said, had stripped them stark naked. They had been sheltering under a tree when a shaft of lightning had suddenly shot down upon them. The doctor's examination revealed no sign of injury and, after reassuring them, sent them home by ambulance wrapped in blankets.

This story is typical of the kind of thing commonly reported of lightning strikes, but a little sceptical caution is called for. Following the precept of the hard-headed Scottish philosopher David Hume, one is inclined, when faced with a highly unlikely story, to consider whether there is an alternative hypothesis which would be easier to believe. Although the electrical current in lightning certainly tends to flow over the surface of the body, the claim that it could actually remove all clothing without inflicting any injury takes a lot of believing. It could do so, presumably, only by burning off the garments! The alternative hypothesis – that the clothes were removed prior to a nearby lightning strike for another purpose and that an explanation for their nakedness was urgently required – would seem adequately to fit Hume's criterion.

The penile pointer

It must not be supposed that doctors are given to superstition. After all, the need for scepticism and for every conclusion to be properly supported by observation or known fact underlies their training. How is it then, that many doctors claim that the penis, as if wishing to assist them in their investigations, always points to the side of the body on which the disease or injury lies?

This extraordinary idea was investigated, in a light-hearted manner, by a group of orthopaedic specialists at Charing Cross Hospital. It seemed to them that the hypothesis might be effectively tested in relation to hip fractures in men – this lesion being close enough to the penis to attract its attention.

Regrettably, the hypothesis was shown to be unfounded. The direction of pointing was to the left in 75 per cent of cases and to the right in 25 per cent. The direction was independent of which hip was fractured. There is, however, another, and more reliable, correlation. The distinguished tailors Gieves and Hawkes confirm that, in cutting the trousers of their very elegant suits they have to allow for dressing to the left in roughly the same proportion of cases.

Breast is best – except in California

Now that we are all enlightened about biology and psychology and know about the health importance of breast feeding and about bonding between mother and baby, there has been a movement in the USA to pass legislation protecting women's rights to breast-feed in public. Several states have gone ahead and done this.

Surprisingly, a bill to provide this right introduced in California has run into trouble. Opponents of the bill described breast-feeding as 'obscene' and the bill was defeated by one vote.

There is evidence that breast-fed babies have, on average, higher IQs than bottle-fed babies. It would be an interesting research project to check whether the Republican party, whose members opposed the measure, had a higher prevalence of bottle-feeding than the Democrats who supported it.

Incredible But True

St Simeon Stylites

So-called because of his extraordinary habit of sitting at the top of a narrow pillar, St Simeon Stylites was an early Christian Syrian ascetic who carried his mortification of the flesh to ridiculous lengths. First he stayed in his cell in the Syrian monastery near Antioch for nine years. Then he spent the next thirty years on top of the seventy-two-foot pillar from which he preached to the crowds who came to benefit from his holiness.

It seems that St Simeon was always on the lookout for new ways to ensure his status in the next life. He bound a rope so tightly around his body that it became embedded in the flesh which was soon deeply ulcerated. Inevitably the resulting sores attracted flies and he was regularly maggoty. For a year he stood on one leg and had an assistant who, when the 'worms' dropped off, carefully put them back in the sores so that the saint could say to them, 'Eat what God has given you.'

Much of the asceticism of these early Christians was based on a near-pathological fear of sex, which was of course, deemed to be sinful. The more it was repressed the more they were liable to lascivious visions. Since many of the anchorites had nothing better to do than to sit around in the desert daydreaming, they were much troubled by these temptations of the devil and went to extraordinary lengths to try to counter them. Keeping clean and fragrant was obviously a spur to sex, so they made a virtue of bodily filthiness. This was regarded by many as a sign of holiness.

Even normal life was hard in those days so for many the promise of future beatitude may have seemed adequate justification for all this unpleasantness. By any reasonable standards, however, such behaviour must be regarded as abnormal.

Wolf children

The legend of Romulus and Remus, founders of Rome is well known, though usually dismissed as pure mythology. However, later research suggests that there may have been some factual basis for the story of the twins who were nourished by a she-wolf. Like many later cases of wolf children, these two were, it seems, remarkably bad-tempered. After deciding to found a new city and then quarrelling over the plans, Romulus murdered his brother Remus. No one seems to have held this against him, and the survivor was drawn up to heaven in a fiery chariot by his father Mars to join the gods, and thereafter was worshipped by the Romans as the god Quirinus.

Most other accounts of wolf children come from India. In 1843, at Chupra in Bengal, a mother was working in a field when her young boy was carried away by a wolf. A year later, at a spot some ten miles away, a wolf was seen, followed by a number of cubs and a strange, ape-like creature. After a long chase in which the creature ran rapidly, apparently on all fours, the oddity was caught and identified as the missing boy. His elbows and knees were densely horny and he would eat nothing but raw meat. He could not be taught to speak but expressed emotion with growls. He never settled down among humans and took every opportunity to try to escape. After seven years he succeeded and disappeared into the forest. He was never seen again.

In another account a large female wolf was seen leaving her den followed by three cubs and a small boy walking on all fours. Attempts were made to catch him but he ran as quickly as the wolf and disappeared into the den with the others. They were then dug out and, in spite of his frantic struggling, the boy was captured. He appeared terrified of adults and tried to attack children. He refused all food except raw meat which he ate like a dog, holding it down on the ground and tearing at it with his teeth.

The issue of March 1888 of the learned journal, *The Zoologist*, contains a reprint of a pamphlet of 1852, citing an account of six cases of boys who had been nurtured by she-wolves in their dens. This account is said to have been written by the celebrated Colonel Sleeman, later Major-General Sir William Sleeman, who was responsible for the suppression of the Thuggi cult in India – an achievement that formed the basis of John Masters' gripping novel *The Deceivers*. In all cases the children would only growl but would not speak. Even one who had been taken by wolves as late as the age of six and who had spoken normally until then, could not be persuaded to speak. They refused to wear clothes even in conditions of extreme cold.

Their elbows and knees were heavily calloused from running on them and they would not touch cooked food but relished raw meat. Locomotion was by elbows and knees with the toes necessarily turned up at right angles to the foot to give purchase on the ground.

A boy was found in the company of wolves in the Etwah district by the river Jumna and was restored to his parents. He never settled but sat howling like a caged animal, especially at night. Once, when chained to a tree near the jungle, he was joined by wolfcubs with whom he played all night with every indication of affection and familiarity. He never spoke and, being kept in captivity, soon died.

Small children are not infrequently taken by wolves and are carried to the den. Most of these children are killed and eaten, but in some cases – perhaps because the animals have already eaten their fill – they survive long enough among the cubs to acquire their scent and for the maternal instincts of the mother wolf to begin to operate. Once hunger has driven the child to copy the cubs and to take to the breast there is no longer any danger that the mother will kill the child.

Modern physiological and neurological research has shown that the personality of the individual is largely determined by his or her early environment. It occasions no surprise to developmental neurologists that wolf children, especially those taken during infancy and nurtured by wolves for a few years, should never talk or be able fully to adapt later to human ways.

It may seem a strange decision, but the available evidence suggests that, in such cases, it may well be best to leave these children with their adopted lupine families.

An enterprising farmer

William was an energetic and highly successful livestock farmer, well up in farming technology and running a profitable and tidy enterprise. Unfortunately, at the very height of his success, when he was beginning to feel that he might risk relaxing a little, he was forced to realize that all was not well with his heart. From time to time he would have attacks of severe palpitations with a very fast pulse and a feeling of such extreme dizziness that he would have to sit down on the ground to prevent himself from falling over.

At first, the attacks occurred infrequently and lasted for only a few minutes. But over the course of a few months they began to come on more often and to last longer. William was a self-reliant man who hated asking for help. He had nothing against doctors but the thought of having to hand over responsibility to someone else for something as important as his health was distressing to him. So he bought a medical book about heart disease and began to puzzle out what he could do. Much of the text was incomprehensible but he was able to make out that he was suffering from something called supraventricular tachycardia. 'Tachycardia' he understood; it meant a very fast pulse. But 'supraventricular' meant nothing. He was also able to work out that the control of the heart beat had something to do with electricity and that occasionally electric shocks were used to put it right.

A week or two after grasping these facts, William was herding some of his cattle out of a grazing field to the byre when he suddenly had a severe attack. He happened at the time to be near the fence and, without a moment's hesitation, he staggered to it and boldly grasped the bare electric wire. He had to let go at once but was gratified to find that the attack had been stopped.

Several times after that William used this convenient method of achieving what the doctors call cardioversion. There came a day, however, when he had an attack so severe that he knew he was on the verge of losing consciousness and probably dying. The electric fence was some yards away but he made for it. Half-way there he fell to the ground. His heart was behaving in an extraordinary manner and he had a strong sense of impending death. How he reached the fence is a wonder. When he did, one hand was in a cow pat and the other was stretched out to the limit so that it only just reached the lower electric wire. He grabbed it. On this occasion, the path of the current was from one hand to the other via the heart. One of the farm hands found him unconscious half an hour later and called an ambulance.

The opinion of the doctors was that he had probably had cardiac arrest, of the kind known as ventricular fibrillation, and that he had succeeded in saving his own life by a do-it-yourself defibrillation. Two more episodes of ventricular fibrillation occurred while he was in hospital and William had to have treatment by more conventional means. A defibrillator machine had to be left at his bedside. Soon, however, definitive treatment was provided, in the form of a special pacemaker, since when he has had no further trouble.

The rat-catcher's remedy

Here is another extraordinary tale of self-help, again with an unexpectedly happy ending.

Livvy was a fifty-nine-year-old rodent control operative and a real expert at her job. She was also an avid reader of popular medical encyclopedias and had acquired a remarkable knowledge of medicine. One summer evening she developed symptoms of faintness and dizziness, most unusual for her, and persuaded herself that she was developing a stroke. Well aware that most strokes were due to clotting of blood in an artery – a thrombosis – and also aware that the principal poison she used to kill rats, warfarin, was an anti-clotting drug – an anticoagulant – Livvy put two and two together and came up with a wet finger dipped into the warfarin powder and sucked.

To her considerable satisfaction the dizzy spells settled and, as far as she was concerned, it was a case of *quod erat demonstrandum*. To prevent any further likelihood of stroke she decided that a daily dose of warfarin was the very thing. A week or two later, however, she was distressed to find that she was bleeding slightly from her rectum. So she went to see her doctor who immediately referred her to a Surgical Outpatient Department.

Rectal bleeding usually means piles but bleeding for the first time in a woman of Livvy's age has to mean cancer of the colon or rectum until proved otherwise. Livvy did try to ask the young surgeon whether it might have anything to do with the warfarin, but a combination of embarrassment and her failure to mention the name of the substance led the doctor to brush aside her extraordinary query as irrelevant. When he carried out the normal routine examination with a steerable fibre-optic endoscope he found that Livvy had an early cancer of the descending colon.

The endoscopic examination was very thorough and showed

no sign of bleeding. The appearances of the tumour, which had not invaded the inner lining of the bowel, were inconsistent with the history of bleeding and the doctors were puzzled. So they took a more detailed history and this time the full truth emerged. It now became apparent that the bleeding was not due to the tumour but to the warfarin.

But for Livvy's extremely dangerous self-treatment, however, the cancer would probably not have been detected for months, during which time it might well have spread dangerously. Livvy had a routine operation in which a segment of colon containing the tumour was removed and the ends joined. She never looked back.

The bacon cure

Myiasis is an unpleasant condition, fortunately almost unknown in Western countries, but not at all uncommon in some of the less advanced parts of the world. It is a form of parasitization with living fly larvae. The larvae of the African *tumbu* fly, for instance, penetrate the skin to produce swellings, each with an opening through which the larva breathes. On maturity, the adult fly emerges. Another fly, the *bot* fly, lays its eggs on a mosquito, which leaves them on human skin while feeding. The larvae then penetrate, producing a painful, itchy spot like a severe mosquito bite. Close inspection may show the tail end of the larva protruding through the skin.

Some fly larvae have the power to penetrate deeply into areas such as the sinuses around the nose and, in the absence of skilled surgical treatment, can cause great destruction to the face. Others may be swallowed and survive in the intestine causing abdominal pain, cramps, vomiting and diarrhoea. Air travel has led to a small increase in the incidence of myiasis in developed countries.

Until recently, myiasis has always been difficult to treat. The usual method was to try to suffocate the larva by sealing off its air tunnel with oil. Often it was then necessary to cut carefully through the skin to gain access to the larvae so that they could be removed. But in 1993 a breakthrough occurred in the Massachusetts General Hospital in Boston, largely as a result of an American tradition that fly larvae are remarkably partial to bacon fat. Dr T. F. Brewer and colleagues, writing in the *Journal of the American Medical Association*, reported that within three hours of the application of small pieces of raw bacon fat the larvae had emerged far enough to allow them to be grabbed with forceps and evicted.

A measure of surgical skill was still required as the larvae, with characteristic suspicion, would withdraw quite quickly into their lairs after the bacon was removed; but if the forceps were held close and the rapid removal of the bacon coordinated with the approach of the instrument the maggot could usually be secured.

An editor in the *Lancet*, commenting on this method, suggested that '. . . the bacon should be discarded after use'.

Antenatal comfort

A new-born baby was found to have blisters on the back of her thumbs. This aroused much medical curiosity and the doctors were gathered around her discussing the possible causes of this strange physical sign when the baby courteously provided the explanation by sticking her thumb in her mouth. The blister was seen to correspond exactly with the position of her upper gum. She had clearly decided to start her thumb-sucking career quite some time before she was born.

Colonic crunch

Physical signs are not the same as symptoms. Signs are objective; symptoms are experienced only by the patient and are subjective. One of the most bizarre physical signs, and possibly one of the rarest, was reported in the *British Journal of Hospital Medicine* in 1993.

A man of ninety-one was admitted to the Accident and Emergency department of a busy London teaching hospital in a state of confusion. When he was examined the most immediately obvious sign was great distention of the abdomen. The skin was tight and drum-like. Careful feeling (palpation) of the abdomen is routine in all such cases. When this was done, the examining doctor was astonished to feel a distinct crunching sensation in the upper abdomen. It was exactly as if there were a bag of granulated sugar inside him.

X-ray showed a markedly widened segment of bowel containing chalky material. Ultrasound scanning showed an obstruction to the bowel consistent with a diagnosis of colonic cancer. At operation, a day or two later, the cancer was confirmed and was found to be virtually blocking the bowel. As a result, the segment of colon above the obstruction had ballooned out markedly and was full of hundreds of small, irregular, stone-like, calcified faecal particles. It was these that were responsible for the crunching sensation on palpation.

A routine operation was performed and in less than two weeks the patient was discharged home, none the worse for his experience.

This case illustrates another interesting point. Calcification is a slow process taking months or years. The bowel obstruction from the cancer must have been present for a very long time. This is often the way with cancers in old people, which are frequently very slow and may never extend outside the site of origin.

Thalidomide is still in use

The thalidomide tragedy thoroughly frightened doctors and for years the drug was completely proscribed. Then it was discovered that it had remarkable powers of controlling and improving a certain form of leprosy known as erythema nodosum leprosum.

When this was discovered, the drug was tried in other similar conditions and it was soon found that thalidomide had considerable value in the treatment of aphthous mouth, genital and anal ulcers. These can occur on their own or as part of the distressing condition of Behçet's disease. Severe mouth and genital ulcers occurring in AIDS also respond very well to thalidomide. Since the discovery, ulcerative colitis has also been treated with thalidomide and found to do well. Quite a range of skin conditions can be effectively treated with the drug. These include post-herpetic pain after shingles, erythema multiforme, discoid lupus erythematosus and pyoderma gangrenosum. Graft-versus-host disease is a serious complication of bone marrow transplantation that can undermine all the efforts of the doctors. Thalidomide was found to have distinctly beneficial effects. Unfortunately about one third of patients suffer severe side effects.

The action of thalidomide is now much better understood. It is a powerful anti-inflammatory drug and has major effects on the functioning of the immune system. It is not without risk as it is capable of damaging nerves, especially sensory nerves. If allowed to go too far, this damage may be permanent, so careful monitoring is necessary. Any woman being treated with thalidomide must, of course, be checked to ensure that she is not pregnant and must be on entirely reliable contraception. Even so, the remote risk of producing severe fetal abnormalities is never taken unless thalidomide is the only drug capable of helping the patient.

A desperate remedy?

Nitroglycerine is a well-known explosive and the basic constituent of dynamite. On its own, it is much too unstable and dangerous to use so it is mixed with kieselguhr, sawdust, or wood pulp – in accordance with the highly profitable formula devised by Alfred Nobel.

Surprisingly, nitroglycerine has been found to be of value as a medication and is widely used by people with angina to relax the coronary arteries, improve the blood supply to the heart and relieve the pain. Naturally, pharmacists and other medical people handling the stuff have to be rather careful. The undiluted compound will readily explode on being tapped or heated and is never stored except in very small quantities. If a solution is allowed to evaporate, a most dangerous situation can arise. For medical purposes, the compound is, of course, greatly diluted.

In trials at King's College Hospital, London, it has been used in the treatment of severe period pains in women (dysmenorrhoea). The drug was administered on adhesive patches applied to the skin. These provided a dose of a few milligrams and the trial was controlled by using placebo patches on the same women in alternate menstrual cycles. It worked.

Main line to gangrene

People who cannot live contentedly without using drugs to change the state of their minds will, apparently, go to almost any lengths to achieve these changes. Here is a story that illustrates this point.

Salvador considered himself of above average intelligence. He was a twenty-three-year-old who had dropped out of university having decided that study was immoral. He had drifted around for a year or two, living on the dole and engaging in petty crime to fuel a heroin habit. He had also found a complaisant GP who seemed unconcerned about signing repeat prescriptions for temazepam capsules, the contents of which Salvador dissolved in tap water and injected intravenously.

Unfortunately for Salvador, the drug manufacturer got on to this widespread practice and started producing the drug in a new gel formulation. When Salvador opened one of the new capsules and saw what had happened, he smiled, thinking this would save him trouble. He had never been particularly worried about sterility but he reckoned that this new form of the drug would not need to be dissolved in water and so would probably be safer.

He found that the gel could be sucked into the syringe most easily with the needle off and that it would pass fairly easily through one of his wider-bore needles. So he sucked up the gel contents of three capsules into the syringe. It was at this point that he encountered a difficulty that had been troubling him increasingly for a few weeks. His veins were beginning to let him down. So many of the accessible veins had become thrombosed and blocked that it was getting to be a problem to find any entry route.

After messing about with arm veins for about ten minutes and getting nowhere, Salvador decided that bolder action was called for. He knew that there was a fairly large artery near the front of the elbow and, sure enough, when he felt carefully for a pulse on the left side he found one and he guided his needle straight in. This turned out to be more painful than he had expected, especially when the point of the needle was passing through the artery wall. There was also a rapidly forming swelling as the blood pulsed out of the vessel. Salvador persisted and soon managed to inject the whole contents of the syringe.

The results were disappointing. Instead of the familiar calming effect, all that happened was that his left hand began to hurt. Soon the pain was unbearable and Salvador crunched up a handful of codeine tablets. These didn't seem to help much so he begged a fix of heroin from a friend and managed to get it into a vein. After that the pain settled a bit and he fell asleep.

When he awoke the next day, his left hand was completely numb. Worse than that, he couldn't move any of his fingers.

He tried to pick up his guitar with his left hand but the hand wouldn't do what he wanted. In fact, it wouldn't do anything. There was no pain, however, and he decided that the best thing to do was to sleep it off and allow nature to do her healing work. So he took three capsules of temazepam, this time by mouth, and achieved the desired effect. He slept for more than a day and, on waking, noted that his hand had turned black.

At this point he panicked and rushed off to the casualty department of his local hospital. Eventually he was seen.

'Sorry, mate,' said the Casualty Officer, 'it's too late to do anything. This is gangrene. The tissues are dead.'

'And how did that happen?' asked Salvador.

'You tell me,' said the doctor.

Salvador thought. 'I guess it must have been that stuff I injected,' he said, 'the gel. It shouldn't be allowed.'

Another doctor came into the cubicle. 'My God,' he said, 'what have you got there?'

'It's another of these temazepam gel cases. That's the third one this week.'

'An arterial injection?'

'Yes.'

'Unbelievable, isn't it?'

'Nothing surprises me any longer,'

Salvador was admitted to hospital and two weeks later his left hand was amputated at the wrist.

Mother knows best

Lilith had wanted a baby for years and now she was sure she was pregnant. Her husband Perce was dubious. It had happened too often and every time she had either been mistaken or she had miscarried spontaneously. But Lilith was absolutely positive. It was more than seven weeks since her last period, but much more importantly than that, she *knew*.

'Don't get your hopes up,' said Perce. 'You know you're always missing periods and it doesn't mean a thing.' He was meaning to be sympathetic but it didn't always come across that way.

Lilith smiled. 'I know,' she said.

A couple of days later she was looking anxious. She had been bleeding slightly and she had pain in the lower abdomen.

Lilith managed to get an appointment with her doctor the same day.

'Well,' said the GP, 'it's what we call a threatened abortion. You really must prepare yourself for the worst. The chances are that you will lose it.'

Lilith wasn't satisfied and went along to the hospital casualty department. Perce went with her. Two hours later she had had an ultrasound scan and was talking to a consultant gynaecologist.

'Look,' he said, 'it could be worse than you think. There's no question but that you are pregnant – '

Lilith smiled.

'But the scan positively shows that there's no fetus in the womb.'

'But that's . . . What do you mean?'

'I'm talking about an ectopic pregnancy. A baby growing outside the womb.'

'Does that matter? I mean, will it be OK?'

'No, it will not. I'm really sorry. An ectopic is a very dangerous situation. The embryo will burrow into anything.

It'll go through blood vessels. You could have massive internal bleeding.'

'So what do you want to do?' asked Lilith.

The procedure is to pass a tube in and take a look,' said the consultant.

'Not likely,' said Lilith. 'you'll kill my little boy. I'm not having it.'

The consultant patiently explained the dangers. 'I've seen women die from untreated ectopics,' he said. 'The real danger is in delay.'

'Come on, love,' said Perce, 'the doctor knows best.'

'Not this time, he doesn't. He's not coming near me. I'm not having that child killed.'

'It's not a child,' said the doctor, 'it's just a lump of very vigorous cells trying to implant itself into some part of your insides. We have to take a look.'

Lilith stood up. 'No, you don't,' she said. 'I'm off. Thanks for telling me about the baby, all the same.'

'Hang on,' said the consultant, 'I'm not taking responsibility for this. You have a right to refuse treatment but I need you to sign a certificate to say I warned you.'

'Come on, love,' said Perce, 'be sensible!'

Neither of them could move her. Lilith signed the disclaimer certificate and went home.

Within a week Lilith was in real trouble. The bleeding had got worse and the pain was terrible. Through it all, however, she remained strangely serene. Smiling mysteriously, she would say, 'My little boy is all right.'

'You're off your head,' said Perce, who was far more worried than he sounded.

Eventually Lilith was persuaded to go back and see the

consultant. He saw her waiting and called her in out of turn.

'Are you going to be sensible?' he asked.

'Yes, she is,' said Perce.

Lilith was admitted, and the same evening had an operation. As the consultant had expected, she was found to have an ectopic pregnancy in one of the Fallopian tubes. Fortunately, it had not yet ruptured but, judging by its size, this would have happened at any moment. The surgeon carefully tied off the tube on either side of the bulge and cut out the affected segment containing the early fetus. There was, of course, no question of saving it.

The next morning the consultant went in to see Lilith, expecting trouble. To his surprise and relief she was calm and smiling. 'Thank you so much,' she said, 'I feel such a lot better. The pain has gone.'

'Good,' said the consultant.

'Now I can settle down and enjoy my pregnancy.'

The consultant's jaw dropped. 'But . . .'

'I'm not mad,' said Lilith, 'and I'm not stupid. I know what you've done. But I also know that my little boy's all right.'

Without a word to Lilith the consultant asked the nurse for a syringe and took some blood from Lilith's arm. Then he said, 'I'm taking this to the lab. Personally.'

Lilith smiled. 'I don't need a pregnancy test,' she said, '*I know.*'

'All the same . . .'

The consultant decided that Lilith should remain in hospital for the time being and two days later he came to see her again.

'Guess what?' he said.

'I don't have to guess.'

'You're spoiling my fun,' said the doctor. 'It's positive, of course.'

'Of course.'

'No "of course" about it. This is practically unheard of. You realize that you are making medical history. You've had an ectopic *and* a normal pregnancy. Only the one in the womb was too small to see on the first ultrasound.'

'I thought it must be that,' said Lilith.

'When you do have your baby, can I write this up for the *British Medical Journal*?'

'Certainly.'

It is hardly necessary to state that thirty-five weeks later Lilith was delivered of a fine, lustily crying baby boy.

Sympathetic sickness

Morning sickness in pregnancy is so well known as hardly to justify mention in a book of this kind. There is an aspect of it, however, that, although almost incredible, is thoroughly well established both by history and by medical research. This phenomenon – morning sickness suffered by the *husband* – was reported as long ago as the sixteenth century by no less an authority than the English philosopher and essayist Francis Bacon (1561–1626), and there have been numerous reports of it by others. It was reported in the *Transactions of the Royal Society* in 1677. In his poetical play *The Country Wife*, the English dramatist William Wycherley (1640–1716) wrote:

'Hows'e'er the kind wife's belly comes to swell
The husband breeds for her and first is ill'

A Dr Hamill, writing in the *Transactions of the Philadelphia Obstetrical Society* and in the *New York Medical Gazette*, both of 1888, reports a case of a man who began to have morning sickness two weeks after his wife missed a period. The wife showed no symptoms whatsoever and was by no means convinced that she was pregnant. During the whole of this time the husband had daily bouts of sickness. In fact, this particular husband had had morning sickness in each of his wife's previous pregnancies and the sickness had always occurred at the same time of day.

A similar case was reported in the *Lancet* in 1878, in which both husband and wife suffered morning sickness at exactly the same time, the disorder beginning and ending simultaneously. The *Dictionnaire des Sciences Médicales* also reports a case in which a man had morning sickness throughout every one of his wife's pregnancies. The remarkable thing about this instance was that the man's father had had exactly the same experience during the pregnancies of the man's mother. At the time, this was taken as unequivocal proof that the condition was hereditary. During World War II many servicemen suffered morning sickness on learning that their wives were pregnant, and some even took to 'eating for two'.

In recent years the condition has become known as the Couvade syndrome. Couvade is an anthropological term describing the custom in certain cultures, dating back at least 2000 years, of treating the husband of a woman giving birth as if it were he who was having the baby. This is not a particularly happy choice of terminology because the couvade is a pure ritual and the husband is expected to act the part. No one imagines that his symptoms are real. In cases of male morning sickness, on the other hand, the symptoms are only too real.

How is one to explain this extraordinary phenomenon? Bacon reported the then extant opinion, without necessarily agreeing with it, that some husbands are so loving and kind that something happens in their own bodies when their wives become pregnant. This view suggests a touching desire on the part of the husband to relieve his wife of distress – a kind of vicarious suffering. But it is by no means certain that the wife derives any great satisfaction from the contemplation of her husband's vomiting, especially if she has to clean up afterwards. Other early suggestions include sympathetic magic; the attempt to expiate a sense of original sin by the husband; male vanity and female submissiveness; natural justice; the desire on the part of the man to possess the child as his own or that of his family; and so on. Some of these theories imply that the condition is fraudulently simulated by the man – a view that is now generally dismissed.

Psychoanalysts and psychopathologists generally have had a field-day with the couvade syndrome. Freud thought it might be an attempt to prove that the man actually was the father of the child. Another psychoanalytic view, typically implausible, was that the husband was really taking pleasure in his wife's suffering but had to repress and conceal this. He could do this most effectively by a dramatic show of sympathy. Some psychologists have suggested that the phenomenon is a manifestation of the man's deep and lifelong envy of the woman's ability to give birth. Others have gone even further and suggested that it is a clear indication of latent homosexuality manifested in 'unconscious feminine reproductive fantasies'.

Empathy is a powerful entity. It is an identification with the emotions and even the physical experiences of others that can be so strong that these emotions and experiences are literally experienced in common. It goes well beyond sympathy. It is worth bearing in mind that emotions and the physiological effects that accompany them are inseparable. Indeed, some researchers believe that the physiological effects *are* the emotions. One cannot feel real rage without having a fast pulse, an increase in respiration rate, flushing of the face, widening of the nostrils, and so on. One cannot feel real fear without a strong sensation in the 'pit of the stomach' that may be so intense as to lead to vomiting. If a man is to share to the full the emotions felt by his beloved partner in early pregnancy, it is to be expected that he may also share her physiological reactions.

Perhaps, in this case, the earliest ideas are the right ones.

A bone in the belly

There is, in the *History of the Royal Academy of Sciences of Paris* for the year 1760, a remarkable account of a seemingly inexplicable phenomenon.

It concerns a Bavarian soldier who died at the age of fifty-one in the Military Hospital in Brussels. He had served for twenty-eight years and had been apparently healthy until the age of fifty when he began to complain of a strange hardness in his belly. This was accompanied by an unexplained inability to urinate which could be relieved by lying down and turning on to his right side. In this position, the urine would flow normally and the bladder could be completely emptied.

The soldier died of an 'inflammatory disease' of unspecified nature and a post-mortem examination was done. To the astonishment of the doctors, they found, lying free in his pelvis, a large bony structure weighing twenty ounces and lodged between the bladder and the back of the pubic bone, a little towards the right side. This bone was 'marbled' and denser and heavier than normal bone. It was enclosed in a thin membrane by which it was hanging down from the apron-like tissue that supports the bowel (the mesentery) and was otherwise freely mobile. This explained the difficulty in urination. When the man was upright, the heavy bone pressed the bladder backwards, kinking the urethra so that it was compressed and closed. When he lay on his right side, the weight moved to the right and away from the bladder, so allowing normal emptying.

The authors of this report were unable to account for the strange structure and, in spite of its appearance, were inclined to doubt whether it actually was bone. When I read the report I was reminded of a case of my own concerning a man in his late forties who, many years before, had, as a schoolboy, suffered a severe injury to his left eye in an explosion in the school chemistry laboratory. When I saw him, the eye was totally blind and felt very hard. It had been persistently inflamed for years and was often painful.

It is an axiom in ophthalmic practice that a blind painful eye should be removed. This point had been put to the patient on a number of occasions by other eye surgeons but he had been reluctant. With a little additional pressure, however, I was able to persuade him. The enucleation was straightforward but I was intrigued by the extraordinary hardness of the eye. This was even more apparent when it was removed. It is not widely known that blind, painful eyes commonly contain a melanomatous tumour. So the first thing I did after I had stitched up the conjunctival membrane and inserted a sterilized artificial eye, was to cut open the eye I had just removed.

The reason for the hardness now became apparent: the whole of the inside of the eye had turned to bone. I was, perhaps, a little less astonished than the soldier's doctors, because my elementary studies in pathology had taught me that a tissue that is the seat of long-persistent inflammation will often calcify and that calcified tissue will sometimes turn to bone. This patient had clearly, years before, had an abscess within his eye. This had calcified and in the fullness of time had ossified.

In the light of this knowledge, the soldier's case is readily explained. The probability is that many years before his death he had suffered an inflammatory disorder in his abdominal cavity. It may be that he had sustained a penetrating wound, perhaps from a bayonet, pike or bullet and had had a leak of intestinal contents into his peritoneal cavity. Such leaks are not necessarily fatal and are sometimes walled off by the peritoneal membrane so that generalized peritonitis does not occur. In such cases an abscess forms in the area. It is even possible that the whole trouble might have stemmed from a ruptured appendix. The attachment to the bowel mesentery, however, suggests that the development was associated with some trouble higher up. Alternatively, he might have developed a rare, benign fatty tumour in the abdomen. Such tumours can also calcify. At first, the abscess would be soft, but gradually, as calcification occurred and bone-forming cells moved into it, the mass of hard material would enlarge until it began to produce symptoms.

Death of a cook

After Johnson had been in OC Medical Reception Station, Johore Bahru, for a few weeks he had a message from the adjutant of the 2nd Tenth Gurkha Rifles. Captain Ffoulks-Jolliffe sent his compliments and asked if he would drop in to see him on a matter of some urgency! So as soon as the morning sick parade was over Johnson went along to Battalion Headquarters.

'Thank you for coming along, doctor. Have a pew. Rather a nasty matter, I'm afraid.'

'What's up?'

'It's 'A' Company *bhanse* – the cook, y' know. Found dead in bed this morning.'

'Oh, bad luck. What have you done with him?'

'Strict orders that no one is to go near. No one to touch a thing till you had seen him.'

'Quite right.'

'But in this weather . . .'

'Quite so. I'd better take a look at him. Do you want to come with me?'

'Rather busy, old boy. Do you mind?'

'Not at all.'

The adjutant called for the Regimental Sergeant Major who summoned the company Sergeant Major to accompany him.

The company cook had been a corporal and had had a small room of his own at the end of a long barrack-room. He was an unusually obese soldier for a Gurkha – indeed he was the first fat Gurkha Johnson had ever seen. Apart from that, there were no signs of external injury or of violence and nothing to indicate the cause of death. So Johnson phoned the pathology department at the British Military Hospital,

Singapore, just across the causeway, and had him sent off in an ambulance.

While waiting for the post-mortem report Johnson thought he should make some enquiries. First he asked the adjutant to send a few of the deceased's friends to him.

'Drawn a bit of a blank there, old boy. It seems cookie had no friends.'

'OK. Let me talk to some chaps who knew him. Anyone who was with him in the corporal's Mess yesterday. I have to find out how he was then. Whether he had been drinking last night. That kind of thing.'

Eventually a small squad of junior NCOs were marched up to the Station. Their response to his questioning – through an interpreter – was strange. Clearly no one was willing to say anything in the least significant about the cook. Johnson knew that the pathologist would expect him to be able to give him some kind of a medical history, but there were no medical notes on the NCO and, so far as he could judge, he had been perfectly normal the day before. He had served up the evening meal entirely as usual and had shown no signs of illness.

Finally, on a sudden suspicion, Johnson asked whether the cook had been popular. To his surprise, as soon as he had asked this question, all the men standing before him stiffened. No one would, however, answer the question.

He called the adjutant. 'I think you should look into this yourself,' he said. 'I've been subjected to a conspiracy of silence. I suspect that dirty work is afoot . . .'

Late that afternoon Johnson had a call from a pathology colonel, 'Well, the fact is that we haven't succeeded in establishing the cause of death. It's a well-nourished body

and entirely free from any form of organic pathology. You
see the problem.'

'Indeed.'

'So? Is there anything in the F Med.4?' He was referring
to the individual's medical envelope in which all the medical
documents were kept.

'I'm afraid not, sir. There's just the F Med 2 and there's
nothing on that. He has never reported sick or been in hospital.
He's had all his jabs and was categorized fit for front-line service
anywhere.'

'When was the last inoculation?'

'About four months ago.'

There was a long silence. Then Johnson said, 'I've asked for
further enquiries to be made here.'

'Aye. Well. Let me know if anything turns up.' He put down
the phone.

A day or two later, rumours began to reach the doctor.

'About that cook – ' said the Warrant Officer II in charge
of the MRS.

'Yes, Q?'

'You did gather, sir, I suppose, that he was the most hated
man in the battalion.'

'Oh really? I had wondered about that.'

'Yes. Don't know how it all started but he was completely
beyond the pale, sir. They say he used to spit in the curry.'

'I see. You're very well informed. Presumably you also know
the cause of death.'

'Oh yes.'

'Come on then. Let's have it.'

The WO II looked straight at the doctor's left ear then said
portentously. 'The Evil Eye, sir.'

'The evil eye. What nonsense is this? An intelligent man like you – '

The WO II was unabashed. 'There are more things in heaven and earth, sir – '

'Quite so. Are you telling me that this was a community psychosomatic homicide.'

'Something of the sort, sir. Only not community. Just the *boksi*. Your counterpart in the battalion.'

'What *do* you mean?'

'The witch doctor, sir.'

Feeling slightly threatened, Johnson decided to pursue the matter no further. A gulf had opened beneath his feet and it seemed to him best to pretend that it wasn't there.

'Thank you Q. That will do.'

Johnson heard nothing more of the case.

Safely pinned

In the days before Elastoplast, a doctor who was tightly bandaging up the chest of a man with a fractured rib once inadvertently passed a safety pin through the man's skin. A month later the patient returned for a checkup and the doctor was horrified to see what he had done.

'Why on earth didn't you say something?' asked the doctor.

'Well, sir, I just thought that was the right thing to do. I assumed it was essential that the bandage shouldn't slip.'

Helen Lanes' immortal cells

Normal body cells can divide and reproduce themselves many times before they decide they have had enough. One way to investigate this is to take a few cells – just by lightly scraping the inside of the mouth with a wooden tongue depressor – and set them out on the surface of a suitable culture material in a flat glass dish, keep them warm in an incubator and let them grow and reproduce. If you do this with the active little cells that make protein, fibroblasts, you will find that they will divide a number of times that depends roughly on the age of the person from whom they were taken. If you take them from a baby they will probably divide about fifty times before they pack up; if you take them from a very old person they might not divide at all, or perhaps just once or twice.

There is a very strange and distressing disease called progeria in which young children grow old prematurely. A child of ten with progeria might look like an old man – with lax, wrinkled skin, sparse grey hair, cataracts and all the other characteristics of old age. If you culture cells for such a child, they just refuse to divide.

A weird feature of this business is what happens when you take cancer cells and culture them. Many types of cancer cell can be cultured very easily. One of the best known in scientific circles is a culture of cells that were taken from a cancer of the cervix many years ago. This culture is named HeLa after Helen Lane, from whom they were taken. The HeLa culture grew so well and so easily and proved to be so useful for all sorts of laboratory purposes that the news soon got around. The HeLa culture spread all over the world and is now used in most laboratories where viruses are grown or cancer studied.

So long as suitable nutrient material is provided HeLa cells grow rapidly, spreading across the surface of the nutrient and heaping up in mounds.

Probably the most extraordinary thing of all is that, like many cultures of cancer cells, HeLa cells are immortal. So long as they are fed and kept free of infections, they simply refuse to die. Of course, HeLa cells are pretty abnormal human cells with a quite different pattern of chromosomes from normal human cells and a much more limited repertoire of functions. They are no good for Dr Frankenstein experiments like making new human beings. But they are certainly very much alive and are all set to go on for ever. There is no theoretical limit to the total amount of HeLa material that could be produced. No one knows for certain how much there is currently in the laboratories of the world but it is certainly substantial.

Scientists have learned a lot about the nature of cancer by studying cultures like the HeLa cell culture and comparing them with cultures of non-cancer cells. One interesting fact is that when normal cells reproduce and get too crowded they stop reproducing. This is called *contact inhibition* and it is, of course, an important factor in preventing excessive tissue growth. Cancer cells, on the other hand, have lost the property of contact inhibition. HeLa cells don't mind being crowded, and are not in the least discouraged by jostling from reproducing themselves. Normal cells in culture need to be anchored to something, so they will only grow in a single layer across the surface of the culture medium. When the surface is covered, growth stops. HeLa cells, on the other hand, are happy to reproduce without anchorage and will heap up on top of one another. This ability to undergo uncontrolled growth is, of course, exactly what makes cancer dangerous.

like. Fair torture. Jist burstin' for a pee and no able to do a thing.'

The doctor tried to amend his expression to one of concerned sympathy. 'Out there on the hills,' he said, 'and not a boogie in sight.'

'No,' said Joseph dryly, glancing at him speculatively, 'so I jist got in the way of using a bit o' paling wire – '

The doctor winced.

'Well, of course, I would rub down the end of the wire on a bit of stone. Get it nice and smooth, ye understand.'

The doctor nodded.

'Worked a treat,' said Joseph. 'Spit on the end and then work it in nice and easy.'

'I'm sure,' said the doctor, 'but what about the snake?'

'I'm coming to that,' said Joseph. 'Well, yesterday I got stappit again and I didna' have my wee bit wire – '

'Don't tell me – ' said the doctor.

'There wisna a fence within miles and I was getting desperate. I didna' know what to do with maself. I was pacin' up and down, real fashed.'

'Then,' said the doctor, 'your eye fell on this snake – '

'Man, ye've got it exactly. It wis a wee adder – '

'Alive?'

'Dead. But fine and flexible. Jist right. Worked pairfectly. Better than the wire. There was jist one snag. It would only go in one way and it wouldna come out. Something to do wi' the scales, ah suppose. So I had to . . .'

'And now you've got a snake in your bladder?'

'Aye. Like I said at the beginning.'

Joseph was taken to X-ray and his diagnosis was confirmed.

There were more people than usual in theatre when the retrieval operation was performed, and a small cheer went up when the adder was pulled out through the abdominal incision on the end of a pair of sponge-holding forceps.

'Enterprising chap,' said the professor of surgery, who had dropped in to observe this unusual case. 'Deserves our best efforts. Do you mind if I scrub up and put in a cystoscope? I'd like to take a look at that stricture. Maybe we can . . .'

Urethral stricture has always been a very difficult surgical problem, but the surgeon was resourceful. The narrowing was triply incised longitudinally and a rubber catheter was left in place to prevent re-closure while the epithelial lining grew sideways to fill the spaces between the cuts. The outer end of the catheter had a little boxwood plug. So whenever Joseph needed to empty his bladder he just pulled out the plug.

A couple of months later Joseph was back on the hills, *sans* catheter and stappit-free. He was duly grateful to the surgeon but was not unmindful of his own ingenuity. As he said to his sheepdog, 'Well, there's no denying he is a cliver man, but he has plenty of tools to work wi'. I wonder how he would manage on a bare hillside without so much as a snake to help him.'

Pinocchio

The story of the little wooden puppet the tip of whose nose grew a little longer every time he told a lie is well known. Such a case has been reported in real life. Not, I must hasten to add, that the growth was associated with prevarication, but the phenomenon was remarkable enough without that.

This three-year-old child had had to put up with a great

deal of teasing because the tip of her nose had been growing progressively longer and more bulbous for a year. She was referred by her family doctor to a plastic surgeon who found that the nasal tip was soft, elongated and covered with skin of normal texture and appearance. Her parents were anxious to have something done before she went to school.

Cosmetic surgeons operating on noses do it all from the inside and this case was no exception. At operation, once the skin had been peeled upwards from the incisions in the nostrils, the surgeon found that the child had a benign tumour of lymph vessels known as a cavernous lymphangioma. This was carefully dissected off the cartilaginous skeleton of the nose, the unneeded extra skin was cut off and the incision closed with catgut. The result was excellent. Had this not been done, there is no reason why the unfortunate child's nose should not have continued to grow.

Nail in the heart

There are many different ways of committing suicide. One of the more unusual ways documented is the use of a nail gun – an industrial device that drives in nails at high speed and with great force. This method was used in 1995 by a thirty-two-year-old man who directed the nail gun at his heart, just to the left of the breastbone. The attempt was not immediately fatal as might have been expected and he was admitted to a hospital emergency room. There it was found that his heart was still beating but that its action was seriously impeded because there was interference with the contraction of the lower chamber on the right side. An X-ray showed the nail, apparently in the heart, but a more accurately localizing echocardiograph showed that it was in fact in the aorta, the massive main artery of the body that springs directly from the heart.

An emergency operation was performed, at which it was confirmed that the nail had indeed passed through the heart, missing the right coronary artery by a hair's breadth and entering the aorta. The right ventricle was virtually nailed to the aorta but the higher pressure blood in the aorta was flowing into the right ventricle, thereby short-circuiting part of the general circulation. After careful consideration of the situation, the surgeon made a small incision and was able to pull out the nail to which were stuck some pieces of the patient's shirt and a large blood clot. At once the normal action of the right ventricle was restored and the man's condition rapidly improved.

A week later, the patient was able to go home. He had had time to think and all the indications were that his mental condition had improved.

The redundant brain?

Everyone knows that we have two cerebral hemispheres that largely duplicate each other. They are not, of course, identical because each has its special emphasis. In right-handed people, the left side of the brain is concerned with speech, writing and other verbal skills and the right side with more creative functions. The right hemisphere controls the left side of the body and the left hemisphere the right. The nerve fibres running to and from the spinal cord cross over to the opposite side at the top.

An American boy, whom we will call Homer, was born with a

severe abnormality of blood vessels in his brain that so affected his left hemisphere that he was hardly able to speak at all. The best he could do was to say 'mama'. There was no question of him ever being able to communicate intelligibly in speech. The arterio-venous abnormality – the Sturge-Weber syndrome – was also triggering off severe motor discharges so that the unfortunate boy was having regular epileptic seizures. It was clear that Homer's left brain was not much good to him and, after lengthy investigation and considerations, Homer's doctors decided that it should be removed. Homer was then eight.

The results were almost incredible. Soon after the operation Homer began to speak exactly like an infant. He started by uttering single words, then phrases, then sentences. It was clear that he was having to learn to speak in the same way as a toddler has to learn. By the time Homer was ten he was able to speak like a normal eight-year-old. Today, although his speech is not quite up to that of the average adult, teenager Homer's ability with language is better than would have been expected from him had the whole of his brain been entirely normal. The possibility of this happening would have been dismissed as nonsense by almost all neuro-physiologists a year or two ago, who would then have insisted that the brain always loses its ability to learn anything as fundamental as speech by about the age of seven. It would appear that even half a brain has more tricks up its sleeve than are dreamt of in the medical profession's philosophy.

There is, unfortunately, a negative side to this extraordinary case. Because the left side of the brain controls the right side of the body, Homer will remain permanently paralysed, and without sensation, on his right side.

Bits in the brain

Medical literature contains numerous references to foreign bodies in the brain and it seems that this remarkable organ, for all its complexity, is strangely tolerant to such intrusion.

A post-mortem examination of the brain of a Viennese man revealed a rusty iron nail. The man had been epileptic and the only incident in which he could have acquired this foreign body dated from his childhood. Another unexpected post-mortem finding was that of part of a knife blade projecting a full inch into the brain. There was no sign of a wound either in the soft tissues or in the bone and it was therefore concluded that the blade must have been driven in during childhood before the sutures of the skull had closed. The metal was corroded and blackened and was surrounded by a sheath of fibrous scar tissue half an inch thick. This was the way the brain had protected itself. The surrounding brain substance appeared entirely normal.

Other foreign bodies known to have been acquired by the brain, without obvious ill effect, include ice picks, skewers, slate pencils, wooden pencils, ball point pens, arrow heads and even crowbars. There are many reports of safely retained bullets in the brain. Any number of hand gun and rifle slugs of all calibres, shapes and sizes are currently being carried around in the brains of seemingly unaffected people. Indeed, reports of such cases date from the beginning of the use of firearms. It has to be said, however, that these surviving cases represent a very small minority of gunshot wounds of the brain, most of which are fatal, usually from involvement of the major blood vessels and internal bleeding.

Some of the reports mentioned clearly indicate that the

brain substance was not actually involved. There is an old report of a prostitute who, in a drunken affray, had a long thin knife driven into her head. She appeared to suffer no permanent ill effects and when she died years later from fever a large piece of knife was found lying between the inside of the skull and the dura mater covering of the brain. The dura is a tough fibrous membrane, the outer of the three layers of the meninges. Although the metal must have indented the soft brain substance in this case, there was probably no direct contact between the two.

A similar report is that of a Greek soldier who was wounded in the temple by a dart at the siege of Colchis and was captured and enslaved for twenty years. Five years after being freed he had a great fit of sneezing and discharged from his nose the long iron point of the dart. In this case, if it is to be believed, the metal probably migrated from its point of entry round and under the brain and broke though the thin perforated plate on the roof of the nose through which the olfactory nerve fibres pass. If all this is true, the loss of the sense of smell would have been the least of this man's worries. Along with the dart would have come cerebrospinal fluid and it would be only a matter of time before he developed an almost certainly fatal meningitis.

Surgeons

Self-surgery

Surgery is a job calling for close concentration and a total
absence of distraction. In most cases these requirements are
easily achieved, but there is one rather rare form of surgery in
which it is hard to see how the surgeon is able to focus all his
or her attention on the task, and that is surgery in which the
surgeon is also the patient. Of necessity, self-surgery precludes
the use of either general anaesthesia or any other ameliorative
measure, such as half a bottle of brandy, that might tend to
reduce the level of surgical skill. Effective local anaesthesia
by injection was unknown until the properties of cocaine were
discovered in 1884. Before that, notable self-surgeons really
had a hard time.

Incidentally, self-surgery should not be confused with self-
mutilation; this story deals with known cases in which people
have felt obliged to operate on themselves because no other
help was available, or possibly because they didn't trust anyone
else to do it properly.

Throughout the ages men have suffered agony from stones

that form in the bladder. Until modern times, the only resource to relieve these frequent episodes of recurrent pain was the operation of lithotomy, or 'cutting for the stone'. This was a crude but speedy procedure in which a very deep incision is made in the perineum in front of the anus and behind the root of the scrotum. This incision must penetrate so deeply that it is continued right up through the base of the bladder, and it must be wide enough to allow a free gush of urine that will, hopefully, carry out the stone, which could be very large. The operation is performed in what is still called the 'lithotomy position', with the patient lying on his back, knees drawn up and feet wide apart.

Millions of men have undergone lithotomy without anaesthesia but usually with the assistance of alcohol or opium. Auto-lithotomy has been reported by various early writers including Nicolas Tulp, the surgeon immortalized in Rembrandt's famous picture *The Anatomy Lesson*, and in the case of a surgeon in the French Royal Guard, Monsieur Clever de Maldigny, who performed lithotomy on himself with the assistance only of a mirror. De Maldigny achieved the desired urinary flush through the incision and was gratified to find stones in the dish. He then swabbed the wound with lint and a soothing lotion and, relieved of the pain of the stone, fell into a deep sleep. The next day he was right as rain and, apparently, never looked back.

Another hero of the lithotomy was a retired draper who had suffered from the stone for twenty years until, in 1872, he had decided to do something about it. The very unusual feature of this case was that this man had, as a youth, fallen down a well and landed across an iron bar, causing a deep wound in his perineum. So it was not particularly difficult for him to push a sharp chisel through the small opening in his perineum and try to chip some bits off the stone. He was able to get about an ounce off it but this caused so much pain that he decided to call a surgeon. The horrified doctor hurried off to get his lithotomy forceps and while he was absent the patient strode up and down the room in agony. Before the surgeon returned, however, an enormous stone burst through the perineum, fell to the floor and broke in two. The total weight of stone of which he was thus relieved, was 14^1/$_2$ ounces. Its longest dimension over 10^1/$_2$ inches. The draper made a good recovery and lived for another eleven years.

One of the most remarkable recorded instances of self-surgery concerns Caesarean section. This was documented by one Thomas Cowley in the *London Medical Journal* in 1785. Cowley related how a negro woman who, after prolonged labour and unable to tolerate the pain any longer, took a sharp knife and made an incision in her lower abdomen so deep that it opened the womb and even injured the baby's buttocks. She then extracted the baby and placenta. Unable to proceed further, she was then sewn up by a horse-doctor. There is no indication of the fate of the woman but it is likely that she died from infection.

A Dr Barker, writing in the *New York Medical Journal* in 1830, describes the case of a pregnant woman who, to spite her husband who had been abusing her, cut open her abdomen with a weaver's knife. When Dr Barker arrived she was drenched in blood and was moribund. He extracted a dead baby and bandaged up the wound, but the woman died two days later.

In another case, reported in the *Lancet* in 1884 by a Dr Madigan, a woman, pregnant for the seventh time, used an open razor to make a five-inch vertical incision in her abdomen and womb and brought out a male child. The incision was elegantly made, presumably by pure chance, and there was hardly any bleeding. Unfortunately, her friends panicked and instead of sending for a doctor or a midwife, wasted three hours looking for a clergyman. By the time medical help arrived, the baby, with the placenta, was lying dead by her side.

Perhaps the most horrible case of this kind was reported in a *Milan Hospital Gazette* in 1886 by two Italian doctors Serpieri and Baliva. It concerned a young unmarried servant girl at full term who, at dawn one day, cut through her abdominal wall with a kitchen knife. She then opened the womb and tried to pull out the baby. This proved difficult and she managed only to pull out an arm. So she cut this off. Still unable to extract the infant she then cut off its head and, after that, was able to empty the womb completely. To close the incisions she bound a bandage tightly round her body, got dressed and, having hidden the dismembered baby and the placenta in a straw mattress, went about her domestic duties.

This remarkably stoical woman then travelled to a city some hours' journey away, taking with her a blood-stained cloth which she showed to her suspicious sister purporting it to be menstrual blood and a proof that she was not pregnant. Having walked back, taking five hours, she became ill, vomited and fainted. The doctors were called and, on examining the girl, found that most of her intestines were protruding through the wound. These were cleansed and the abdominal cavity was washed out and the wounds closed. Extraordinarily, this woman survived.

The Cooke indictment

On 22 March 1827, the Exeter surgeon William Cooke appeared as defendant before Mr Justice Park at Devon Assize Court charged with two offences: the felony of stealing the grave clothes of a corpse; and, a lesser offence, the misdemeanour of stealing the body. The co-defendant, Mr Giles Yarde, was a gravedigger.

The terms of the indictment were that Cooke, having required a body for the purposes of giving a public demonstration of anatomy and having failed to acquire one by more orthodox means, had approached Yarde and requested his assistance. The result of this conversation was that Yarde had, during the night of 8–9 November 1826, opened the grave of one Elizabeth Taylor who had been buried on 8 November and abstracted the corpse.

The prosecution quickly established that Cooke had not actually participated in this unpleasant activity.

It was an open and shut case and the jury was not out long. Both Cooke and Yarde were found guilty. Cooke was allowed bail and was sent for sentencing by Mr Justice Bayley at the King's Bench Division in London where he appeared two months later. Professional colleagues confirmed that he was a distinguished member of the College of Surgeons, and commended his surgical abilities and his kindness to patients.

Here Cooke spoke for himself. 'My Lord, a knowledge of anatomy is the basis of all scientific surgery. Anatomy can be learned only by dissection, and for that purpose, cadavers are required. While I have been, of course, profoundly distressed at the pain caused to the relatives of Elizabeth Taylor, I have to say that it was never my intention that they should ever know what had happened. This deceased lady could have benefited science and humanity and no one a whit the wiser had it not been for the incompetence or idleness of the gravedigger Yarde. I am not a rich man. I have no reserve of capital. My unfortunate wife and unhappy children are wholly dependent on me for support. If you send me to prison, they will starve.'

Mr Justice Bayley seems to have been impressed by this appeal and saw his way to temper justice with mercy. He decided against imprisonment and fined Cooke £100. Pending payment of the fine, Cooke was to be detained in the Marshalsea. The *Lancet* of 26 May 1827 contained an account of this affair and a remarkably outspoken leading article. Here is an extract from it:

'Had Mr Cooke, from a lack of surgical skill, rendered these prosecutors or any of their relatives the victims of injury or deformity, how loud and bitter would have been their complaints! how vigorously would they have sought for heavy damages, and have punished him for his want of skill! while they now punish him for endeavouring to possess and communicate it! The cant, of which we hear so much on these occasions, about attachment, respect, and veneration for the dead, (as respects the animal frame), is truly despicable, mere undertaker's sentimentality. No one more sacredly respects the memory of the moral reputation of our departed brethren than ourselves; and we are at a loss to discover how respect can be more effectually displayed towards the deceased than by removal to the dissecting-rooms. A plan similar to this is adopted in Paris, where subjects are always procurable in the medical schools, at from two to six francs each.

Our present law relating to this subject is so truly disgraceful and injurious, and the difficulties that beset the teachers of anatomy so numerous and perplexing that we think it advisable that a public meeting of the profession should be held as soon as possible, for the purpose of petitioning Parliament for an Act to render it legal to remove to the dissecting rooms all unclaimed dead bodies from either public or private institutions. We believe that such a measure would receive the strenuous support of our present enlightened government.'

In spite of this kind of support, Dr Cooke had to remain in the Marshalsea debtors' prison until November when a subscription fund, set up by the *Lancet*, had raised enough money to release him.

That is one version of the case, but it is by no means the whole story. The fact is that Cooke wanted the body, not to demonstrate anatomy to medical students or other doctors, but for a demonstration to the general public. He had inserted an advert in the *Exeter Flying Post* of 29 June 1826 announcing his intention of delivering a course of lectures on anatomy for the purpose of '. . . the development of those leading features of the science with which it concerns every gentleman to be acquainted, as a branch of general education. The lectures will be gratuitous . . .'

It is hard to imagine what purpose Cooke must have had in delivering free lectures on anatomy other than to promote his own reputation as a surgeon.

The campaign by the *Lancet* met with little encouragement from the 'enlightened government' and it was not until after other prosecutions for body-snatching, including the notorious

Burke and Hare case, that the Anatomy Act of 1832 was passed, allowing unclaimed bodies to be used for dissection.

Subjects or objects

There is a tendency for busy (or insensitive) doctors to refer to patients in terms of their disease or of the affected part: 'Sister, the colostomy in bed three needs a sleeping pill.' Or, 'The hernia in bed seven is breaking down. Could you give it a Eusol soak?' A busy surgeon in the Outpatient Department, on the phone to the X-ray Department, might say: 'I'm sending you a femur. There's also a hand. Oh, and there are three collar bones waiting. Can you do them this afternoon?'

Some doctors have been known to carry this principle to extreme lengths. One well-known British surgeon of the old school is reputed to have said, while operating, 'Sister, this patient has died. Bring me another.'

A Bedouin beauty

During the whole of 1970, Richardson, on secondment from the army, worked in the St John Ophthalmic Hospital in Jerusalem. For most of the time there were only three other doctors and the workload was heavy. Between them they saw about 65,000 patients during that year, all of them Arabs. Many were desert Bedouin. Some days in the summer they had as many as 500 patients to see, so they were not particularly patient with the garrulous or the uncooperative and their tempers tended to run short. There was no air-conditioning and the crowded outpatient department was hot and very noisy. Each of the doctors sat at a white-painted desk at the side of which was one chair for the patient. There was an Arab nurse at each desk. To try to maintain discipline and keep down noise it was the rule that adult patients were brought to the desks one at a time. Otherwise they would have whole families crowding round with several people trying to explain what was wrong.

One day, towards the end of Richardson's year there, three or four men came up to his desk escorting a young woman. They were all in black robes. The woman's face was entirely covered except for a narrow slit between her head-dress and a fold of her robe. 'Tell them to clear off.' he said to the nurse.

'They will not go, doctor,' she said, 'they are very jealous of the girl.'

'OK. Next patient, please,' said Richardson, waving them away.

The four went off into a corner to discuss the situation. When he had seen the next patient they came back. 'They say the Hakim can talk to the girl,' translated the nurse, 'but they must stand close. The Hakim must not remove her veil.'

Eventually he succeeded in getting the girl to sit down leaving the relatives in the corner of the room. 'Ask her to take off her veil,' he said.

'You cannot do that, doctor,' said the nurse, 'they will not allow it.'

'Get Abu Achmad,' said Richardson. Abu was the senior nurse who ran the treatment room. He was very experienced and wise. Richardson explained the difficulty and Abu took them all away, returning in half an hour. The girl now agreed to sit down by the desk and, with lowered eyes, unfastened her veil. Richardson was astonished. She was stunningly beautiful.

With an effort he collected his thoughts and asked her what was troubling her. She explained that she was continually seeing bright flashing lights in her left eye. A quick examination showed that she had a rare condition known as pathological or malignant myopia. Her eyes were enormous and, in consequence, she was exceptionally short-sighted – needing lenses of nearly 20 dioptres to correct the myopia. As a result of the increase in the front-to-back dimensions of her eyes, the retina on the left side was being dangerously stretched. This was the cause of the flashing lights. The real danger, however, was that the retina might tear and detach. Obviously something had to be done, and soon, or she would lose the sight in the eye. And there was no particular reason to suppose that the same would not happen to the other eye.

While Richardson was examining her he remembered that, not long before, he had read a paper about an operation for this very condition, written by a Russian ophthalmic surgeon and published in the *British Journal of Ophthalmology*. When he explained to her that she would have to come into hospital she looked very dubious and said that her brothers and father would never allow this. Richardson stressed that the problem was a serious one and that he could not guarantee success. Abu Ahmad was despatched to try and make her relatives understand the gravity to the problem and what needed to be done.

A few days later he was told that the girl was in the ward. The only feasible treatment for this condition involved reinforcing the back of the eye with a graft of strong, white tendinous tissue taken from the outer side of the thigh, just under the skin. This tissue, called *fascia lata*, forms a shining white sheet covering the muscles, and it is used as a natural graft material for various operations. Nowadays, one can get preserved cadaver fascia lata in packets ready to use, but at that time one had to take it from the same patient. Removing a strip of fascia lata does no harm, except, of course, to leave a scar.

Richardson went to see the girl in the ward and through an interpreter he explained to the girl that he had to strengthen her eye using tissue from her leg. She would be put to sleep and would not feel any pain. She would have to sign a paper agreeing to the operation. Shyly she confessed that she could not write. The nurses explained that it would be sufficient if she made a mark, such as a cross. Again, Murdoch made sure she understood that he could not guarantee success. This was a most unusual operation. There was, however, very little choice in the matter. If he did nothing, it was almost certain that she would go blind.

Before he could operate he had to have a special instrument made and this took several days. During that time, the girl became very friendly with a young woman in the next bed who had had a corneal graft and who was convalescing. Soon the two were inseparable. This helped her confidence. Even at that stage Richardson was conscious that the extraordinary experience of being in hospital and away from her family had a greater emotional effect on the girl than fear of surgery.

The instrument he needed was a curved, flat, steel bodkin, with an elongated slit near the tip, that could be passed right round behind the eyeball. No such instrument appeared in the catalogues, but Richardson drew a sketch, based on details in the Russian paper, and a craftsman in the old city made one up for a few shekels. This instrument worked very well. While he was manoeuvring it very gently round the back of the eyeball, anxious to avoid damaging the many small blood vessels that enter the back of the globe, an experienced operating nurse was harvesting the fascia lata from the girl's thigh. Murdoch needed a strip about six inches long and about an inch wide. When this was obtained he got the nurse to cut it longitudinally halfway along its length from one end, so that it would make a Y-shaped piece. He then threaded one of the half-width ends through the eye of the instrument, fixed it with a stitch, and pulled it round above the optic nerve. Then he passed the instrument round again and pulled round the other half-width end below the optic nerve.

All this sounds much easier than it was. The eye socket behind the globe is full of fat and contains a network of blood vessels. Murdoch had to be careful to keep the tip of the bodkin well above and below the optic nerve so as to avoid damaging the ring of small arteries that enter the eye around the nerve. The nurse had sewn up the gap in the fascia of the girl's leg and had neatly closed the skin incision long before he had succeeded in getting the fascia in place. In the end, however it was snugly applied to the globe and all he had to do was to trim the three front ends and stitch them securely to the white of the eye underneath the eye-moving muscles.

Within a day or two after recovering from the operation the beautiful girl had become completely relaxed in her dealings with Richardson and always greeted him with a warm smile on his daily visits to the ward. She had completely lost all her shyness. Although her eye was bruised and discoloured, she insisted that there was no pain. From the time of the operation the flashing ceased. The girl was discharged from hospital about two weeks after the operation. She was clearly reluctant to go and took a tearful farewell of her new friend.

When Richardson saw her a month later in the Outpatients

he was delighted to find that her myopia had been reduced by about four dioptres. Clearly, the fascia had healed firmly to the globe and was contracting as it did so. This was a gratifying result and he felt confident that the outcome would be good. He told her to come back and to see them if she had any trouble with her right eye.

This experience of comparative freedom and insight into strange Western ways and attitudes had clearly been emancipating for the young woman and, so far as he could judge, she had enjoyed a kind of freedom. He thought it more than likely, though, that, once back with the menfolk of the family, she would once again be forced into servility.

A surgeon's temptation

Daryl was the son of a British tea planter who had decided to remain in India after independence. He was an intelligent and lively boy who worked hard at school and nearly always came out top in the exams. To his parents' delight he easily passed matriculation for Delhi University and enrolled as a medical student. Gold medals and other prizes followed and in due course he graduated with honours.

After two years of preliminary hospital work Daryl decided to specialize in surgery and in due course, after satisfactorily filling a succession of surgical appointments in Delhi, flew to London to sit, and pass, the examination for the Fellowship of the Royal College of Surgeons. As Daryl well knew, this was an examination to separate the men from the boys, and the effect, on his opinion of himself, of passing it, was considerable. A certain slight arrogance of manner began to creep into his behaviour and with it, a growing discontentment with the rewards of his work. As a government employee he was salaried and there were almost no opportunities for private practice.

After discussing the matter with his parents and obtaining their approval, he resolved to move to Britain. This turned out to be more difficult than he had anticipated. The competition for surgical jobs in Britain was keen and it seemed that there were already plenty of well-qualified young general surgeons in Britain. After a dozen refusals, Daryl decided that there was nothing for it but to embellish his CV using a bit of imagination.

His new, updated CV quickly yielded results and a tentative offer of a job in a busy provincial hospital in the north of England soon followed. The job description required that applicants should certify that they had been vaccinated against hepatitis B and that they should submit a sample of blood for testing. Unfortunately, some years before, Daryl had had the bad luck to prick his finger with a needle while taking blood from a patient with hepatitis. He had suffered an acute attack but had made a good recovery. The strain was, however, a virulent one and by continuing to operate, Daryl was undoubtedly putting his patients at risk. Still, there was no way he was going to terminate a promising career just because of an accident that was not his fault.

So Daryl duly certified that he had been vaccinated and, to comply with the requirement for a blood sample, sent some blood from a healthy patient. His documents seemed to be in order and his qualifications impeccable, so he got the job. Things were hard at first and, as far as he could see, the only difference from Delhi seemed to be that the patients treated him with rather less respect. But Daryl was undaunted and worked long hours without complaining. He was a very determined young man and had his sights on the upper reaches of the profession. In order to improve his experience and to lengthen his CV he then applied for, and obtained, a succession of progressively better surgical jobs in other hospitals. The reports on his work were uniformly excellent. In due course, he obtained a Mastership in surgery and eventually, after again certifying fraudulently and sending in someone else's blood, he was able to move to London where he became a senior registrar in one of the great teaching hospitals. There seemed no reason why he should not, in a year or two, be appointed consultant. Once he had achieved that it would be a simple matter to get into the private practice business.

After he had been in London for three years and his prospects were steadily brightening, the blow fell. Unexplained cases of hepatitis B were occurring among surgical patients in the hospital in which he was working. Altogether more than twenty patients developed hepatitis and most of them had been treated by Daryl. There was no definite proof, however, that they had been infected by him, but the circumstantial evidence against him was strong. Along with all the other surgeons, he was asked to provide a blood sample. He agreed to do so and, having obtained a routine sample from a healthy patient, sent it to the lab labelled as his own blood. Unfortunately for Daryl a conscientious laboratory technician ran various other tests on the blood provided and checked the results against the recorded facts about Daryl's blood. The groups were different.

The authorities at the hospital were reluctant to accuse Daryl of such a serious offence but they made discrete enquiries at the hospitals at which he had worked and found, to their horror, that unusually large numbers of cases of hepatitis B had been occurring. When these were investigated it was found that most of them had been Daryl's patients. It was decided to send a lab technician to Daryl's department who would insist on taking a sample of the doctor's blood. The technician was courteous and diplomatic and explained that a repeat check was necessary. He did not say why. Daryl refused to allow him to take blood, but said that he would deliver a sample to the lab later that day. This sample was of yet another blood group.

At that point the head of surgical division paid Daryl a visit. He quietly outlined the known facts of the case and asked Daryl for an explanation. Daryl was forced to acknowledge his guilt. The surgical chief was sympathetic but firm. The offence was unpardonable and the matter must go to the General Medical Council. Daryl appeared before the disciplinary committee and had no valid defence. His name was struck off the medical register so that he could no longer engage in any form of orthodox medical paractice. The papers were sent to the Director of Public Prosecutions.

Ten months later Daryl appeared before a London Crown Court and was duly convicted. He was sentenced to imprisonment for one year.

Self-help

In the early 1960s Collins was a medical administrator in the garrison headquarters in Gibraltar. Out of boredom, he volunteered to take his turn as after-duty orderly medical officer in the Military Hospital. One evening he was on duty in the hospital when a light aircraft connected with a British film company crashed in the Campamento area of Spain. The pilot was brought into the hospital in a pretty poor state. He was in surgical shock and there were clear indications of severe internal bleeding, probably from a ruptured spleen.

Blood transfusion was started and he was taken at once to theatre for an exploration of the abdomen. As soon as he was opened, blood started to pour out of the incision. Obviously a large artery – probably the splenic artery – had been torn. The trouble was that the bleeding was so rapid that the surgeon simply could not see what was happening. This is a classic horror situation for a surgeon. The assistant tried mopping with large swabs and the theatre sister was using a sucker, but the faster the blood was removed from the abdominal cavity, the faster it continued to fill up. A second transfusion was set up, not without difficulty for the patient's veins were collapsed, then a third, then a fourth.

The surgeon was trying to apply internal pressure to control the bleeding while the others used swabs and suckers. Collins was horrified to see the level of waste blood rising in the glass reservoir of the sucker pump. A nurse was hanging up used swabs on a rack for the later swab count and the rack was already completely covered. The situation was getting desperate. The patient's blood pressure was too low to give any reliable reading, and his pulse was fast but thready and could barely be felt. There was an imminent risk that his brain would pack up for want of a blood supply or that so little blood would get along his coronary arteries that his heart would stop beating.

Collins started squeezing two of the plastic blood bags with his hands and got the circulating nurse to squeeze the others. As soon as the bags were empty, new bags were connected.

There was a shuttle service running between the theatre and the pathology lab and before long a message came back that they had just used the last two units of suitable blood. The injured man had had no less than 30 units and nearly all of that had come straight out again.

Just at that moment the surgeon managed to see enough to get clamps on the splenic artery. Within minutes the abdomen was mopped dry and the operation could proceed. But by then the patient's condition was desperate and the immediate priority was to maintain his blood circulation. Severe surgical shock from inadequate blood volume is rapidly fatal and they all knew that it was touch and go. The anaesthetist deliberately had him so light that he was actually moving a little and groaning. They were now transfusing with saline, but what the man really needed was blood. They all kept looking at the full sucker reservoir.

'This patient is going to die if he doesn't get blood,' said the surgeon. 'We have no choice. OK, so it's not sterile, but we'll worry about that later.'

So they poured the blood from the sucker reservoir into transfusion bottles and connected these to the drip tubes instead of the saline. Five minutes later the anaesthetist said: 'BP 60/40.'

'Bloody good,' said the surgeon. 'Maybe we can get on now.'

That patient made a complete recovery and was soon none the worse for his near-death experience. Of course they gave him antibiotics in case of infection of his twice-used blood, but he didn't even run a fever. In view of the lightness of the anaesthesia, Collins was interested to know whether he had been aware of what had been happening and asked him if he remembered anything.

'Not a thing,' he said. 'I remember you when I came in. And I remember some guy starting an injection into the back of my hand and asking me to count up to ten. I think I got to three and then I was back in the ward and it was all over.'

He had been in theatre for nearly six hours.

The demented surgeon is operating

Ernst Ferdinand Sauerbruch (1875–1951), Director of the Surgical Clinic at the Charité Hospital in East Berlin, was one of the most celebrated surgeons in the world. He was a man of complex personality, an autocrat of unpredictable moodiness and explosive temper, yet capable of great charm and compassion. He had been a bold innovator in surgery. Prior to his work, surgeons had operated within the human chest only in dire emergency or to deal with penetrating wounds. As a result of Sauerbruch's innovations and advances, especially an ingenious negative pressure chamber, surgeons were able to undertake definitive surgery on the heart, the lungs and the gullet. These were procedures which, previously, had been deemed impossibly dangerous.

Sauerbruch had also pioneered a number of major advances in the surgery of tuberculosis, advances that often allowed a complete cure of this dreaded and then prevalent disease. He developed and perfected the method of removing a short length of rib to collapse a lung and allow healing, and established the feasibility of actually removing diseased lung lobes. He was the first to operate successfully on the heart to relieve the constricting effect of inflammation of the outer membrane. He saved a patient's life by stitching up a ballooning swelling in the muscular wall of the heart itself. This patient lived for many years after the operation. Sauerbruch wrote a definitive multi-volume textbook on the surgery of the chest organs – a work that was enormously influential all over the world.

At the end of World War II Sauerbruch was in his early seventies. Most of the major surgical honours had been conferred on him and he was at the height of his reputation. It was then that Sauerbruch's colleagues began to suspect that something was terribly wrong. On one occasion, Sauerbruch was operating to remove a spleen. This organ is supplied with blood through a very large artery and it is vital to ensure that this artery is firmly clamped and tied off before the organ is removed. Sauerbruch started the operation with all his customary aplomb, but at a critical stage he appeared to be unaware of what he was doing. Without first tying off the vessel, he released the clamps on the cut splenic artery and the patient bled to death. Those present were horrified, but because of the power of medical discipline and their respect for Sauerbruch, did and said nothing.

As the number of serious mistakes multiplied, and patient after patient died, Sauerbruch's associates tried to arrange that the most difficult and dangerous operations were listed for other experienced surgeons. Ironically, Sauerbruch's reputation was so great that most of the patients insisted that only he should operate on them, especially those with more serious conditions.

Sauerbruch's colleagues were terrified to suggest to him that he had become unfit to operate. His symptoms clearly indicated that he was suffering from an intermittent loss of intellectual power and that he was completely unaware that anything was wrong. It was, of course, obvious to Sauerbruch that more of his patients were dying, but it was easy to rationalize this by telling himself that these were especially difficult cases, of a type that naturally carried a high mortality.

In April 1949, Sauerbruch was summoned before a Denazification Tribunal in West Berlin. Like many other prominent Germans, he was required to show whether or not he had had any significant dealings with the Nazi Party. Before the tribunal he took violent exception to some remarks and questions and after making a long, rambling speech, he entirely lost his temper, shouted that he was being insulted, and walked out of the room. This incident, together with the verdict of acquittal, was duly reported in the Berlin newspapers. But even then, no one outside his immediate group of professional associates suspected the real cause of his inappropriate behaviour – progressive brain damage from hardening and narrowing of the arteries supplying the brain with blood. Sauerbruch was suffering from incipient dementia.

He continued to operate and patients continued to die. This horrifying situation dragged on for months. Sauerbruch's colleagues were caught in a terrible dilemma. If they now made the matter public, they would be accused of failing to take action sooner. If they warned Sauerbruch's patients of their danger, they would probably not be believed.

There was also another obstacle. Berlin had suffered terrible damage during the war and East German medical science was at a low ebb. Many of the best doctors, attracted by the improving economic and social conditions on the west side, had moved to West Germany. The one jewel in the East German medical crown was Sauerbruch with his worldwide reputation. Politically, it was very important that the authorities should be able to continue to use Sauerbruch's name with pride. The best the surgeons at the Charité could hope for was that Sauerbruch, now at an age when many surgeons would already have retired, would simply do so, quietly and gracefully and without scandal. Their hopes were to be dashed.

At this juncture Sauerbruch operated on a young boy with a rare intestinal cancer. A senior colleague, Professor Madlener, who was well aware of his chief's problem, was also present. Part of the child's bowel was affected and had to be removed, but instead of re-establishing the connection between the stomach and the intestine, Sauerbruch simply sewed up each open end separately, leaving no connection between them. Madlener was well aware that the outlook for the boy, even with correct surgery, was very poor and that a good operation would at the best have only briefly extended his life. This fact, he felt, justified his continuing silence. Not long afterwards the boy died.

Mysteriously, a report of the case was leaked to a medical official of the Central Administration for People's Education, Dr Friedrich Hall. Horrified, Hall visited the Charité and challenged Professor Madlener. He remained silent and, in spite of Hall's appeals, refused to incriminate his chief. Finally, however, he suggested that Hall should speak to the pathologist who had done the post-mortem examination on the child. Here Dr Hall was more successful and the autopsy reports, showing what Sauerbruch had done, were eventually handed over. 'Don't hurt the old man,' said the pathologist.

The next day Hall went to see the President of the Central Administration for People's Education. Here he ran up against a brick wall. In President Wandel's eyes neither medical ethics nor the fate of a few unfortunate patients were as important as the maintenance of Sauerbruch's reputation in the interests of the advancement of the Communist ideal and its socialist development. Medical ethics were bourgeois concepts.

In desperation, Hall pointed out that the matter was bound, sooner or later, to become public knowledge. When it did, the newspapers would learn that he, Wandel, had been appealed to and had done nothing while patients died. Wandel finally agreed to consider the case.

In due course it was announced that the Central Administration had agreed that Sauerbruch should be required to retire – provided the doctors could find some way of arranging this without scandal. In the end a new Ministry rule was instituted under which professors over seventy should be automatically retired. Madlener went to see Sauerbruch and broke the news to him. At first seemed to accept the ruling quietly, but in a short time, convinced that he was the victim of a conspiracy, refused to give up his appointment or to stop operating. In Madlener's absence Sauerbruch operated again, and another patient died. At this, the doctors tackled Sauerbruch, *en masse*, but he was deaf to any suggestion that there was anything wrong with him, and categorically refused to give up operating.

In desperation, Wandel and the other doctors invited Sauerbruch to have a few drinks with them at a private house. The wife of one of the doctors, a young and attractive woman whom Sauerbruch admired, was present. After three hours of discussion and an appeal to Sauerbruch's pride by the woman and her husband, Sauerbruch was finally persuaded to agree that it was undignified to continue to cling to his post in the face of so much opposition. Muttering about conspiracy, malice and ingratitude, he promised that he would tender his resignation the next morning at the Ministry.

In spite of the misgivings of his colleagues, Sauerbruch turned up at the Ministry. While he stood stony-faced, Minister Wandel enquired whether Sauerbruch's resignation was a free decision, made without pressure or influence. Sauerbruch paused. Everyone sat tensely. Reluctantly and slowly Sauerbruch agreed to retire. The Minister then made a speech of appreciation on behalf of the German Democratic Republic for Sauerbruch's years of effort. The general relief was almost palpable.

Not long after this Sauerbruch was invited to address a medical meeting in Hanover on the subject of the philosophy of medicine. Few of the many doctors present had any idea that there was anything wrong with the great surgeon. The lecture was one that Sauerbruch had delivered often to students and it started well. But after he had turned the first page he became confused. Soon he was incoherent. Nothing he said conveyed any meaning. The audience was horrified. At once the reason for his unexpected retirement became apparent. Out of sympathy for the old man the doctors decided to hush up the matter and implored the few reporters present to keep quiet about it.

Soon after this the doctors were shocked to learn that Sauerbruch had taken up an appointment as surgeon to a small private clinic in Grünewald near his home. Some of the events during Sauerbruch's short sojourn at the Grünewald clinic were bizarre. On one occasion a film crew came along to photograph the great surgeon in action. By then, however, the chief of the clinic was alive to the dangers and was allowing Sauerbruch only to assist him. In the course of the operation – for the removal of a kidney – Sauerbruch became more and more impatient with the slowness of the operating surgeon. 'Why are you messing about? Get on with it. Let's have some cutting.'

The surgeon was furious. 'I can't see the vessels,' he muttered. 'If I cut blind, we could have a disaster.'

'Rubbish!' shouted Sauerbruch, 'None of you people are any good.'

'I am responsible for this operation,' hissed the surgeon, 'Kindly restrict yourself to assisting.'

The members of the film crew, who could clearly hear all this, were astonished. How was it possible that anyone should speak to Sauerbruch like this?

Suddenly Sauerbruch flung his retractor onto the floor. His face was scarlet with rage. Complaining incoherently, he flung out of the theatre. An assistant immediately took his place and the operation was uneventfully completed.

The surgeon turned to the film people. 'Professor Sauerbruch specializes in boldness,' he said, 'but blind cutting is bad surgery.'

Soon after this, patients presenting for treatment by Sauerbruch at the Grünewald clinic began to find that the great surgeon was no longer available. Tactfully, the old man was eased out of his appointment. But this was not the end of his surgical career. Denied access to proper operating facilities in hospital Sauerbruch took to operating, sometimes under local anaesthesia, in the kitchen of his own home. His novocaine injections were not always properly given. In his urgency to get on with the operation he did not always have a clear diagnosis or unequivocal reasons for operating. As his mental condition continued to deteriorate he did not even wash his hands or sterilize his instruments properly. The results of these macabre procedures were, predictably, disastrous – infection, haemorrhage, shock and high operative mortality. The Berlin Board of Health issued a series of orders attempting to restrain Sauerbruch from practising surgery, but these were ignored. For months he went on treating patients in this way.

During this time Sauerbruch was also occupied with a new project – the writing of his memoirs. Alone, he was now quite incapable of undertaking such a task, but the potential profits from such a book were considerable and Sauerbruch, once affluent, was now almost a pauper. So a publisher proposed that a skilled ghost writer, Hans Rudolf Berndorff, should do the job, and Sauerbruch agreed to dictate the text.

Berndorff soon found that the matter was not so simple as he had expected. Often Sauerbruch was unable to distinguish fact from fancy or imagination. Events were described that could not have occurred, dates were confused. For much of the time Sauerbruch would simply ramble on reporting matter of no possible interest. A succession of secretaries were needed to get the material down on paper. Berndorff, who knew a good story when he heard one, was determined to include as many Sauerbruch anecdotes as possible. Some of these were less than complimentary to the great man. To try to distinguish truth from fiction, Berndorff had to recruit the help of Sauerbruch's wife, Ada. She, however, wished to omit anything that might detract from her husband's dignity and fame. For a time, it looked as if the book was going to be impossibly dull. In spite of all these difficulties, however, Berndorff succeeded, by vigorous research and writing skill, in putting together a work that was an outstanding popular and commercial success. Nearly a million copies of *Aus Meinen Leben* were sold. Unfortunately, Sauerbruch did not live to hold the book in his hands.

In June 1951 he had a small stroke and was taken to hospital to be under the care of Professor Madlener. There he lay quietly for a time then attempted to escape. He got as far as the car park where he tried to start a car that had been left with the keys in the ignition. But the nurses and doctors ran out and brought him back. Repeatedly he dressed himself and insisted on being taken home to attend to his patients. As his condition deteriorated and his mind clouded, his hands would often go though the motions of operating, even as he lay in bed. Finally, on 2 July 1951, he died. He was buried in his best operating gown.

Courage

When Jenkins was working as an ophthalmic specialist in the British Military Hospital in Singapore in the mid-1960s, a Chinese sea cook was brought in off a merchant navy vessel. He was a small, wizened man in dirty white shorts and a singlet, who spoke no English but who bowed politely and repeatedly whenever he was addressed. He was seen first by one of the general surgeons who asked Jenkins to consult with him.

In the centre of the patient's left lower lid was a large, jet-black swelling and, on either side of this, along the lid margin, were conspicuous splashes of black. Through an interpreter he explained that this 'blood blister' as he called it, had been growing for months and that he had been squeezing it every day. When Jenkins heard this his blood ran cold.

He could see that the black area, although irregular, was continuous and extended to the lid from the white of the eye. A check with an ophthalmoscope showed that there was a large mass inside the eye. So, under local anaesthesia, they took a small piece of tissue from the lid for microscopic examination. As expected, the pathologist reported that they were dealing with a highly malignant melanoma. Full general examination

problem and constantly tried to manoeuvre him into agreeing with her that there was very little wrong. Rathbone had always disliked being manipulated by patients – even charming old ladies – and his response was to inform her, as kindly as he could, that she should have had her name on the waiting list for surgery long ago.

Finally she came to him to say that she had decided that he should operate. She showed no sign of nervousness but Rathbone was aware that she had something else on her mind – something she badly wanted to say but was hesitant about. It was not until he went to see her in the ward the evening before her operation – often an emotional occasion for the patient – that she finally unburdened herself. The matter surprised him.

'Doctor,' she said with a shy smile, 'you will think me an old silly, but there is one thing I very much wanted to ask you.'

'And what is that?'

'While you are at it tomorrow, do you think . . . would it be possible for you to cut off these horrible bags around my eyes?'

'Ninety-two . . .' he thought. He had hardly noticed that the skin of her eyelids was, as is common with the elderly, somewhat redundant. In the upper lids, the loose skin hung down a little over the lid margins. He had to make a quick decision.

'No problem,' he said.

She threw her hands in the air and sank back on her pillows.

'Wonderful!' she said.

Rathbone wondered whether it was superstition on his part, but he believed that he could always tell when a cataract operation was going to go smoothly and easily and when he was going to have trouble. There were patients who were so screwed up and anxious that it seemed to have an effect even through a general anaesthetic. Such patients were fighting him. On the other hand, there were patients like this one. As anticipated, the operation went like a dream. When he was finished, he gently pinched up the loose skin of each lid to form a kind of vertical wall, based on a skin crease, snipped off the redundant skin with sharp scissors, and closed the gap with a few interrupted virgin silk stitches finer than a hair. Each lid took only a few minutes.

He saw her in the ward on the evening of the next day. She had been waiting impatiently for his visit. Her sister was by her bedside. When he took off the plastic shield and the eyepad she gave a little gasp and said, 'Oh, it's you, doctor.'

'How's the vision?' he asked.

She looked around the ward. 'Very good,' she said, as if this were nothing remarkable. Then she turned to her sister. 'Have you got it?' she asked.

Her sister opened her large handbag and took out an old-fashioned, silver-bordered, oval mirror with a handle. The old lady grabbed it and gazed at her face in the mirror. There was a moment's tense silence. It was as if the whole ward were in suspense.

'Oh,' she cried in a tone of extreme gratification, 'that's lovely!'

'Always was as vain as a peacock,' grumbled her sister.

Arrow wounds

For centuries, the bow and arrow was one of the most important weapons of war. The wounds this weapon caused were often horrifying and commonly fatal. Many arrows had a heavy, sharp, barbed-iron tip or a tip of sharp stone and passed easily through soft tissues such as the abdominal wall. They could also penetrate bone, such as the ribs and the skull, and although penetration was much less deep in these cases, the barb must often have made removal difficult or impossible. Arrow wounds of the limbs were very common and, in general, were the least serious. Quite often an arrow would pass right through the soft tissue of a limb and out again.

Arrows entering the abdomen were always very dangerous, partly because of the risk of opening a major artery and giving rise to massive internal bleeding and partly because of the risk of cutting into the intestine so that the infected contents spilled into the normally sterile abdominal cavity to cause peritonitis. The mortality rate from penetrating arrow wounds of the abdomen was about 90 per cent. Penetrating chest wounds were usually fatal.

An army surgeon, Major Joseph B. Bill, has left an interesting record, dated 1862, of the treatment of wounds caused to US army personnel by red Indian arrows. Major Bill had had plenty of experience of these and had designed an ingenious pair of long-handled forceps for extracting arrows. These had circular metal guards to surround the barb so that the arrow could be withdrawn with minimal damage to tissue.

All in the brain

Neurology is full of surprises. Jennifer put her uncharacteristic loss of interest in housework down to the menopause. In any case, now that the kids were gone why should she worry about a bit of dust? It was time she had a life of her own. Her husband Michael was not so sure. He knew that something was wrong. There was a subtle, indefinable difference in Jennifer's personality. Nothing you could put your finger on but, to him, very obvious.

Eventually, after about three years of gentle but persistent nagging, he persuaded her to see a doctor. The GP was unimpressed and told her that there was nothing wrong with her. But Michael was nothing if not determined. So he went to the doctor and made such a fuss that the GP, really to get rid of him, promised to make an appointment with a neurologist.

Eventually the time for the appointment came. The consultant was very thorough and carried out a full examination. All the routine clinical tests came out normal and there was no indication of intellectual deficit, as he called it in his letter to the GP. He was, however, a canny man and thought it would be just as well to have a CT scan of Jennifer's head. He was glad he did. The picture took his breath away. Jennifer had a really enormous tumour, about half the size of her whole brain, situated centrally and towards the front.

At operation the neurosurgeon was delighted to find that it was a meningioma – a benign tumour arising from one of the membranes surrounding the brain. The brain substance was not actually invaded but was, of course, considerably squashed. Because of its upper location, the tumour was fairly easy to remove and the whole thing was taken away. His opinion was that the tumour had been growing slowly for many years and that Jennifer's brain had had time to get accustomed to its unwanted companion.

Needless to say, Jennifer never looked back. Nor did she resume her interest in housework. But Michael knew that everything was now OK.

A generous surgeon

In July 1996 the fifty-three-year-old German transplant surgeon Professor Jochem Hoyer voluntarily donated one of his kidneys to a patient whom he did not know. This remarkably altruistic act was performed because the professor believed that it was inappropriate for doctors to try to persuade healthy people to donate kidneys unless they were willing to do it themselves.

Surgical prejudice

Until the beginning of the twentieth century there was still some residual prejudice, in the medical profession, against surgeons. This presumably dates from earlier times when the surgeons were barbers and the physicians gentlemen. The same notion underlies the odd tradition of calling physicians 'doctor' and surgeons 'mister'. As late as the 1870s, the great but autocratic Dr Howship Dickinson of St George's Hospital referred to 'these eviscerations and dismemberments that surgeons regard with such complacency, their patients with such inquietude'.

In his campaign against the surgeons Dickinson put forward at a committee meeting the proposal that only one of the

St George's surgeons should be allowed to do abdominal operations. Most of the staff were too much in awe of him to object, but one intrepid junior surgeon who had recently been appointed stood up.

'Dr Dickinson's proposal', he said, 'is a most interesting one. It is an idea that might well be extended. So I am now proposing that only one of the physicians should be allowed to treat typhoid fever.'

There was a moment's horrified and electric silence. Dickinson turned his devastating glare on the impertinent junior and it was hard to judge whether his anger or his astonishment was the greater. Then Dickinson's face changed. His expression slowly returned to its accustomed calm and, to the surprise of all present, broke into a charming smile. 'My young friend has eloquently made his point,' he said.

Nothing more was heard of the suggested restriction on the surgeons.

Medical eminence is sometimes apt to be damaging to the character, and pundits do, occasionally, arrive at the conviction that they are infallible. Dr Dickinson was not immune to this delusion. On one ward round, after he had been discoursing on the then prevalent syphilitic disorder, general paralysis of the insane (GPI), and had emphasized that a prominent symptom was an inflated sense of importance, he came to the bed of a crossing sweeper.

'Would you say that you were a very good crossing sweeper?' he asked the man.

'I hope so,' said the sweeper timidly.

'There you are,' said Dickinson to the students, 'Megalomania. Unquestionably GPI.'

Ununited fractures

A late nineteenth-century surgeon was puzzled that a succession of simple fractures of the leg bones in his patients stubbornly refused to heal. None of these fractures were infected and all had a good blood supply and there was no apparent reason why they should not do well. After some weeks the reputation of the surgeon was well-nigh ruined. He was distraught, his friends were concerned, and his rival colleagues were smiling.

One night the surgeon was called to his ward to see a patient who was in great pain. After dealing with the case he turned to go when he noticed that there were screens around the bed of one of his cases of ununited leg fracture. Curious to know why, he went to the bed. Two night nurses, whom he had never met, were washing the patient's back and had so twisted the leg at the fracture site that the foot was pointing backwards. Enquiries revealed that the nurses were washing *all* the patients during the night and were quite unaware that there could be any harm in doing so. This practice was instantly stopped, whereupon all the fractures quickly healed.

It is hard to credit that as late as the end of the nineteenth century it was not appreciated, even by the best surgeons, that proper splinting to achieve immobilization was one of the essentials of the elementary management of fractures. The story also illustrates the power of respect for authority in that none of these patients dared to complain to the surgeon. Most of them must have been aware of the reason for the failure of their fractures to heal.

Nothing palsied about Bell

Sir Charles Bell (1774–1842), professor of surgery at Edinburgh, was the greatest experimental and investigative neurologist of all time. Almost alone, he placed the science of neuroanatomy on a sound basis by a series of brilliant studies and demonstrations. The advances he made in the elucidation of the human nervous system were of inestimable value to medicine. His recognition of the disorder caused by cutting or paralysis of the seventh cranial nerve to the muscles of the face – now known as Bells' palsy – was but one tiny element in the great volume of essential knowledge he bequeathed to the medical canon.

Happily, Bell's contributions were recognized in his lifetime and he was showered with honours. When he was in Paris and was taken to a class of students by the neurologist M. Roux, the latter said 'Gentlemen, enough for today. You have seen Charles Bell!'

An operation evolves

When Murdoch started to study eye surgery in the early 1960s, the operation for cataract was, by present-day standards, crude. Nearly all cases were done under local anaesthesia and drops were used to widen the pupil to a maximum so as to expose as much of the lens as possible. The surgeon wore magnifying spectacles and the main instrument used was a slim knife with a long, narrow, pointed blade that had been invented by the great German ophthalmologist, von Graefe. Every surgeon treasured his Graefe knives and treated them with scrupulous care. One knife might do for half a dozen operations and then it had to be sent in its case to the cutlers to be re-sharpened.

The eye was held firmly with toothed forceps that gripped the uppermost eye-moving muscle and the point of the knife was passed in from the outer side of the cornea, pushed right across to emerge at the other side and then used to cut upwards with a slight sawing action. The most embarrassing thing a surgeon could do would be to put the knife in with the sharp edge downwards. Right-handed surgeons preferred to operate on right eyes, left-handed on left. Right-handed surgeons had to use the left hand for left eyes. This was because the Graefe knife had to be passed in from the outer side; the nose prevented an approach from the inner side.

Once the Graefe knife had done its work and the eye was opened, a blunt metal hook was used to apply external pressure to break the fine fibres – the suspensory ligament holding the cataractous lens in place. Special forceps were then used to grasp the capsule of the lens and carefully tumble it out of the eye. Some surgeons simply squeezed out the lens with the hook, but this was considered rather second-rate. Removing the lens called for great skill as it was a final disaster if any of the jelly of the eye – the vitreous humour which lies immediately behind the lens – escaped. This usually led to loss of the eye. If all this had been successfully accomplished there was still another risk of loss of vitreous when attempts were made to sew up the incision. At the time, needles and stitches were so crude that it was almost impossible to stitch up the wound without distorting the eye and squeezing out vitreous. Many surgeons, therefore, made no attempt to do so and the patient had to lie still for two or three weeks with the head between sandbags until some healing had occurred.

Murdoch's chief had a clever ways of putting in a stitch *before* opening the eye and pulling the loops out of the way so that the Graefe incision could be made between them. Once the lens was out the suture could be carefully pulled tight and tied. This chief, incidentally, was a man with a very short fuse. On one occasion, just as the cataractous lens had been beautifully removed, the patient, a fat old lady gave a great sigh and most of the vitreous welled out of her eye.

'You silly old fool!' shouted the surgeon, 'You've ruined your eye!'

'Oh, I'm sorry! I'm sorry!' cried the woman.

Murdoch, who was assisting, was shocked. This woman was actually apologizing to the surgeon for spoiling his operation.

About a week later the chief said to him, 'You remember that unfortunate lady that lost her vitreous? Well, I want you to take her eye out. Do it today.' The eye had never settled down and was acutely inflamed and painful and quite blind. The chief was worried about a condition known as sympathetic ophthalmia that often affected the other eye, causing it to become blind, following such events. At that point Murdoch had a new insight into the emotional problems of his chief and saw that he had been tortured by regrets since the time of the operation. The chief could not, under any circumstances, bring himself to apologize to the patient, and he could not bear having to remove the eye himself.

Happily this was near the end of the Graefe era and there were better things to come. By the time Murdoch was doing his own cataract operations, methods had enormously improved. Within a year or so the Graefe knives had been relegated to the museum and the incision was being made with tiny chips of razor blade held in a special handle. In those days, the razor blade market was dominated by the Blue Gillette – a wonderfully sharp blade made of very hard, brittle blue steel that broke easily. The later stainless steel blades, although rustless, would bend but would not break, so they were no good for this purpose. Old blades had to be obtained.

The razor-blade knife could be used with great precision to cut an incision around the edge of the cornea, from 10 to 2 o'clock, just where the cornea meets the white of the eye. This could be done deliberately and carefully, by gradually deepening a groove along the whole length of the incision until the water of the eye – the aqueous humour in front of the iris – escaped. It was fairly easy to do this without indenting the eye. The tip of the blade could then be slipped a fraction of an inch into the eye and the incision completed by cutting outwards.

A blunt needle was now used to inject into the eye a solution of a protein-splitting enzyme called alpha chymotrypsin. Once this was done everything had to stop for a couple of minutes while the enzyme got to work breaking down the delicate fibres of the suspensory ligament of the lens. The assistant then held open the incision while the surgeon retracted the iris and touched on to the lens a fine probe the end of which was at a temperature of about –20° C. The lens immediately froze on to the probe and could easily be removed. Probes could be cooled by pouring highly volatile liquids, such as freon, into them or by various other methods. Murdoch used an Amoils machine that cooled the tip by the expansion of laughing gas (nitrous oxide) through a small hole. This worked very well but was rather clumsy and there were flexible pipes attached to the top of the handle of the probe that made it awkward to manoeuvre. Fortunately, the escape of laughing gas caused no problems. Cataract surgery is no laughing matter.

The other great advance that Murdoch enjoyed was the production of a superb suture called 7–0 virgin silk to which was swaged a remarkably fine and sharp needle. The suture was so delicate that, if dropped, it just floated down. The needle, together with tiny toothed holding forceps called Collibri forceps, allowed the incision to be closed with little or no risk of vitreous loss.

This operation, known as the intracapsular cataract extraction, was the standard for about ten years. It was very successful but had a number of disadvantages. About one patient in 100 developed a retinal detachment within a year or two of the operation. A more general disadvantage was that once the lens was removed the eye was, of course, grossly defocused and it was necessary to prescribe spectacles that were very strong, thick, heavy and uncomfortable. They also caused great enlargement of the image and serious peripheral distortion.

Murdoch was distressed by the problems many of his elderly patients had with their glasses and he badly wanted to do something better for them. So he bought a range of contact lenses of 12 to 15 dioptres power and, one day, having selected a suitable patient, decided to try one out. He did a refraction to determine the power needed, checked the corneal curvature for the proper fit and, without saying anything, slipped the appropriate lens on to the eye.

'Read the chart,' he said.

The patient quickly read half-way down the chart and then stopped. 'My God,' he said, 'It's a miracle!' He looked around the consulting room in astonishment and confusion.

Murdoch explained what he had done and told him that the

lenses were a possible alternative to glasses. The improvements were due to the fact that the optical correction with the contact lens was, in effect, part of the eye – an almost normal situation. Soon after that Murdoch was busy fitting his cataract patients with contact lenses. Many of them had trouble handling the lenses but their motivation was so strong that nearly all succeeded.

By the time Murdoch became a consultant, cataract surgery had reached a further stage that had largely eliminated both these major disadvantages of the intracapsular extraction. By then the operating microscope had become ubiquitous and was universally used by eye surgeons. This allowed a new dimension of precision and delicacy and, although operations took a little longer, the results were just about as good as seemed possible. Many of the operations were being done under general anaesthesia.

The major advance was the use of intraocular lens implants. These were little masterpieces of optical precision. The first implanted lenses were inserted in front of the iris or were clipped on to the iris with delicate plastic loops. Murdoch put in many of these iris clip lenses after doing a standard intracapsular lens extraction. Patients were asked to use drops for a time to keep the pupil small. Wide dilatation would lead to the risk of the lens becoming displaced.

Iris clip lenses were by no means ideal and were eventually replaced by lenses so tiny that they could be inserted into the capsule of the lens after all the cataractous material had been removed. Access to this material was gained by cutting away only the front part of the capsule of the lens. The preservation of the rear wall of the lens capsule allowed the dynamics of the vitreous to be left unaffected and the incidence of retinal detachment dropped to normal. This type of lens and operation became definitive and the extracapsular operation completely replaced the intracapsular procedure.

The power of the implant lens was determined by measuring the internal length of the eye using an ultrasound measuring device and by measuring the curvature of the cornea. These figures were used in a computer calculation that came up with the required power.

Murdoch reviews this evolution of an operation with mixed feelings. Young men and women coming into eye surgery today are certainly spared a great deal of anxiety but, as surgeons, they are unlikely to experience the unique satisfaction of being able to progressively and radically refine their methods, reduce their operating anxiety and improve their service to their patients.

To cut or not to cut – that is the question

It is a little-known fact that American boy babies apparently suffer from a disorder that is rare in British boy babies. In America, between 80 and 90 per cent of boy babies have their foreskins removed; only about 5 per cent of British boy babies suffer this fate. The critic might suggest that the difference is based on religious conviction. At least two of the great religions of the world require ritual circumcision. But this would mean suggesting that over 80 per cent of the American population consisted of Muslims and Jews. This does not accord with the known facts.

Alternatively, there may be quite a different explanation. In the United States, the surgeon gets paid, usually by the patient or parents, for each operation performed; in Britain – with the exception of those in private practice – the surgeon gets paid an NHS salary which is unrelated to the number of operations performed. It is quite hard to get a circumcision on the NHS. This is largely because British surgeons believe that God got it right.

Of course, if you want to go to Harley Street – that's quite a different matter.

A surfeit of Caesars

A report by the US Public Citizens' Health Research Group states that nearly a quarter of all births in the United States in 1992 were by Caesarean section. The figure of 22.6 per cent was, apparently, almost twice what it ought to have been if the clinical indications for Caesarean section had been strictly followed. The rate had been 5.5 per cent in 1970 and had peaked at 24.7 per cent in 1988.

On close examination the report revealed some truly remarkable figures. One hospital in Michigan had a Caesarean section rate for births of no less than 63.7 per cent. Interestingly, the states with the highest figures for Caesarean sections were all in the south: Arkansas (28.4 per cent), Louisiana (28.2 per cent), Mississippi (27.7 per cent) and Texas (27 per cent). The state with the lowest figures was Colorado (16.3 per cent). According to the authors of the report, the rate ought not to be higher than 12 per cent anywhere in the USA.

It would be unfair to assume that these high figures are mainly related to the fact that gynaecological surgeons are paid more for performing a Caesar than for conducting a vaginal delivery. But there may be something in this; the authors recommend that doctors should be paid the same for either procedure.

Improving the palate?

The soft palate is the loose flap at the back of the roof of the mouth. In the centre of the soft palate there is a hanging floppy part called the uvula. In many parts of Africa it is believed that removal of the uvula is an effective treatment for sore throats and coughs as well as for vomiting and for various other symptoms. The operation is performed on children without anaesthesia and using the crudest of instruments. The surgeon is usually an itinerant barber. In one series of 530 children, studied in northern Cameroon, 78 per cent of the children had had the operation.

It is hardly necessary to say that there is no medical basis whatsoever for this practice and that it has no useful effect on the conditions for which it is performed.

A toe for a thumb

A 38-year-old woman accidentally suffered the total amputation of her left thumb by the propellor of a boat while she was scuba-diving. Unfortunately, the thumb was never found and she was left with a severely disabled hand. The thumb is essential to allow gripping and a hand without a thumb is far more seriously disadvantaged than might be supposed.

Advances in microsurgery now allow surgeons to perform procedures of a previously unthinkable delicacy. Tiny cut blood vessels can be stitched together, end-to-end, so effectively that a full blood supply is maintained. Nerves and tendons can also be precisely and strongly approximated. Four months after the injury one of this lady's toes was surgically detached with its blood vessels and was used to replace the lost thumb. After healing, the new digit had full movement, adequate power and almost normal sensation. The appearance of the toe in its new position so resembled a thumb that no one would suspect what had been done. Her walking ability was virtually unaffected by the loss of the toe.

Another factor making this kind of surgery possible is that because the tissue is recognized by the immune system as 'self' there are no problems with immunological rejection. Healing is rapid and complete.

Suing for life

Doctors are commonly sued because they have, by negligence or default, caused the death of a patient. Recently a very sad case arose in which doctors were being sued by a patient because he did not die. In 1992, a British patient was told that he had cancer and that he could only expect to live for a period of months. It appears that this prognosis was too pessimistic, for in 1996 the patient was granted legal aid to bring an action claiming that he had suffered unnecessary distress and, because he had stopped working, he had sustained considerable loss of earnings.

Doctors in the Making

His future in their hands

When Taylor was a medical student at Aberdeen, one of the most popular lecturers was a senior surgeon called Mr Andrew Fowler, a short, tubby, jovial man with a passion for his subject, and a wonderful talent for teaching.

One day in surgical Out-patients Andie, as he was known, was talking about the hand and pointing out to the students the importance of comparing the two sides of the body. He stopped before a middle-aged lady, picked up both her hands, turned them palm upwards, compared them, and said, 'Now gentlemen, tell me, is this lady right-handed or left-handed?'

He was looking at Taylor, who immediately said 'Right-handed.'

'Well done, laddie,' he said. 'Now tell the others how you know.'

The point of the exercise was that the muscle bulk at the base of the thumb is often better developed on the right side than on the left in right-handed people. This fact had entirely escaped Taylor. He was, however, in possession of some other information. 'This lady', he said, 'is my mother.'

This episode greatly amused Mrs Taylor, who was attending Out-patients for a minor finger infection, but Andie was speechless and was placed in a quandary. He was a very kind man and much too concerned about the young man's feelings to apply the deserved censure in the presence of his mother, so he passed the matter off as a joke. At the time, Taylor was rather pleased with himself, but on maturer consideration it occurred to him that he might have committed a dangerous tactical error. The final examinations were rapidly approaching and there was a real possibility that Andie would recount the incident to his friend Wilson the professor of surgery. The approach to the final examinations for the degree of Bachelor of Medicine and Bachelor of Surgery is a period during which, for the worried candidate, paranoia certainly rules. It was distinctly on the cards that Taylor would fail this examination, not being one of the brightest students.

When the time came for his surgical viva (oral examination) Taylor found himself faced by their own Professor Wilson and by an external professor from Glasgow. The external examiner started with some pretty tough questions and he was not doing too well. He, managed to stumble along for about ten minutes without actually coming to a complete stop until, to his horror, the examiner asked him which movement of the hip joint was the first to be limited in a tuberculous infection. Needless to say, Taylor did not have the remotest idea. In desperation, he glanced at Professor Wilson who was sitting there impassively. To his astonishment he saw him clench his right fist and turn it slowly in the palm of his left hand.

He turned to the external examiner. 'Rotation,' he said.

The examiner's eyebrow shot up. 'Very good,' he said, grudgingly, then turned to Professor Wilson and said, 'Do you want to ask any questions?'

With what seemed to Taylor unseemly haste, the Professor said, 'No, no. I think that will do very well.'

Taylor never knew what it was that prompted the professor to resort to such an unprofessional yet generous act, but he blessed his memory from that day on. He passed.

A green doctor

A few months after qualifying as a doctor and before being called up for military service, Taylor took a job as a trainee assistant in a country family practice in Aberdeenshire. Although appallingly ignorant, he had a high opinion of himself and this was rapidly reinforced by the respect and submissive compliance of most of the country folk who were his patients. Their kindness and tact was remarkable. It was an almost daily occurrence for him to find, on paying a domiciliary visit, that some little gift of eggs or other farm produce had been left on the front seat of his car.

Soon after starting that job, his principal went off with his family for two week's holiday and he was left to run the practice as well as he might. For a time all appeared to go well and then a mysterious epidemic of slight fever, diarrhoea, vomiting and abdominal pain struck the region. Some days he had as many as twenty calls to make and most of these patients had the strange disorder. He had no idea what it was and never thought of scientific investigation, but was consoled by the fact that none of the patients were seriously ill. They all seemed to derive great comfort from a standard mixture of kaolin and morphine known as Mist. kaolin sed. and he soon got into the way of prescribing this as a routine. The local chemist was kept busy making up gallons of this pleasant-tasting elixir.

Towards the end of the epidemic, and two or three days before his chief was due to return, he had a call from the 'big house' – a substantial mansion occupied by the one aristocratic family in the district. The lady who answered the telephone in the surgery interrupted Dr Taylor's morning clinic to pass on this portentous news to him, and it was clear that she was deeply impressed. 'Oh doctor,' she said, anxiously, 'do you no think you should go straight away?'

Such cringing servility annoyed him. 'Certainly not,' he said. 'The people who have come to see me here have as much right to my immediate attention as anyone from the big house.' So he finished the clinic before setting out on his rounds in his little blue Austin 7. He did, however, put the big house on the top of his visiting list.

When he got there he was shown into an enormous bedroom where a very pleasant middle-aged lady was lying in a huge four-poster bed. She greeted him courteously and apologized for troubling him. His enquiries elicited that she had been troubled by abdominal pain and felt feverish. He asked if she had had diarrhoea and after a moment's hesitation she agreed that her bowels had been 'a bit loose'. He asked her to pull up her nightie and felt her tummy, but without deriving much information except that it seemed generally a little tender. Unhappily, he had made the disastrous mistake of deciding in advance what was wrong. He reassured her, wrote a prescription for Mist. kaolin sed. and told her that he would look in again in a day or two to make sure she was all right.

When his chief returned, the first thing he did was to take a look at the domiciliary visits lists. At once he spotted that Taylor had been at the big house. 'Who was it?' he asked, looking annoyed.

'Mrs Duke-MacDermoid.'

'The elder?'

'The younger.'

'What was wrong?'

'Oh, the same as everyone else. Epidemic diarrhoea.'

'Was she all right?'

'Oh yes. I was going to see her again this evening.'

'Don't bother.'

With that, he threw his bag into his Daimler and went off to the big house. Glad to be relieved of sole responsibility for the practice, Taylor went home.

Two hours later his phone rang. It was his principal. His voice was tight, barely controlled. 'Will you come across straight away?' he said.

It was the first time Taylor had known him really angry and it was not a pleasant experience. The chief motioned him into his consulting room and shut the door. Then he turned to face him. 'Because of your stupidity and uselessness,' he said, 'that woman will probably die.'

Taylor felt his face go white. 'You mean Mrs Duke-MacDermoid?'

'Of course. Who else?'

'But . . . I thought . . .'

'She is gravely ill. She is now on her way to Aberdeen in an ambulance. She is suffering from acute peritonitis from a burst appendix that you . . . you ignoramus . . . failed to diagnose.'

'But . . . I thought . . .'

'I know what you thought. Did you take a proper history? Did you examine her? Did you take her temperature? Did you even put a hand on her belly? Did you do a rectal? Did you do anything?'

Taylor tried to defend himself, but his protests were brushed aside.

'It absolutely defeats me how anyone could miss a thing like that,' the principal said in a tone of utter disgust. 'The signs must have been obvious when you saw her. Central pain moving to the right iliac fossa. Localized tenderness. Rebound tenderness. Haven't you learned anything?'

'How bad is she?' asked Taylor, horrified.

'Just about as bad as she could be. It's a matter of touch and go.'

Taylor didn't sleep much that night and first thing in the morning he called the Aberdeen Royal Infirmary. Eventually he got through to the senior registrar in the appropriate surgical ward.

'How is Mrs Duke-MacDermoid?' he asked, his mouth dry.

There was an agonizing pause during which Taylor expected him to say that she had died during the night. Then he said, 'Interesting case that. Thank you for sending her in. We were nearly three hours in theatre.'

'But how is she?'

'Oh, she's fine. Much better this morning. She'll be all right.'

'Thank God,' said Taylor, feeling incredibly relieved.

'You a relative?'

'No, just her doctor. And I feel a right fool. I completely missed the diagnosis. It was my chief that sent her in. Peritonitis, was it?'

'Yes. I suppose we were quite lucky to get her in time. Another twenty-four hours and I doubt if we could have pulled her through.'

'Well, I must say I'm very grateful – '

'Don't mention it.' The specialist must have sensed Taylor's anguish, for he then showed him a kindness that he was never to forget. 'Incidentally,' he said, 'you shouldn't blame yourself for missing this one. I'm not surprised you had a problem.'

Taylor was astonished. 'Really? How is that?'

'It was a rather long retrocaecal appendix. We found the tip right down in the pelvis – no doubt irritating the rectum and causing diarrhoea. I don't suppose the signs were at all classical. No cause to blame yourself.'

Taylor muttered some further broken thanks. This generous man was actually finding excuses for him, where no excuses were possible.

Later in the day his chief called him in again. 'I may have been a wee bit hard on you,' he said. 'I gather it was atypical. Well, no hard feelings, I hope. We live and learn, laddie. One thing we can be sure of – you're not going to miss a straightforward appendix in the future, are you?'

The reluctant placenta

The Gurkha Families Hospital at Majeedee Barracks in Johore ran like clockwork. It was staffed by Gurkha midwives who had been carefully selected and trained in the maternity department of the British Military Hospitals in Singapore or Hong Kong. Johnson was not expected to attend on routine confinements but was supposed to be on call for emergencies.

When he went to Majeedee he was acutely conscious of his ignorance of obstetrics. He had passed his finals in the subject and had delivered the statutory twenty babies as a student, but he really knew very little. So he decided to use his position to gain more experience and asked the sister-in-charge to call him for deliveries. This was not a very popular move and the women were very modest and, even in labour, shy with a white doctor, but he insisted and, as a result, learned quite a lot.

One evening he was in the Officers' Mess and was just finishing dinner when he had a phone call from the Families Hospital. A woman was having a severe post-partum haemorrhage and he was needed urgently. He ran.

There was blood everywhere and he saw at once that she had a retained placenta. When this is accompanied by severe bleeding it is a grave emergency. The placenta remains partly adherent and prevents the womb from contracting down to stop the bleeding. Fortunately the midwife had recognized what was happening and had not waited but had called him at once. He did not know how much blood she had lost but he did know that he had to get that placenta out at once.

So he rolled up his sleeves and quickly washed his hands. This procedure is usually done under general anaesthesia but there was no one to help him and he didn't know how much time he had. So he got down on his knees by the bed. Just then Johnson had a vivid recollection of a lecture on manual removal of the placenta by Professor Dougald Baird at Aberdeen. In his inimitable way the professor had told a story about a Scottish country GP who had had to do this and who had failed to follow the umbilical cord with his fingers all the way up to the placenta. He had put his hand into the vagina, felt a free edge and had succeeded in doing a digital hysterectomy. The woman had died and the doctor had been struck off.

Hastily Johnson encircled the cord with thumb and forefinger and worked his way up. The baby had recently been born and both the vagina and the cervical canal were still widely dilated. There was plenty of room for manoeuvre. It was very hot in there, and it was very slippery and bloody. Johnson found the placenta and felt for its edge. By good fortune he first encountered a separated edge and was able to get his fingers between the placenta and the wall of the womb. In a few minutes the whole placenta was freed and he brought it out. The midwife was ready with a syringe of ergometrine. Johnson thought it best to give the 0.5 mg dose intravenously. Almost at once the womb contracted down tightly and the bleeding stopped.

A pint of blood spilled from a kicked-over kidney dish makes a large showing and the woman had lost less than he thought. Her blood pressure was OK. He asked the midwife to give her a penicillin injection, washed his hands and phoned the senior specialist in obstetrics and gynaecology at the British Military Hospital, Singapore. She agreed to take the case and Johnson called an ambulance. So mother, baby and a very pleased-with-himself young doctor made the twenty minute trip to the hospital.

The specialist was a hard-bitten lady Lieutenant-colonel called Mary Saunders and Johnson saw at once that, so far as she was concerned, this was just boring routine. So as soon as the patient had been delivered to the ward, he hopped back into the ambulance and was driven back to Johore Bahru.

Dislocation

Late one evening Collins was duty medical officer in the Military Hospital, Gibraltar, when three naval officers came rolling into casualty tenderly supporting a fourth. These officers were off a ship anchored in the naval base and had clearly been celebrating. Two of them were ships' surgeons and the other two were executive officers. One of the officers was clutching his right arm to his chest with his left hand and Collins was told that he had a dislocated shoulder. This had been acquired, over the border in La Linea, in a 'slight misunderstanding' with a Spanish gentilhombre over the relative merits of football and bullfighting.

The naval doctors had had several attempts at reducing the dislocation but without success, and the injured party, having lost confidence in their abilities, had insisted that they bring him to see an orthopaedic specialist. Collins had a look at the patient, confirmed the diagnosis and checked that there was no nerve injury. It was a point of honour never to call out a specialist unless the matter was beyond one's competence, so Collins asked them to wait while he went next door to his tiny bedroom where he had secreted a copy of Pye's *Surgical Handicraft* – the casualty officers' vade-mecum.

Having consulted this invaluable book he returned to the consulting room where he asked the patient to lie face down on a narrow examination couch with the affected arm hanging down over the edge. He knew that the patient was in a fairly relaxed state and, indeed, appeared to drop off to sleep. According to Pye, if a patient was placed in this position and given a large dose of powerful pain-killer, such as pethidine, the relaxation of the muscles and the weight of the arm should effect the reduction without more ado.

By Collins estimate, this patient had already had an effectively analgesic dose of alcohol. So he chatted to the officers for a few minutes, keeping a wary eye on the patient in the meantime. Finally he said, 'That should do it,' and gave the sleeping officer a gentle shake. He sat up, looked around, and then allowed his jaw to drop open. 'I say, old boy,' he said, 'that's bloody marvellous!'

Collins was conscious of the chagrin and embarrassment of the two doctors but was not yet man enough to resist a further minor triumph. Instead of coming clean about his methods, he remained silent until one of them said, 'That was pretty good. You must be an orthopod.'

'Well no,' he replied, with becoming modesty, 'actually, I'm an eye man.'

The gas man cometh

While he was working in the army in Gibraltar in the 1960s, Collins had the misfortune to be ordered to take over the job of hospital anaesthetist for a period of about three months. The regular anaesthetist had been posted away on some other duty and there was no available qualified replacement. As his experience in this line of business was limited to the required minimum of twenty inductions done under supervision as a medical student, and a few casual anaesthetics since, he was rightly dismayed. His protestations of ineptitude were brushed aside. There was no one else to do the job. That was an order.

At once all other matters became trivial by comparison with the urgent necessity for him to assimilate the entire contents of the cram book *Aids to Anaesthesia* – the only text basic enough for him to master in the time. From that moment until three months later, Collins knew hardly a moment's peace of mind. Every time the phone rang his heart raced, his mouth went dry and he was oppressed by a sense of impending disaster. Phone calls during the night were especially alarming, as they implied emergency and possibly a patient in poor shape. He had always considered the administration of general anaesthesia to be an extraordinary responsible task – a kind of balancing of a patient in the narrow gap between life and death – and he seriously doubted his ability to perform this delicate function without erring in one direction or another and either having a patient wake up at the wrong time, or killing someone.

All this was, of course, a pure panic reaction. It is actually quite hard to kill someone with modern general anaesthetic agents. And unless one is totally ignorant or inept, or criminally careless, it is most unlikely that the patient will come to any harm. Nevertheless, this is not how Collins saw it at the time and it was with an almost overwhelming sense of emancipation that he reached the end of his stint without getting himself or anyone else into any real trouble. The period was not, however, totally free from embarrassment.

Out of anxiety over getting patients too deep, he was rather inclined to keep them too shallow and he had a few caustic remarks from surgeons of the type: 'Better give him some more halothane, Bob, or he'll be walking out of theatre.' Or 'I'm not sure which of us is more sleepy – me or the patient.' Happily, none of his patients actually woke up during an operation, but there were certainly some he had difficulty in putting to sleep.

One particular case is engraved on his memory. The patient was a large, plethoric lieutenant commander from the naval base, to whom Gibraltar must have seemed an ideal posting. Just across the causeway from the bodegas of La Linea de la Frontera, Gibraltar was a dangerous posting for the bibulous in those days. You could fill the boot of your car with demijohns of brandy for a few pounds worth of pesetas. In his pre-operative examination, Collins had naively failed to appreciate that, as is usual in such cases, the commander had grossly understated his alcohol intake. There were, to his untutored eye, no obvious signs of over-indulgence. The significance of the officer's dilated veins all over his face had entirely escaped him.

The relevance of all this is that people with a high alcohol tolerance also have a high anaesthetic tolerance. For such a patient Collins should probably have used 5 per cent Pentothal solution for the induction of the anaesthetic. But, out of caution, and on the advice of the experts who wrote the books, he had standardized on a 2.5 per cent solution. The result was that he was stuck in the anaesthetic room, slowly emptying syringe after syringe of dilute pentothal into the commander's veins while he stubbornly refused to go to sleep.

Instead of cooperating, he simply lay back chortling. Meanwhile, in theatre, the surgeon, assistant, scrub sister, circulating nurses and others were impatiently waiting to get on with the operation. It is not in the nature of the average surgeon to repress impatience and when, as red-faced as the commander, Collins finally pushed the trolley with the snoring victim into theatre, he was greeted with the comment, 'What an unnecessary waste of thiopentone, Collins! Another half hour and it would have been his bed-time.'

Historical Tales

The Hippocratic facies

Modern doctors seldom give much thought to a man who, for well over 2000 years, has been revered by many as the 'father of medicine'. Hippocrates of Cos, who was born around 500 years BC, knew nothing about antibiotics, genetics or immunology and very little about anatomy and physiology, but he knew how to observe and record phenomena and some of his reports are as valid today as they were when he wrote them.

Here is what he said about the facial appearance of a gravely ill person: 'If the appearance of the patient be different from normal, there is danger. If the nose be sharp, the eyes hollow, the temples collapsed, the ears cold and contracted, and the lobes inverted, whilst the skin of the forehead is hard, dry and stretched, and the colour of the face pale or black or livid or leaden, unless these appearances are caused by watching or diarrhoea, or under the influence of malaria, the patient is near death.' The reference to diarrhoea relates to the effects of dehydration.

Hippocrates suggested that useful information could be

obtained by listening to the breath sounds as heard through the chest wall; in some of his writings he gives details of what to listen for. Most historians have forgotten this and claim that auscultation started with the French physician René Théophile Hyacinthe Laennec (1781–1826) who invented the stethoscope.

Hippocrates insisted that a doctor should not be ashamed to call in a colleague for a second opinion if he found himself at a loss in the management of a case. He is, of course, best remembered for the set of rules for the conduct of doctors, known as the Hippocratic oath, which he required his pupils to take: 'The doctor will reverence his teacher as a father; he will use his art to the benefit of his patients and never to their injury or death, even if requested by them; he will never attempt to procure abortion; he will be chaste and never divulge any professional secrets.'

How many doctors of today can put a hand on the heart and claim to have kept all these rules?

Celsus and Paracelsus

The dates of the Roman Aurelius Cornelius Celsus are unknown as he is confidently stated by various historians as having been a contemporary of Augustus (63 BC – AD 14), Tiberius (42 BC – AD 37), Caligula (AD 12–41), Nero (AD 37–68) and Trajan (AD 53–117). He was a man of many interests and a great writer who produced works on military matters, agriculture, usage of language (rhetoric) and medicine. Unfortunately, all of his writings have disappeared except for a fragment on rhetoric and one important medical treatise called *De Medicina*.

It is this work on which Celsus' reputation depends and it was this that influenced medical thought in Europe for centuries. *De Medicina* consists of eight books, respectively on the history of medicine; healthy living; diet and outlook in disease (prognosis); treatment of disease by diet; treatment of poor health; medicines; surgical operations; and diseases, fractures and dislocations of bones. Quite a lot of the book was cribbed from Hippocrates and Aesculapius, sometimes word-for-word, but Celsus had a mind of his own and applied a good deal of judgement to the ideas of the ancients, from which he selected what he considered right.

The book contains much remarkable detail on surgery and describes the operations of lithotomy (cutting for the bladder stone), lens displacement (couching) for cataract, tapping the abdomen for fluid, removal of goitre, the use of the catheter to relieve urinary obstruction, the management of fractures and even plastic surgery to restore a foreskin after circumcision. Celsus had an excellent knowledge of anatomy.

Unfortunately, his judgement was sometimes faulty. Hippocrates had, wisely, been very cautious about the merits of bloodletting, but Celsus went completely overboard on this. He advocated bleeding for almost everything – for paralysis, fever, full veins, redness of the skin, severe pain, convulsions, pleurisy, breathlessness, suffocation, spitting blood and terminal weakness. Celsus had an enormous influence and his advice on bleeding, together with that of his successor Claudius Galen, must throughout the centuries have killed millions.

This apart, Celsus was a fine doctor and an honest man. The same, regrettably, cannot be said for another successor who chose to compare himself with Celsus. The self-styled Philippus Aureolus Paracelsus (Theophrastus Bombastus von

Hohenheim) was an extraordinary person, generally thought to have been born in 1493 at Einsiedeln. He had no formal education but made up for it by the remarkably high opinion he had of himself. He adopted 'Paracelsus' as part of his name simply to indicate that he was a greater man than Celsus.

Paracelsus spent many years wandering all over Europe picking up miscellaneous information, for which he had an insatiable appetite and a remarkable memory. He was undiscriminating in the sources of his information and consulted quacks, conjurers, old women, as well as responsible physicians and philosophers. He was an eloquent man, very entertaining in his talk, and never troubled by the fact that his expressed opinions were often in conflict with each other. He might justly be described as the arch-eclectic of all time. He was also the arch-egotist and a pathological liar who never ceased to make claims for his wonderful cures.

People of this kind of disposition have always been successful because others will often take them at their own valuation. So it was with Bombastus, and in 1526 he was actually appointed professor of medicine and natural philosophy at Basle. There he was extremely popular with the students largely because of the vituperative scorn he cast on his predecessors and rivals and because he often lectured in German. At the time it was considered proper to lecture in Latin, which was harder to understand.

Paracelsus was an alchemist who insisted that, by chemistry, he could cure almost any disease. In fact, his contributions to chemistry were negligible. He did, however, draw attention to the possibility that some chemical substances might have pharmaceutical value. At the same time, he boasted that he possessed the elixir of life and the philosopher's stone. The former could maintain health and indefinite life and the latter could turn any base metal into gold. These claims, too, added to his popularity. Some of his other claims were equally fantastic. He taught that the human body was made exclusively of sulphur, mercury and salt. He stated that every physician ought to be able to indicate, in the human body the location of the points of the compass and the signs of the zodiac. He gave detailed instructions for the creation, by a man, of a miniature living child. He was a great enthusiast for inventing new words and for applying new meanings to existing words. This habit makes some of his works almost impossible to understand. This may have been his intention.

His stay in Basle lasted for only a year and, as a result of a quarrel with the authorities over the size of a fee which he demanded from a churchman, he had to leave. So he resumed his wanderings, never staying long in one place and living mainly in taverns where he consorted drunkenly with the lowest company. It is said that he never took off his clothes, day or night. In spite of possessing the elixir of life and the philosopher's stone he soon sank into poverty and destitution and died at Salzburg in 1541 at the age of forty-eight.

Paracelsus was a man who contributed nothing to medicine or to any other branch of learning, misled thousands of serious students and probably retarded the progress of science for many years. His fame – which was and is considerable – was based on nothing more or less than his own inflated opinion of himself. He is worth studying as a prime example of the power of self-confidence and suggestion.

Paré the great

Ambrose Paré (1509–90) is regarded by many as the father of modern surgery. He was born into a poor French family and had a scanty education, but one day, watching the operation of cutting for the bladder stone (lithotomy), he immediately resolved to be a surgeon and went to Paris to study. After learning the elements of his craft he joined the French army in several campaigns in Italy where he did such excellent work that he was appointed surgeon in ordinary to King Henry II.

This was the start of his royal patronage which continued throughout his life, successively under Francis II, Charles IX and Henry III. Paré was an excellent and pious man and a great favourite of the monarchs. During the St Bartholomew's Day massacre, when over 3000 Huguenots were slaughtered in Paris at the instigation of Catherine de Medici, the mother of Charles IX, the king sent for Paré, insisted he join him in his bedroom and kept him there the whole night. 'It is not right,' said the king, 'that a man so useful to the whole world should be murdered.'

Paré was a thinker who refused blindly to follow the surgical dogmas laid down by his predecessors. Instead, he believed in close observation, reason and experience. He was responsible for radical changes in the management of gunshot wounds and abandoned the damaging practice of pouring boiling oil into them. He stopped the horrifying cautery of the stump with a red-hot iron after amputation and advocated the tying off of arteries to control bleeding. He wrote some excellent papers on the proper management of difficult labour and described how accumulated fluid in the abdomen (ascites) could be safely removed.

His works, which are full of good and reasonable advice were published in twenty-eight volumes. This body of knowledge formed an excellent basis for the development of modern surgery and was widely followed. His life was a triumph of reason over superstition. The French are justifiably proud of him.

Felt upon the pulses

The celebrated Persian physician Avicenna (980–1037), while escaping from Mahmud of Ghazna, paid a visit incognito to Gurgan by the Caspian Sea. A close relative of the ruler of that region lay sick with an illness that had defeated all the local doctors. When it was known that Avicenna was a physician, he was taken to see the patient – a young man.

After examining him, Avicenna asked those present to send for someone who knew the geography of the local area intimately. Such a person duly arrived. Avicenna then put his fingers lightly on the young man's pulse and asked the man to recite the names of the surrounding towns. As one name was mentioned Avicenna cried 'Stop!' He then asked the relatives to send for someone who knew, in detail, the geography of that town. This was done. Avicenna, again feeling the pulse, asked the man to name the quarters and streets. Again, at one point he cried 'Stop!' Another person was sent for who was able to name the families of a particular street and the process was repeated. Finally, the names of the inhabitants of a particular house were enumerated.

Then Avicenna said, 'It is finished. This young man is in love with so-and-so who lives in such-and-such a house. The cure lies in that girl's face.' Avicenna then prescribed the appropriate hour for the marriage and the cure was completed.

It's obvious

William Harvey (1578–1657) was a short-tempered, irascible man who had a hard time building up his medical practice. Fortunately, his father was rich and his brothers were doing well in business, so they helped him. This was just as well because when he came up with the ridiculous, almost heretical, suggestion that the blood did not ebb and flow as that almost divine authority Galen insisted, he was immediately regarded as a complete crank and lost nearly all the patients he had.

Fifteen hundred years before, Galen had stated that there were two kinds of blood: arterial blood and venous blood. When the heart contracted the blood pulsed out into the veins and the arteries; when it relaxed, the blood ebbed back. So much was obvious. Galen's ideas were accepted by the Church, and anyone who questioned them came close to being considered a heretic – a dangerous state of affairs.

Harvey tied a string around his upper arm. When this was tight enough to close off the arteries and thus stop the pulse at the wrist, the veins did not stand out and the hand did not swell. But when the string was just tight enough to obstruct the veins at the top of the arm without closing the arteries, the veins lower down became congested and the hand became swollen. There was only one possible explanation; the blood was coming into the arm by way of the arteries and was leaving by the veins.

So Harvey wrote a book about this with a description of

the valves in the veins, showing that the blood could only go one way. There were also some other completely convincing arguments. Convincing, that is, to anyone with an open mind. Unfortunately none of his contemporaries had an open mind and they just treated his demonstration with the scorn they thought it deserved. It wasn't until long after he was dead that it was generally realized that Harvey was right and that the unthinking veneration of Galen's writings had been misleading humanity for a millennium and a half.

The really important thing, however, was not the discovery by William Harvey of the circulation of the blood. What mattered, and what made a fundamental difference to medical science, was the recognition that it was much better to look, think, experiment and discover than to accept the dogma of a pundit who believed that something was right just because he said it was. This was Harvey's real breakthrough and this is why he is still venerated by scientists.

A doctor at court

Dr Roderigo Lopes, born around 1520, was an excellent Portuguese Jewish doctor who was forced by the Inquisition to renounce his religion. Not content with this, the Inquisition applied such strong anti-Semitic pressures against his family that they had to leave Portugal. Lopes settled in England where he flourished. He was a scholarly and hard-working man and a capable and popular physician. A skilled linguist, he was fluent in Portuguese, Spanish, English, Dutch and Hebrew. In 1565 he took up a resident appointment at St Bartholomew's Hospital in London where he worked for sixteen years. Four years after this appointment he was elected a Fellow of the Royal College of Physicians.

While at Barts, Roderigo was consulted by a number of Queen Elizabeth's courtiers, including the Earl of Leicester and Sir Francis Walsingham, and it seems likely that they carried good reports of his work to the Queen because in 1575 he was appointed physician to the royal court. There he did well and came to the notice of Elizabeth I. In 1586 he achieved the ultimate accolade when he became physician to the Queen.

Roderigo was very popular with Elizabeth and this was not only on account of his medical competence. The Queen found it very convenient to have to hand a mature, reliable and experienced man who could speak several of the languages important in her foreign affairs. Needless to say, in a context of jealousy and conspiracy there were certain dangers in becoming such an obvious favourite of the Queen's. Human nature being what it is, the fact that Lopes was both a foreigner and a Jew, simply added to the mistrust and envy with which he was regarded by his fellow courtiers. He was particularly disliked and distrusted by the scheming Robert Devereux, 2nd Earl of Essex. At this stage, Essex had achieved a great deal of power in the court and was acting as a kind of Foreign Secretary.

When Sir Francis Drake defeated the Spanish Armada in 1588 some members of the court were in favour of making peace with Spain; others remained suspicious of Spanish motives. Philip II of Spain had already taken over Portugal and showed other territorial ambitions – in America as well as in Europe. Arguments raged and spying was rife in both courts. The situation was further complicated by the presence in England of one Don Antonio who was the illegitimate son of the rightful heir to the Portuguese throne. Don Antonio had hoped to become King of Portugal but Philip's aggressive response had forced him to flee to England. He was supported by various courtiers who were antagonistic to Philip, including the Earl of Essex. The last thing Roderigo Lopes wanted was to get involved in all this. He was content with his situation in the court and in his friendship with the Queen. He was happily married and had five children.

In 1593, one of the secret agents of the King of Spain approached Roderigo and offered him a valuable diamond and ruby ring – a present from King Philip. The quid pro quo was that Roderigo should poison Don Antonio. Roderigo was horrified and uncertain what to do. However, he played the situation coolly, equivocated with the spy and then went to see the Queen. Unfortunately, Elizabeth did not take the matter seriously, and brushed aside Roderigo's concerns. Roderigo offered her the ring but she refused to take it.

The Spanish agent was encouraged however, and the next thing Roderigo knew was that he was being propositioned by three other Spanish spies and offered a fortune of 50,000 crowns to do the deed. Roderigo immediately refused. By an extraordinary misfortune, the Earl of Essex got to know of the conspiracy. If seemed to him that if Philip of Spain could plot to have Dr Lopes poison Don Antonio, he might just as easily plot to have him poison Queen Elizabeth. So Essex had two of the Spanish agents arrested and tortured. It is hardly surprising that, to try to please him and avoid further torture, they confessed that Roderigo had agreed to poison Elizabeth.

It is no credit to the Earl of Essex that he was willing to accept evidence obtained under torture. On New Year's Day

1594 Roderigo was arrested by Essex, questioned severely and threatened with torture. Lopes was now in his seventies and did not have the stamina of youth. Under the importunate questioning of Essex he eventually broke done and actually confessed to implication in a plot to poison the Queen. It never seemed to occur to Essex that Roderigo had no possible reason to wish to assist King Philip against Elizabeth and every reason to support the latter who was his friend and benefactor. Roderigo was immediately locked up in the Tower along with the Spanish agents.

At the end of February Essex mounted a trial in the Guildhall. The only evidence available against Lopes was that of the Spaniards – evidence that had been obtained under torture. Roderigo insisted he was innocent; the spies insisted that he was guilty. All three were convicted and sentenced to death. Elizabeth stood by her doctor, believing him to be innocent, and refused to sign his death warrant. Essex was not going to be baulked, however, and had the three prisoners moved from the Tower to the prison at Southwark where they could be treated as common criminals whose death warrants did not require the Queen's signature.

On 7 June 1594, Roderigo Lopes and the two Spanish agents were dragged through the streets to Tyburn. Roderigo was hanged until he was almost dead but cut down while still conscious. He was then castrated, his belly cut open and the bowels pulled out. His body was then cut into four quarters. All this was in accordance with the standard sentence that he should be hanged, drawn and quartered.

Elizabeth mourned her lost doctor and never accepted his guilt. She managed to get hold of the ring that Lopes had offered her and, for the rest of her life, wore it on her belt so as to remember him. She provided financial support for his widow and children and sent one of his sons to Winchester College.

The bezoar

A bezoar is a hard, compacted and concreted body, such as a calcified hairball or gallstone, found in the stomach and intestines of ruminant and other animals, especially goats, and occasionally in humans. The term derives from two Persian roots: *bad* – 'against' and *zahr* – 'poison', and the bezoar, at one time, had a wonderful reputation, not only as a sure antidote to poisons, but also as a universal panacea. The ideas started with Arab physicians and spread from them to Europe where it persisted right up to the eighteenth century. Such was the belief in the power of the bezoar that any specimen was worth a good deal of money. Rich men carried them with them wherever they went, and there was a brisk trade in counterfeit or fraudulent articles.

The most prized specimens were those showing concentric rings when cut across. Such a stone would have taken a long time to form. The value of a bezoar seems to have been relative to the rarity of the animal from which it was taken. Especially prized were those from the chamois. Best of all was a bezoar from a Peruvian llama.

Bezoar was considered to be a medicine and either had to be taken by mouth or rubbed on the affected part of the body. There is a story that the great French surgeon Ambrose Paré (1509–90) tried to disabuse King Charles IX of his belief in a very expensive bezoar of which he was proud. Paré knew the value of experiment and suggested to the king that they carry out a trial of the power of the stone. The king agreed. So a cook who had just been condemned to death for stealing silver plates from his master was brought before them. He was told that, rather than being publicly strangled, he could have the choice of taking poison and then being cured of it by means of a miraculous bezoar. Needless to say, the felon agreed.

An apothecary was summoned and was told to give the man a strong poison. He did so, using a large dose of bichloride of mercury. This was immediately followed up with the bezoar stone. Within an hour the cook was in agony. Bichloride of mercury (mercuric chloride) taken in more than trace quantities is a corrosive poison causing severe nausea, vomiting, abdominal pain and bloody diarrhoea. There is a rapidly destructive effect on the kidneys. In this case the cook is reported as having taken seven hours to die and said to have cried out in the course of his agony that he would rather have been strangled.

Paré, no doubt pleased with the result, carried out a post-mortem examination and retrieved the bezoar which he presented to the king.

'Burn it,' said his Majesty.

The doctor is touched

When he was a child, the great Dr Samuel Johnson (1709–84) was, quite naturally, given milk to drink. These were the days before Louis Pasteur had shown how to make milk safe from infection and some of the milk that Johnson drank came from cows with tuberculosis of the udders. The milk was infected with the *Mycobacterium tuberculosis* and this germ settled in the boy's tonsils where it flourished. The infection spread to the lymph nodes in his neck and these, too, became infected with bovine tuberculosis.

The nodes became inflamed, swollen, enlarged and tender and some of them, lying just under the skin, broke down and discharged externally on to his neck. The sinuses that formed were kept open by the constant discharge of tuberculous pus and the infection spread to involve the skin as well as the lymph system. The unfortunate boy now had a chronic condition known as scrofula.

Because of the number of cows that were infected at that time, scrofula was very common – so common, indeed, that it was known as the 'king's evil'. The origin of this name remains obscure but it must have been related to the then widespread belief that the condition could be cured if the sufferer could only be touched by the sovereign. It is just possible that the emotional effect of the event might somehow have influenced the immune system to attack the infection more vigorously. Only a few of such cures would have been sufficient to establish the belief.

Be that as it may, the infant Samuel Johnson was taken to be touched by the then sovereign, Queen Anne. Johnson was a great sceptic all his life and, perhaps because of that, or perhaps because he made no secret of his contempt for the generality of women – whom he considered manifestly inferior to men – the touching had no useful effect and the scrofula stayed with him for the rest of his life.

Le malade imaginaire

The great French dramatist Molière (1622–73) was a confirmed hypochondriac as well as being a writer of genius and a talented actor. It was his habit to take the leading part in each of his major dramatic productions. He wrote a number of excellent plays of which the best known are *Le misanthrope*, *Le médecin malgré lui*, *L'avare*, *Le bourgeois gentilhomme* and *Le malade imaginaire*.

In spite of his hypochondriasis Molière never missed an opportunity to attack members of the medical profession. He did so, with sharp malice, in the plays *Féstin de Pierre*, *L'amour medecin, Le médecin malgré lui* and in his last play *Le malade imaginaire (The hypochondriac)*. This play was one of his most entertaining pieces and his most savage attack on the doctors. It contains an ironical ballet burlesquing the ceremonies of French medical graduation, with the members of the chorus brandishing enema syringes.

Molière had been having chest pains and was convinced that he was having a heart attack. Although very worried about himself, he was so engrossed in the part that he insisted on going on stage. During the third performance the pain became worse and his wife and fellow actors tried to persuade him to let an understudy take the part, but Molière refused and continued to the end. He was a real trouper and, when he had a particularly severe spasm of pain, passed it off as a laugh. As he staggered off the stage he felt terrible and was barely able to make his way home.

Irony followed him to the last. There was nothing wrong with Molière's heart, as was soon to become apparent. That evening he began to cough blood and the flow of blood from his mouth rapidly increased to a severe haemorrhage. This became so severe that he was unable to breathe and he died from suffocation.

The cause of his death remains obscure. Today, the most likely diagnosis would be cancer of the lung. Or Molière may have had tuberculosis or an aneurysm of a large artery that burst. He was said to have 'consumption' but it would be unusual for tuberculosis to bring about death in this way. Whatever the cause, there is no possibility that any form of medical treatment could have been of any avail. Judging by results, Molière was entirely justified in his opinion of the doctors.

Pectoral honey of liverwort

'Experience has amply confirmed the utility of this preparation for coughs, colds, spitting of blood, and all affections of the lungs, etc. The unparalleled success with which this justly celebrated medicine has met, has induced some ignorant pretenders to attempt to palm off a counterfeit article on the public; which in outward appearance so much resembles the original as easily to deceive the unwary. To escape this miserable imposition, remember the GENUINE bears the signature of the proprietor and inventor, JAMES D. NOWILL in full on the outside wrapper.'

This advert appeared on the front page of the *New York Tribune* in 1841. It raises an interesting point of logic and a nice question of ethics. According to Culpeper: 'Liverwort is under the dominion of Jupiter and the sign of Cancer. It is a rare herb for all diseases of the liver, to cool and cleanse it, and subdue inflammation in any part, and to cure yellow jaundice ... It is a first-rate remedy for such whose livers are corrupted by surfeits, which cause their bodies to break out, for it fortifyeth the liver exceedingly, and makes it impregnable.'

According to modern pharmacology, liverwort is devoid of any medicinal value whatsoever, either for disorders of the liver or the lungs. To be charitable, we must suppose that both Nicholas Culpeper and James D. Nowill were suffering from the common *post hoc, ergo propter hoc* delusion. Someone has an illness; you give a concoction of liverwort. Afterwards the patient recovers; therefore it was on account of the concoction that the recovery took place. This logical fallacy is as alive and well today as it was in the times of Culpeper and of Nowill. The probability is, however, that James D. Nowill was as cynically aware of the uselessness of his product as are most snake oil merchants.

The ethical question is whether the fraudulent nature of the original attempt to separate the gullible from their money can excuse plagiaristic competitors from trying to dilute the profits of the first racketeer.

The mercury cure

Barton Booth was a distinguished Shakespearean actor and tragedian of the early eighteenth century, and an associate of Wilks and Colley Cibber. Among his finest interpretations were those of King Lear, Brutus, Hotspur and Henry VIII. At the height of his career in 1727, he developed a serious illness with fever that lasted for over six weeks. He was able to return to the stage but soon afterwards became ill again and this time developed severe jaundice.

From that time on Booth was a chronic invalid terrified of succumbing to illness and constantly consulting doctors and reading medical books. One of these was *The Ancient Physician's Legacy to his Country* by one Thomas Dover. Dover was a remarkable man, a Bachelor of Arts of Magdalen Hall, Oxford, a Bachelor of Medicine of Caius College, Cambridge, and a privateering ship's captain. In 1708 he had sacked Guayaquil in Peru and, on the same voyage, rescued Alexander Selkirk from the desert island Juan Fernandez, where he had been marooned for four years and four months, thereby providing Defoe with the idea for *Robinson Crusoe.*

Dover was known as the 'quicksilver doctor' because of his advocacy of mercury as a panacea for all sorts of ills including, to quote his own words, 'leprosy, rheumatisms, the Itch, inflammations and fluxions of the Eyes, all Cutaneous Foulness, White Swellings, Tumours, internal ulcers, sharp Humours in the stomach and guts, stone, Gravel and Gout'. The book that Barton Booth read was largely concerned with this claim. There is little in it of worthwhile medical knowledge but plenty of unsupported claims. It was impressive to uninformed people partly because of its disingenuous claim to 'the power of art without the show.'

There had been numerous criticisms of Dover's mercury cure by members of the medical profession, some pointing out that mercury compounds were very poisonous. It was well known that workers in mercury mines suffered severely from shaking palsy and general weakness. To these Dover replied: 'It is a generally received notion, nay even among many Gentlemen of the Faculty, that quicksilver is a poison.

If such persons are not ashamed of their being no better natural philosophers, I have no reason to be under confusion if faced with them.' Dover was right about one thing. Quicksilver – metallic mercury – is fairly innocuous. The salts, however, are extremely dangerous.

Booth decided to consult Dover. The doctor was as confident as ever and assured him that the wonderful medicine would 'effectively cure him of all his complaints'. Booth was impressed and decided to do the job in style. He consumed almost two pounds of mercury. Dover's predictions soon came true and within two weeks the patient was permanently relieved of all worldly cares. Sir Hans Sloane, who was called in shortly before he died, forbade further mercury, but this advice came too late.

A post-mortem examination was carried out which quickly showed the cause of the unfortunate actor's illness. Numerous gall stones were present in the gall bladder and bile duct, and a particularly large one had completely obstructed the duct so that bile was unable to escape into the intestine. The accumulation of bile in the blood was, of course, the cause of the jaundice. The surgeon who carried out the autopsy reported that the intestines were blackened from mercury and the rectum 'so rotten and blackened that it broke between my fingers like tinder.'

In spite of the furore that this case aroused, Dover remained unperturbed. For the rest of his life he continued to promote and prescribe his mercury cure and his book went into edition after edition. When he died, he had won fame, fortune and an international reputation. The twenty-ninth edition of the highly respected *Martindale's Extra Pharmacopoeia*, 1898, still contains a reference to another remedy of the distinguished doctor – Dover's powders. This preparation, composed of ten grains each of opium, ipecacuanha, and potassium sulphate, but no mercury, has been in use for over 200 years. Ipecac is a highly effective emetic so it may be that many of Dover's patients were saved from the effects of one of his prescriptions by the effects of another.

Wharton's duct

Thomas Wharton (1614–73) was an eminent physician and anatomist who took MD degrees from both Oxford and Cambridge and was physician to St Thomas's Hospital, London. He was a courageous man who was one of the very few doctors to remain in London throughout the whole of the great plague outbreak of 1665. This was not entirely disinterested; King Charles II promised him the appointment of Physician in Ordinary if he attended all the plague patients from the guards at St Thomas's. Wharton was faithful to this agreement but the king was not and the job went to another. So Wharton had to console himself with fishing. Isaak Walton described him, in the *Compleat Angler*, as 'a dear friend that loves both me and my art of angling'.

Wharton's name is well known to generations of medical students for his description of the duct of the submaxillary salivary gland in the floor of the mouth. The twining relationship of the duct to the lingual nerve has been described in the immortal mnemonic, never mentioned by lecturers but well known to all students: 'The lingual nerve, it took a swerve,

across the hyoglossus. And Wharton's duct said "I'll be f — d,
the b — r's double-crossed us!"'

Giving leave

John Coakley Lettsom was a Quaker physician of the eighteenth and early nineteenth centuries. At twenty-three he inherited a property in the West Indies and immediately freed all the slaves, leaving himself penniless. He returned to Britain where he set up the first out-patient clinics for the poor – a thing unheard of at the time. In 1773 he founded the Medical Society of London and the following year he attended the first meeting of the Royal Humane Society, and became a member of the committee. Lettsom then became interested in prison reform and, through his writings, speeches and support for and editing of a long succession of letters on 'Prison Visitations' in the *Gentleman's Magazine*, did much to ameliorate the horrors of the eighteenth-century prisons. His interest in this had been aroused after being called to attend the notorious Lord George Gordon (see Dickens' *Barnaby Rudge*) who was dying of typhus in Newgate.

In 1791 Lettsom founded the Royal Seabathing Hospital in Margate, primarily to provide the children of the poor with the benefits of sea breezes, open air and healthful exercise. He was one of the first to recommend sunshine and cleanliness as important elements in hygiene and to insist – against the tide of medical opinion – that these would lower the incidence of typhus and smallpox. He was also an ardent supporter of vaccination and fought vigorously against the anti-vaccinationists. He founded the Royal Jennerian Society. By 1800 Lettsom was so well known and successful that his income from medical practice was about £12,000 a year. In those days this was a huge sum. But he was a man of such generosity that he gave it all away to charity. Indeed he was so generous that he ran into debt and had to sell his beautiful villa in Camberwell Grove and his museum, library and gardens.

Because he made no very dramatic contribution to medical science, hardly anyone has heard of Lettsom nowadays. His only original finding was the neuritis caused by alcoholism. But the influence of this remarkable man was far greater than that of many who are renowned for their scientific discoveries. His example helps to remind us what medicine is all about. It is not about making clever diagnoses and rising higher in the profession than our rivals; it is about the relief of human suffering and the promotion of human happiness.

Ironically, Lettsom is best remembered by an epigram which, although witty, could hardly be less appropriate or justified. It goes:

> When any sick to me apply,
> I physics, bleed and sweats 'em.
> If after that they choose to die,
> Why, verily
>
> I. Lettsom

Scheele's 'fire air'

The Swedish apothecary and chemist Karl Wilhelm Scheele (1742–86), was a remarkable man, the extent of whose chemical discoveries is almost unrivalled in science and is matched only by his inexplicable obscurity. In 1771, while heating mercuric oxide, Scheele discovered a new gas with remarkable properties. It was colourless and odourless and could keep small animals alive and frisky. A glowing wood splint plunged into it would burst into flame. Scheele called the gas 'fire air' and wrote a book about it in which he described his experiments. Unfortunately, his dilatory publisher did not get the book out until 1777 and by that time the English scientist Joseph Priestley (1733–1804) had reported his own similar experiments and had taken the credit – still generally acknowledged – as the discoverer of oxygen.

In a life devoted exclusively to the pursuit of science, and probably shortened by his habit of tasting all the new substances he came across, Scheele isolated the elements barium, chlorine, manganese, molybdenum, nitrogen and oxygen, and produced scores of important new compounds. His contributions to chemistry probably exceeded those of any other scientist of his time.

Neither Scheele nor Priestley fully grasped the vital role of oxygen in keeping humans and other animals alive and in combustion. Priestley visited the French scientist Antoine-Laurent Lavoisier (1743–94) in 1774 and told him about his experiments. Lavoisier immediately repeated these and soon saw the importance of the newly discovered gas and its relation to air. He gave oxygen its current name and showed that air contained two main gases, one which supported combustion and one which did not. He studied the heat produced by animals breathing oxygen and demonstrated the relationship of respiration to combustion. Lavoisier, anxious to be known as the discoverer of an element, did not acknowledge the help of Priestley, whom he regarded as an amateur. Scheele, the real hero, was sadly ignored and forgotten.

Priority

Edward Jenner is almost universally regarded as the discoverer of vaccination against smallpox for his experiments carried out in 1796. He was certainly so regarded officially and handsomely rewarded. But historical research shows that the efficacy of vaccination was well known to Dorset farmers some years before Jenner came to fame. There is clear evidence that, twenty-two years earlier, a farmer called Benjamin Jesty was carrying out vaccination using cowpox. Later in 1805, as proof of his success, Jesty was presented with two gold-mounted lancets and a certificate crediting him with the discovery.

Jenner was a part of the establishment and a fellow of the Royal Society. He was also patronized by the Duke of Bedford and the Lord Mayor of London. It seems that credit for scientific discoveries often rests with the person who make the most fuss rather than with the genuine originator.

Elephantiasis

When the great tropical medicine specialist Patrick Manson was working in Amoy, 300 miles north of Hong Kong, a young man was brought to him with an enormous, sack-like elephantiasis of the scrotum. This was so large that the man could not work and was a great burden to his family. The young man had been advised to kill himself and had tried three times to do so by taking arsenic. However, he had been somewhat over-liberal with the dosage and as a result had; on each occasion, vomited it all up again.

By now desperate, he decided that if he could not kill himself, he might as well let Manson do it for him. Amputation of an elephantiatic scrotum is a simple and straightforward operation and Manson, although not primarily a surgeon, had no great difficulty in relieving the young man of his embarrassing burden. Recovery was complete and the young man, much to his surprise, was restored, only slightly attenuated but fit for full duty, to his family. History does not record whether they were pleased to see him.

Manson's interest in elephantiasis was now aroused so he undertook some research. He soon discovered that the disease was caused by blockage of the lymph drainage channels by millions of tiny microscopic parasitic worms called microfilaria. Later he was to demonstrate that these worms reached people by way of mosquitoes who were intermediate hosts to the parasite. This was but one of the many discoveries Manson made in tropical medicine. His contributions to medicine were legion, not the least being his founding of the London School of Tropical Medicine. His textbook, *Manson's Tropical Diseases*, became a classic and went through numerous editions.

Broca susses out the brain

The most important of the early attempts to find out which parts of the brain did what and to show how the mind and the brain were related was that of Pierre Paul Broca (1824–80). Broca was a distinguished surgeon, anatomist and anthropologist, with degrees in surgery, pathology and anthropology and simultaneous professorships at the Paris Faculty of Medicine and the Anthropological Institute. In 1861, in a lecture at the Paris Anthropological Society, Broca demonstrated the brain of a former patient. The medical history of this man, M. Leborgne, revealed that he had lost the ability to speak or to write although his intelligence and comprehension had been unaffected.

Prior to his death Leborgne had been able to communicate only by gestures, nods and facial expressions. Broca had conducted a post-mortem examination and had found an area of damage the size of a golf ball in the left hemisphere of the brain. Broca was convinced that this damage was the cause of the language defect. Many of his medical colleagues believed he was talking nonsense. Broca's claim, however, aroused interest in the possibility that certain parts of the brain had particular functions and within a decade other neurologists began to discover that other people with brain damage in the same general area had suffered various kinds of language difficulties. This area of the brain is still called 'Broca's area'.

When Broca's findings were fully substantiated, neurologists started to search for other correlations between loss of function of all kinds and subsequent observable brain damage. Later, in the course of brain surgery it became possible to discover the effects on the body of mild electrical stimulation of the cortex of the brain. By the end of the nineteenth century the functions of most of the different areas of the brain were established.

The cure and the disease

Robert Bentley Todd was a professor of physiology at King's College at the age of twenty-seven, and was one of the prime movers in the foundation of King's College Hospital in 1839. He wrote extensively on physiology and neurology and produced, with William Bowman, a four-volume *Cyclopaedia of Anatomy and Physiology*. Todd was a highly religious man who thought nothing of reminding his students regularly of the religious and moral duties of the doctor. He was also a great advocate of the use of alcohol in medical practice. He wrote: 'Alcohol, in some form or other, is a remedy whose value can scarcely, I think, be overestimated, and upon which, when carefully administered, I rely on with the utmost confidence in a great number of cases of disease which are at all amenable to treatment.'

After a distinguished career at King's he retired in December 1859 to go into private practice. Six weeks later he started to vomit blood but continued to see his patients at home. The vomiting persisted, however, and within two days he was dead. The post-mortem examination revealed that the bleeding came from grossly varicose veins at the lower end of the gullet (oesophageal varices). These were caused by advanced cirrhosis of the liver.

Mad dogs and Frenchmen

Louis Pasteur (1822–95) was nothing if not courageous. He knew better than almost anyone how dangerous rabies was, how universally fatal and how horrible the death from the disease. Yet he was willing to bring his nose within a couple of inches of the slavering jaws of a mad dog held by his assistants so that he could suck out some saliva to get a specimen of the organism of the disease.

In people who have been bitten by a rabid animal, the disease begins, usually after a long incubation period, with a low fever, loss of appetite, headache, and often a recurrence of pain or tingling at the site of the bite. During the next few days there is growing anxiety, jumpiness, disorientation, neck stiffness, and sometimes epileptic seizures. Within a week the characteristic fear of swallowing starts. The patient may be consumed with thirst, but any attempt to drink at once induces violent spasms of the diaphragm, pharynx and larynx, with gagging, choking and a growing sense of panic – hence the term hydrophobia. As the condition worsens, even the sight or sound of water prompts these reactions and there are intervals of maniacal behaviour with thrashing, spitting, biting and raving. Delusions and hallucinations develop. These attacks alternate with periods of lucidity in which the patient suffers acute anxiety and mental distress. The nerves controlling eye movement and facial expression become paralysed and coma and death occur, usually within a week of the onset of the severe symptoms

Pasteur knew all this but persisted, even though the germ he found and which he took to be the cause of the disease was also present in the mouths of healthy dogs. It was not until some time later that Pasteur decided that rabies was an infection of the nervous system and that the germ had to get into a nerve. At the time, viruses were unknown, and even if they had been identified, they could not have been seen with any of the microscopes of the time. It was not until the electron microscope was invented that viruses could be seen.

Acting on his hunch about the brain infection, Pasteur and

his assistants injected some brain material from a rabid dog into the brain of a healthy animal. Two weeks later the animal developed rabies. The next step was to get an animal to survive the injection. This seemed impossible. No one had ever survived an attack of rabies. The germ was one of the most deadly known. This dangerous work went on for months as they tried again and again. At last one dog developed the disease but after a short illness made a complete recovery. Excitedly Pasteur again injected the animal with deadly rabies germs. The dog was immune. Pasteur now knew that vaccination against rabies was possible.

Now it was necessary somehow to modify the invisible germ so that it could be made safe and used as a vaccine. After endless experiment they succeeded by taking some material from the spinal cord of rabbits dead from rabies and letting it dry out for fourteen days under sterile conditions. They then powdered, suspended and injected this material. The dogs showed no ill effects. Pasteur then injected material that had been dried for progressively less time. He reasoned that the shorter the period of drying, the more virulent the germ. And he was right. Dogs that had had a full course of fourteen injections were completely immune to rabies.

Pasteur wanted to try out the new vaccine on himself and was dissuaded only with difficulty by his colleagues. At that point a mother brought him her nine-year-old son who had been extensively bitten two days before by a mad dog. The wounds were deep and were beginning to fester.

That evening they started giving the boy the course of fourteen injections. He remained healthy.

Victims of rabid dogs and wolves beat a path to Pasteur's door. They came from all over the world, often dying *en route* because they came too late. Nineteen peasants who had been bitten by a mad wolf came from Smolensk. Some of them were so mangled that they could hardly walk. Sixteen of them were saved and returned to Russia healthy. The Tsar sent Pasteur the diamond cross of St Anne and 100,000 francs to build a laboratory, which became known as the Pasteur Institute.

Fourteen years before this astonishing achievement, Pasteur, at the age of forty-six had suffered a devastating cerebral haemorrhage – a stroke that left him completely paralyzed down his left side. He was not expected to recover. It was fortunate for the world that Pasteur bled on the right side of his brain, the side that controls the left side of the body. Had the stroke been on the other side his speech and language would probably have been seriously deranged and his scientific career brought to an untimely close.

Burke and Hare

William Fergusson, who was later to become a major figure in British surgery was a student of anatomy in Edinburgh in the winter of 1828–9. One of the bodies brought in for dissection was that of a young prostitute who was immediately recognized by the students as a Mary Paterson. The body was 'very well formed' and the anatomist, Dr Knox, seemed to be rather taken with it. So he directed that it should not be dissected but should be preserved in spirit. He called in the artist Samuel Joseph to make a drawing of it.

Fergusson was not at all happy about how Mary came to end up in the dissecting room, and began to make enquiries. At that time not too many questions were asked about the source of these bodies and it was well known that grave-robbing was one way they were procured. This was not considered a particularly heinous offence as there were no property rights in a dead body. Dr Knox was quite ready to turn a blind eye to the exact circumstances of how the bodies were obtained. And some time before the arrival of Mary Paterson, the anatomist had found a new source of subjects for his students.

William Burke and his mistress and William Hare and his wife lived together in a sleazy Edinburgh boarding house for vagrants run by Hare. When one of the vagrants, a man called Donald, died owing four pounds, Hare was furious and resolved to get his money by hook or by crook. A cheap coffin was provided by the parish and Donald was duly put into it for burial. Realizing that there was a market for bodies, Burke and Hare opened up the coffin again, hid the body in a bed and weighted the coffin with bark from a tanners' yard. They did quite well out of this transaction because Dr Knox paid them seven pounds ten shillings.

This was an eye-opener for these unsavoury characters and immediately suggested to them a ready source of income. However, grave-opening was hard and dirty work. So Burke and Hare began to look out for people who would not be readily missed. Their methods were crude but effective. Simulating friendship, they enticed the victim into the boarding house. Burke's mistress was particularly good at this. The unsuspecting person was plied with drink and then suffocated by Burke and Hare. This form of murder, which came to be known as 'burking', ensured that there were no suspicious marks. No less than sixteen men and women were killed in this way and all were sold to Dr Knox for dissection.

As is often the case, the two murderers became both greedy

and careless. It was a serious mistake to do away with Mary Paterson, a girl who was well known to the students. Burke and Hare also killed a cheerful imbecile known as 'Daft Jamie' who was also well known and whose disappearance could not be accounted for. The pair were soon arrested. Fergusson was called as one of the witnesses at their trial.

There is no honour either among thieves or murderers. Hare, ever the opportunist, turned Queen's evidence and so was spared the gallows. Burke was convicted and sentenced to death. Dr Knox did not come out of all this too well and, although he defended himself boldly, it was fairly obvious that he had not been too particular as to where the bodies came from. Burke was hanged and the event was witnessed by an approving crowd of over 20,000 people. The mob then turned their attention to Dr Knox's anatomy school and the police had to intervene to save his life. His reputation was destroyed, nevertheless, and he was ostracized and had to leave Edinburgh.

The Burke and Hare scandal aroused so much public outcry that Parliament was driven to enact legislation controlling the supply of bodies for dissection. The Anatomy Act of 1832 ruled that institutions having lawful custody of the bodies of inmates with no known relatives may provide them for schools of anatomy. The Act also covered the bequeathing of bodies for medical purposes.

Banting knew best

The Canadian Frederick Banting was seriously injured at Cambrai during a heavy artillery bombardment in World

War I. He recovered consciousness in a field hospital to be told by the surgeon that it was necessary to amputate his arm. Banting objected weakly but the surgeon was insistent. Finally Banting said 'Look. I'm a doctor myself. Put yourself in my position. What would you want?'

The surgeon shrugged his shoulders and moved on to the next patient.

Banting survived the war and recovered the use of his arm. After the war, the decorated hero returned to medical research where, working with a medical student called Charlie Best, he conducted a series of classic experiments to prove that the then fatal disease of diabetes was caused by lack of insulin from the pancreas and that insulin could be used to keep diabetic patients healthy.

Later, Banting and the head of his laboratory – a Professor MacLeod who seems to have done little but discourage the work until its success was obvious – were awarded the Nobel Prize. Charlie Best was ignored. Banting protested and immediately gave half of his prize money to Best. Happily, history has remembered and has coupled the names of Banting and Best. No one now remembers MacLeod.

The first hormone

Ernest Henry Starling (1866–1927) and William Maddock Bayliss (1860–1924) were two English physiologists who formed a lifelong intellectual alliance based on their interest in research. Starling was educated at Guy's Hospital, London, and became head of the department of physiology there. In 1899 he became a Fellow of the Royal Society and the same year was appointed

Professor of Physiology at University College, London. Bayliss started training as a doctor at University College but decided that medicine was not for him and went to Wadham College, Oxford, to do research in physiology. A man of some wealth, he decided to return to University College to join forces with Starling.

In 1902 Starling and Bayliss were investigating the puzzling question of how it was that the pancreas always produced its digestive juice as soon as food passed from the stomach into the duodenum. Pavlov had claimed that this was the result of messages passing along nerves, but Starling and Bayliss proved that the pancreas continued to secrete on time even if all the nerves to it were cut. Careful research showed that stomach acid contact with the lining of the small intestine caused a substance, which they arbitrarily named 'secretin', to be produced. This substance entered the bloodstream and was carried to the pancreas where it prompted the gland to start secreting its enzyme juice. Later, as it became clear that there were other chemical messengers of this kind, Starling suggested the general term 'hormones' for these substances, derived from the Greek *hormao*, meaning 'I set in motion'.

Starling's *Principles of Human Physiology* was published in 1912, went into many editions and was read by generations of medical students. In 1903 Bayliss was elected a Fellow of the Royal Society and in 1912 became Professor of General Physiology at University College. He was knighted in 1922.

The Street

Those who work in it affectionately call it 'The Street'. Actually, the name 'Harley Street' is remarkably elastic and really refers to a small medical district that also encompasses the adjoining streets: Wimpole Street, Devonshire Place, Portland Place, Welbeck Street, Queen Anne Street, Weymouth Street and New Cavendish Street.

Harley Street is named after the Harley family, whose most distinguished member was Robert Harley, First Earl of Oxford (1661–1724). Harley was Secretary of State, Chancellor of the Exchequer and chief Minister to Queen Anne, to whom he was inclined to be rather disrespectful, especially when drunk. He had a talent for attracting trouble. In 1711 he was stabbed while interrogating a spy of Louis XIV. He recovered, but three years later was tried and convicted of a treasonous correspondence with the Pretender in France and sent to the Tower. His friends managed to get him out, however, after he had served two years of his sentence.

Harley was not universally admired. 'His slender and pliant intellect,' said Lord Chesterfield, 'was well fitted to crawl up to the height of power through all the crooked mazes and dirty by-paths of intrigue; but having once attained the pinnacle, its smallness and meanness was exposed to all the world.' Be that as it may, Harley certainly achieved greatness. Among other notable achievements, he was the founder of the magnificent Harleian library at Oxford.

Harley's son Edward originated the Cavendish Estate venture in 1717 as a plan to build residences 'for the nobility and gentry'. Most of Harley Street, though, dates from the late eighteenth century and was work of various architects including W.

Thomas Collins and John Johnson from Leicester. One of the largest houses, No. 4 (now No. 10) was designed by the distinguished architect James Wyatt and built in the early 1820s. This house, when new, cost £6000 and was notable for possessing a bathroom with running water.

It is not at all clear why Harley Street and environs became the medical mecca of the world. Possibly its proximity to four major railway stations may have helped, for patients came from far and near. It would be unworthy to speculate that the popularity of the Street could have had anything to do with the extraordinary success of one of its first practitioners. This was the Irish quack doctor John St John Long who made an enormous fortune at 41 Harley Street (now No. 84) in the early 1830s. Patients, especially women, queued at his front door and his income was at least £10,000 a year. Long twice ended up in the Old Bailey charged with causing the death of his patients. In spite of these minor setbacks, this enterprising practitioner, who claimed to be able to cure tuberculosis by rubbing the bosoms of his female patients and getting them to inhale medicated vapours, died a very rich man – from tuberculosis.

When the Medical Register was started in 1858 only 19 doctors were practising in the Street. By 1873 there were 36; by 1880 there were 58. By 1900, the number had risen to 157, of which, remarkably, three of the practitioners were women. One of these was the redoubtable Elizabeth Blackwell, the first British woman doctor to practise openly and, in 1865, to be registered as a medical practitioner. When the horrified members of the Medical Society realized that they had a woman on the Register they took immediate legislative steps to ensure that no such dreadful event would happen again.

In those days, doctors working in the Street actually lived there, and these tall four- and five-storey houses were occupied by single families and their servants. At first the doctors were a somewhat despised minority, greatly outnumbered by noble families, retired senior officers, members of the diplomatic corps, government ministers and successful manufacturers. Gladstone lived at No. 73. The painter Turner at No. 64 (now No. 51).

In the late nineteenth and early twentieth centuries the tall buildings of Harley Street had a dingy, dark appearance. A photograph of the period shows soot-blackened buildings forming, in spite of the considerable breadth of the thoroughfare, a sombre-looking and forbidding chasm. For many patients in the advanced stages of disease, a journey to Harley Street was the last, forlorn hope. Small wonder that in those days it was often known by the macabre nickname 'The Valley of the Shadow of Death'.

Many names, distinguished both for professional brilliance and for downright quackery, have graced the purlieus of Harley Street. Sir Morell Mackenzie, surgeon to the crowned heads of Europe, and a surgeon of great distinction, lived at 19 Harley Street. His book on his management of the throat cancer of the Crown Prince Frederick of Germany, published in 1888 soon after the death of his patient, slated the German doctors for their incompetence and misdiagnosis, and sold 100,000 copies in two weeks. Mackenzie, in spite of adverse criticism of the standards of his medical ethics, was a shining example of the power of advertising. Soon he had the largest and most profitable medical practice in the land, and his international fame really put Harley Street on the map.

Sir Frederick Treves, of 'Elephant man' fame and distinguished for his appendicitis operations, practised in 6 Wimpole Street. In June 1902 Treves advised King Edward VII, who was about to be crowned, to postpone the coronation, as his life was in grave danger and immediate surgery was indicated. The king decided that the coronation must proceed as planned. As soon as the long, agonizing ceremony was over, Treves successfully opened a large appendix abscess and let out the pus, thus saving the king from fatal peritonitis. Recovery was rapid and the whole matter remained a secret to all but a handful of people.

Harley Street can boast of having accommodated more outstanding historical figures connected with medicine than any comparable district in the world. Only a few can be mentioned here. Ernest Jones, who introduced Freud to Britain and wrote his biography, lived at 81 Harley Street. Wilfred Trotter ('The Instinct of the Herd in peace and War') lived at 101. Sir Arthur Conan Doyle, the creator of Sherlock Holmes, set up in practice as an ophthalmologist at 2 Devonshire Place, failed miserably, and took up writing instead. Sir James Mackenzie, a pioneer in the treatment of heart disease, lived at No. 133. The handsome Sir Bertrand Dawson, later Lord Dawson, Physician-in-Ordinary to King George V, lived and worked at 32 Wimpole Street. Lionel Logue, CVO, speech therapist to King George VI, who successfully overcame the King's shyness and painful stammer, was at 146 Harley Street. Lord Horder, known to his colleagues as 'Tommy Horder', world-famous doctor to kings, prime ministers and many lesser mortals, lived at 141 Harley Street. Harold Gillies, later World War II pioneer of plastic surgery, worked at 188 Upper Wimpole Street as assistant to the ENT surgeon Sir Milsom Rees.

By the end of the 1920s there were few non-medical residents in Harley Street. However, with the arrival of the National Health Service in 1948, the medical monopoly of Harley Street went into a temporary decline. Houses were sold or let to solicitors, consulting engineers, quantity surveyors, even (shock, horror) manufacturers. But the setback was short-lived. Soon it became apparent that there was one way of combining a career in the NHS with the joys and rewards of high-class private practice. Consultants on 'maximum part time' had one or two free afternoons each week which could conveniently be spent in private practice. Others decided not to join the NHS at all.

Gradually, confidence in the magic of Harley Street recovered and more and more doctors decided that a few regular sessions in the Street were exactly what their patients, and their own bank statements, wanted. The result was multiple renting of consulting rooms. At one time some of the doors bore as many as twenty brass name plates indicating who could, at the appropriate time, be found within.

By the early 1950s anyone owning a house in the Street and foolish enough to want to sell such a gold-plated investment would be told by the local town planning authority that the property could be disposed of only for medical occupation. A leading article in the *British Medical Journal* at the time stated that the Street 'consorted well' with medical practice and should, if possible, be kept purely medical, or at least professional and residential. In 1948 there were about 800 doctors practising in the Street, including those consulting and working in the London Clinic; and by 1958 there were about 1000. By the 1960s the demand for consulting rooms had greatly outstripped the supply and there were waiting lists of specialists of all kinds, both medical and dental, orthodox and 'alternative'. Many were psychotherapists, osteopaths, acupuncturists, herbalists, naturopaths and faith healers. Not all were British; even at that time a number of foreign doctors were keenly aware of the opportunities. The 1960s and 1970s saw a remarkable rise in the popularity of Harley Street among wealthy patients from abroad, especially from the Middle East. Rich oil sheiks would charter aircraft to come to London for medical attention. The Street was lined with Rolls-Royces.

Today, few doctors practising in Harley Street are fortunate enough to own the properties in which they work. Nearly all of them have to rent, and most of the premises, and even individual consulting rooms, are shared by many doctors. Harley Street is flourishing as never before and is a veritable hive of medical industry. Patients come to Harley Street from the ends of the earth, many to be treated in the London Clinic. Contrary to the popular view, the London Clinic is a non-profit-making institution. This is not to say that it is cheap, but that all surplus income is ploughed back into the clinical and other facilities.

Nineteen claps for Jamie

Dr Samuel Johnson (1709–84) was a pillar of rectitude and the most outstanding commentator on moral questions of the eighteenth century. Ironically, little would have been known of this great man had it not been for one of the most sexually promiscuous scamps of the same period – the Scottish man of letters, diarist and biographer, James Boswell (1740–95).

Boswell was the descendant of an old Scottish family possessed of the estate of Auchinleck in Ayrshire. He was educated by a private tutor and at Edinburgh High School and Edinburgh University. In childhood he claimed to be a Jacobite but was persuaded, by the offer of a shilling, to change his allegiance and pray for King George. In the early 1750s he began to keep a journal and to publish short pieces in magazines. In 1759 he went to Glasgow to study civil law, and to make the intimate acquaintance of a number of actors. He also met some Roman Catholics and immediately decided to become a priest. At the request of his distressed parents, however, he agreed to abandon this ambition if they would allow him to give up the law and join the army. The Duke of Argyll, asked to get him a commission in the guards, refused on the grounds that he liked him and 'that boy must not be shot at for three-and-sixpence a day'.

Boswell was an amusing, well-read, entertaining and engaging fellow and knew how to make himself popular. As a result he had many associations both in the *beau monde* and in the *demi-monde*, and many friends among soldiers, actors and the horse-racing fraternity. Wherever he went, he cultivated the acquaintance of the aristocracy; he was friendly with the Duke of York, Lord Eglington, Lord Somerville and many others. He also knew the philosopher David Hume. Boswell loved London and, from his first taste of the city at the end of 1762, resolved to spend most of his time there. He met Johnson in May 1763 and the two were soon close friends. Boswell spent many evenings alone with Johnson and with him in the company of many of the notable literary and artistic figures of the day including Oliver Goldsmith, Edmund Burke, Joshua Reynolds and Charles James Fox. From the first he made careful notes of the sayings and conversations of the great man. These, however, were not the only notes he made.

Boswell was too interested in the gay life to waste time studying, and his father, enraged by his son's idleness, threatened to disinherit him unless he pursued his legal studies. So Boswell, to his disgust, went abroad to study civil law at Utrecht. Instead of settling down to work, Boswell went to Berlin where he cultivated the acquaintance of the British ambassador. He wrote to his father asking for funds to make a voyage to Italy. This was refused, but he did succeed in visiting Paris and Geneva, where he met Voltaire and Rousseau. His father then relented and he was able to visit Italy and Corsica where he met and became intimate with the great Corsican patriot Pasquale de Paoli (1725–1807). Boswell also entertained the peasantry by singing Scottish airs.

On his return to England, Boswell, to his great regret, was prevented by necessity from remaining in London and had to settle in Edinburgh where he worked at his legal practice. At every possible opportunity he returned to London. In 1773 he and Johnson made their celebrated journey to the Hebrides. Apart from this journey, Boswell met Johnson on a total of only 180 days. Nevertheless, on the basis of this acquaintance, he was able to write the most celebrated biography in the English language – the *Life of Samuel Johson*.

During the whole of his acquaintance with Johnson and during his time abroad, Boswell, whose appetite for promiscuous sex was apparently insatiable, was engaging in an endless succession of sexual encounters with a great variety of women. Often, as he said, he felt 'carnal inclinations' raging through his frame. He was, it seems, partial to prostitutes, and as a result of his commerce with them and others succeeded in infecting himself with gonorrhoea no less than nineteen times. In London he was, in his own words, 'surrounded with numbers of free-hearted ladies of all kinds: from the splendid Madam at fifty guineas a night, down to the civil nymph . . . who tramps along the Strand and will resign her engaging person to your honour for a pint of wine and a shilling.'

Boswell was not one to fight too hard against temptation, and his practice was to take his pleasure where it was offered, whether in a dark doorway, on Westminster Bridge ('with the Thames rolling below us'), in the park or in my lady's chamber. In an attempt to avoid the clap, Boswell sometimes used a condom, or, as he put it, 'engaged in armour'. In those days, however, these articles were less delicate than they are today and Boswell found this 'but a dull satisfaction'.

Boswell married in 1769 and for a time tried to avoid sex with other women. For almost three years he remained faithful, but after a drinking bout he resorted to a woman of the town. Thereafter, there were many encounters, especially on his visits to London. In 1776, for instance, according to his journals, he had sexual intercourse with London whores on 29, 30 and 31 March and on 1 April.

In the company of Dr Johnson, Boswell was careful to appear respectable. On one occasion while they were walking down the Strand arm-in-arm they were approached by a prostitute. 'No,' said Johnson, 'no, my girl, it won't do.' They then discussed at length how much more misery than happiness was caused by 'irregular love'.

In Boswell's day, little or nothing was known about effective treatment of gonorrhoea, amd no doubt Boswell suffered from some or all of the complications – inflammation of the testicle, narrowing of the urethra, arthritis, hepatitis, and eye inflammation. Boswell consulted numerous physicians and surgeons and was prescribed a variety of useless 'remedies' such as blood-letting, purges, bed rest and special diets. One of his favourite treatments was Kennedy's Lisbon Diet Drink, a mixture of liquorice, sarsparilla, sassafras and guaiac wood. This cost half a guinea a bottle and Boswell was told to drink two bottles a day. Although Boswell had great faith in this concoction, there is no reason to suppose that it was of the slightest value in treating gonorrhoea.

Boswell's favourite occupation is no less popular today, and the disease infects about 60,000 people a year in Britain. Forty per cent of men who have sexual intercourse with infected women acquire the infection. In the USA the disease has reached pandemic proportions. Ninety per cent of cases are occurring in teenagers and young adults.

Medicine does not, of course, have all the answers to this problem. The *gonococcus*, by a process of natural selection, has mutated and evolved to produce an enzyme that interferes with the action of antibiotics. In effect, gonorrhoea has, for years, been developing resistance to our one and only sure treatment. Penicillin, a drug which once was a 100 per cent sure cure, can no longer be relied on to work. Resistance to other antibiotics such as ampicillin, tetracycline, cefoxitin and spectinomycin is also commonplace. Over 20 per cent of gonococci are now resistant to penicillin and tetracycline.

No doubt Dr Johnson would have some appropriate comment. 'Sir, depend on it,' he might say, 'there is a retribution in nature that is not to be avoided, however we may struggle.'

Domagk's daughter

Gerhard Domagk (1895–1964) was a distinguished German bacteriologist. Among other things, he was interested in the dyes used to stain bacteria so that they could easily be seen under the microscope. Domagk knew that these dyes penetrated the outer membrane of bacteria and so probably killed them. This led him to speculate on whether they might be used to destroy organisms in the living body. After trying many of the bacterial stains without success he hit upon an azo compound, prontosil, which had been synthesized in 1932. To his delight he found that prontosil was remarkably effective in killing streptococci in mice, while apparently causing the animals no harm. It looked as if he had discovered an important new drug.

A short time after this, Domagk's daughter Hildegarde pricked her finger and within a day or two had a severe streptococcal infection with red streaks running up her arm. She became fevered and the condition developed into blood poisoning (septicaemia). Soon she was critically ill. None of the conventional treatments were of any avail and her father knew that she was likely to die at any moment. In desperation, he gave her a large dose of prontosil dye. Almost at once her condition improved and in a day or two she was out of danger. Soon she made a complete recovery. Not long after this the dye was also used to save the life of the son of the President of the United States, Franklin D. Roosevelt, Junior.

Domagk was too good a scientist to insist on the efficacy of the drug on the basis of a couple of cases. Four years later, in the Queen Charlotte Maternity Hospital in London, thirty-eight women were seriously ill with the commonly fatal childbirth fever caused by streptococci. Prontosil was tried and thirty-five of them recovered. This was an unheard-of success rate. Another series of infected women were treated and the results were even better.

Domagk was unaware of it at the time, but the effectiveness of prontosil was due to its conversion in the body to the substance sulphanilamide. The knowledge that an azo dye could kill germs in the body started an investigation into many hundreds of related compounds for even greater antibacterial activity and greater safety. The drug company May and Baker, after a great deal of research, struck lucky with the 693rd trial and in 1938 marketed M&B 693 or sulphapyridine. This drug became so famous that medical students used to joke that those who passed their finals, instead of being awarded the degree MB.ChB, should be capped 'M&B 693'. The improved drug, sulphathiazole, appeared in 1940 and sulphadimidine was brought out in 1941. These were followed by scores of other effective sulpha drugs. This range of drugs saved countless lives in World War II and was superseded only by the development of the antibiotics. Several of the sulpha drugs are still in use today.

Domagk was awarded the Nobel Prize in 1939.

Barbara immortalized

The barbiturates are a class of sedative drugs, formerly used in enormous quantities, but now largely replaced by benzodiazepine drugs such as Valium and Librium. Apart from phenobarbitone (Luminal) for epilepsy and thiopentone (Pentothal) for the induction of general anaesthesia, they are now largely out of fashion and are beginning to acquire the same disreputable air in medical circles as the once equally highly regarded amphetamines. Much the same thing, incidentally, is now beginning to happen to the benzodiazepines.

The origin of the term 'barbiturate' is interesting. Johann Friedrich Wilhelm Baeyer (1835–1917), the Nobel prize winner, was working on new derivatives of urea, a constituent of urine. Baeyer, who needed large quantities of urea for his work managed to find a Munich waitress called Barbara who, in the interests of science, collected her entire urinary output into a series of large bottles. In this way the chemist was able to obtain the supplies of urea from which he synthesized the new compound. In appreciation of Barbara's contribution Baeyer decided that Barbara's uric acid should be immortalized. So he shortened it to barbituric acid. The rest is history.

This is by no means the only good story associated with drug naming. The benzodiazepine sleeping pill Mogadon is said to have been tested on moggies, and the antibiotic drug Bacitracin was isolated from a bacillus found in a child called Tracy (Baci-Trac-in). Glaxo's record-breaking drug, Zantac, is an excellent remedy, but it did it no harm to be named in such a way as to remind everyone that it is an antacid. Prior to Zantac, it had long been thought that it was a good idea to choose names at the beginning of the alphabet. This was to ensure that the drug would appear near the top of lists of drug names. Since Zantac's phenomenal commercial success, however, stronger motives than this have prevailed. The attentive student of medication terminology will notice that a remarkable number of new drugs have come out with names beginning with Z.

Once a good drug name has caught on it is commercially sound to try, somehow, to associate similar drugs in the same class with the successful product. ICI came up with a remarkably ingenious way of doing this. After the success of their beta-blocker drug Inderal, they brought out two more winners that they named Alderin and Eraldin. Unless you are a crossword puzzle addict, you may not immediately spot the association.

Who discovered the AIDS virus?

AIDS was first reported in 1981, in Los Angeles and New York. As soon as its significance was appreciated, an immense research effort was mounted all over the world to discover the cause. In September 1983, Luc Montagnier, head of the Pasteur Institute in Paris sent to Robert Gallo, head of the tumour cell biology laboratory at the American National Cancer Institute, samples of a virus which had been isolated in his laboratory from an AIDS patient by Françoise Barré-Sinoussi, C. Cherman, F. Rey and others. This virus had been isolated from a young man with widespread lymph node enlargement from AIDS, and so was called the lymphadenopathy-associated virus (LAV).

Seven months later Gallo held a press conference at which he announced he had discovered the cause of AIDS – a virus he called the human T-cell leukaemia virus, group 3 or HTLV-III. He also announced that he had developed a blood test, an antigen–antibody reaction, using the new virus as an antigen. Gallo was advised to patent the test and did so. In view of the huge number of people who would have to be tested for AIDS, this test was expected to become, and indeed proved to be, a major money-spinner. Gallo, as a government employee, however, had a strict limit placed on his own earnings from it.

In 1985 France sued the United States government, implying that Gallo had used the French virus for the test. For years, the Gallo team had been working on this class of human retroviruses and had described a similar virus, HTLV-I, in 1976. Workers in Gallo's laboratory, notably Mikulas Popovic, had solved the difficult problem of how to culture HTLV-III, so they were able to produce the large quantities needed for commercial exploitation of the test. Much other work of fundamental importance in immunology had come out of Gallo's laboratory. But efforts to trace the real origins of the virus now known to be the cause of AIDS and now called HIV, failed.

Gallo acknowledged the possibility that his virus may have arisen from contamination with LAV. Eventually, the dispute over royalties was settled when President Reagan and the French premier Jacques Chirac agreed that Luc Montagnier and Robert Gallo should share both the credit and the financial profits. But this was not the end of the affair. In 1989 the *Chicago Tribune* published an article implying that Gallo had deprived the Pasteur Institute of credit for the discovery of the virus and concluded that his own claim of priority was based either on 'accident or theft'.

An investigation was ordered and was undertaken by the American Office of Scientific Integrity. Its findings were published in September 1991. This body censured Gallo for self-aggrandizement and for detracting from the French achievement, but concluded that his behaviour did not amount to misconduct. This report was criticized as whitewashing and pressure rose for a further enquiry by the Office of Research Integrity of the US Department of Health. Late in 1992 this body stated that in a research paper published in *Science* in 1984

Gallo had claimed that the French virus given him in 1983 had failed to grow in tissue culture. This, the enquiry had found, was 'knowingly false when written'. Gallo was accused of concealing information, of impeding the advancement of research and of abusing his senior status as a scientist. He was also accused of having a 'propensity to misrepresent and mislead in favour of his own research findings or hypotheses'.

These new findings overturned the previous verdict but the Office of Research Integrity, sensitive to criticism, drafted an appeals process to the Appeals Board of the Department of Health. This Board now instituted new legal standards for establishing misconduct. These required that there should be a genuine intent to deceive and that the consequences of the deception should be serious. Under the new more rigorous standards it was decided, and announced by the Office of Research Integrity, that it would not contest an appeal by Gallo. Gallo claimed that he had been exonerated, but remained at risk of investigation on the same charge by a Congress sub-committee. There have been allegations of a cover-up.

Alternative Medicine

Sun gazing

For a few years Elmer was looking for the meaning of life and got into various cults which promised everything and mostly delivered nothing. One of these was a sun-worshipping group that believed that the Sun God would look after those who allowed him to brand his mark upon them.

At the highest level of enlightenment were those who accepted retinal branding by staring straight at the sun. Elmer was urged to attain this level but fortunately retained some vestige of common sense. Some days before the ceremony, he took to wearing a black patch over one eye which, he said, had been prescribed for conjunctivitis and was not to be removed. So, in the end, one brilliant Californian afternoon, he stared unblinkingly at the sun with his right eye only for a full five minutes.

For about six months afterwards he had a small but dense black spot wherever he looked. This meant that if he shut his left eye he couldn't read normal-sized print. The black spot just moved along the line, blanking out two or three letters at a time exactly at the point at which he was trying to see. With both eyes open he could read but he could still see the black blur jumping about annoyingly all over the page. An ophthalmologist had a look at his retinas with an ophthalmoscope and told him that he had a scar at his right macula. It did not appear immediately obvious to Elmer that the Sun God was doing much for him.

At the end of six months the vision in his right eye seemed to have improved, but a new and even more annoying thing had happened. Everything he looked at directly with his right eye was about 50 per cent larger than the image seen with his left eye. It was also distorted. The two effects nearly drove him mad. His ophthalmologist was interested in this phenomenon and told him that he had made a contribution to medical science.

'The contracting scar has pulled the cones closer together, so more of them get stimulated by a given size of image. Your brain doesn't know that the macula has changed, so it naturally thinks that the object you are looking at is bigger than it really is.'

Swamp rabbit milk

Silent George, of Shawneetown, Illinois, was as enterprising as he was imaginative, and decided to make his fortune. So he took the labels off tins of ordinary condensed milk, sprayed the tins gold, and re-labelled them 'Swamp Rabbit Milk – a balanced product for unbalanced people, rich in vitamins J, U, M and P.'

Swamp rabbits were presumed to be highly sexually active, and so the new product purported to have corresponding properties. The consumer was advised not to drink it 'in the absence of your husband, sparring partner, boy friend or running mate, as the action is fast and it is two jumps from a lettuce picnic to a cruise down the Nile with your dream version of Mark Antony'.

Regrettably, the poetical Silent George, who deserved better, was put out of business by an unsympathetic state government, presumably on the grounds that vitamins J, U, M and P do not exist.

Most of the gaps in the alphabet have, from time to time, been used up by the manufacturers of imaginary vitamins. Vitamin X (also imaginary) was once a great favourite and, but for restrictive legislation, the entrepreneurs would no doubt, by now, be working their way through the J1, J2, J3 series.

Sadly, the facts about vitamins are more prosaic. Those essential for health are the three fat-soluble vitamins, A, D, E and K and the water-soluble vitamins C and the eight B vitamins – thiamine (B_1), riboflavine (B_2), pyridoxine (B_6), niacin, pantothenic acid, folic acid, biotin and vitamin B_{12}. Any reasonably mixed diet (especially one featuring breakfast cereals) will contain far more than the minimum requirements of these vitamins, and some of them are so widely distributed in food that you would have to try very hard to get less than you need to stay healthy.

Wart cures

Medical folklore and anecdote contain many alleged cures for warts, most of them so improbable as to be laughable. Some of these, however, have a sneaking following among the medical profession.

This is because even the most scientific of doctors are never entirely guiltless of the *post hoc ergo propter hoc* fallacy – the failure to appreciate that just because something occurs after something else is done, the second isn't necessarily a consequence of the first.

Just suppose that it was noticed that touching the top of a wart with a glass rod dipped in solution of gentian violet was regularly followed by the disappearance of the wart. Such an experience would be quite likely to induce in the mind of the doctor the idea that there might be something in it. The trouble is that there is no end of substances that you can touch on warts to produce an equally satisfactory effect. These include urine, menstrual blood, tobacco juice, early morning saliva (must be before the teeth are brushed), pig's blood, dog's faeces, celandine ('wartflower'), houseleek, sun spurge ('wartwort' or 'wart weed'), buckthorn, euphorbia, rain water from a rotten tree stump ('spunk water'), etc., etc.

In the southern states of the USA there is a well-known character, the 'Wart Lady of Kansas'. This itinerant healer operates in church on Sunday mornings. All the children with warts line up, and one by one the Wart Lady solemnly touches each wart with the tip of her tongue. Allegedly the procedure never fails.

The number of substances claimed to be effective in this way is rivalled only by the number of procedures recommended to remove warts. Rubbing with a black slug is a sure cure, rivalled only in effectiveness by stroking with the tail of a tortoiseshell cat (but this works only in May), or having the warts rubbed by a man who is the father of an illegitimate child. Other sure cures include selling the warts to someone else; persuading a long-horned grasshopper to chew them off; rubbing them with a wart-charming stone (there is one in the museum of the Royal College of General Practitioners); washing your hands in moonbeams in an empty polished silver bowl; or rubbing the wart in the direction of a passing funeral.

All this is a sad setback to the discoverer of the gentian violet wart cure. So, being scientific, our doctor ponders the question and soon hits on a better explanation. 'Probably a psychological effect on the immune system from the strong mental stimulus of going about with blue warts,' he decides, reaching for his pen.

Fatal astrology

Lim Hock Chin was only forty-nine and was dying, quite unnecessarily, from a perfectly treatable pneumonia. Neither Lim nor his family knew what was wrong or that it could be quickly cured by antibiotics. This was because, although they lived in a large American city and were surrounded by all kinds of evidence of modern medical advances, they were almost completely blind to these. They could not read English and the whole pattern of their lives was founded in Chinese tradition and traditional methods. When sick, they had always turned to an old practitioner of traditional Chinese medicine for treatment.

Traditional Chinese medicine, chung-i, classifies drugs according to the tastes and smells appropriate to the 'four energies' and the 'five flavours'. The energies manifest excess (yang) or deficiency (yin) and the flavours – sour, bitter, pungent, salt and sweet – correspond to the five 'elements' – wood, fire, earth, metal and water. Drugs are used, in balanced formulations, to counter effects which are apparent to the patient. 'Cool' drugs, such as extracts of mint and chrysanthemum, are used for 'hot' disorders such as fevers. Sweet herbs deal with 'sour' symptoms, such as dyspepsia, while sour preparations are given for their astringent or 'solidifying' effect.

Disease is regarded as an imbalance between the forces of yin and yang and recovery is to be obtained by correcting the balance. In the most refined practice, diagnosis is made by examination of the twelve pulses, six in each wrist, three deep and three superficial, each of which is said to inform about the health of an organ or part of the body. Apart from drugs, the most important treatment method is acupuncture. Nine types of needle, each with a different purpose, are used and different disorders call for different angles and speed of insertion, whether the needle is twisted or pumped, and for how long it is left in place. Another means of treatment is moxibustion. This involves the burning of a cone of dried leaves close to the skin.

Unfortunately for Hock Chin, symptoms are not disorders, and metaphors are not facts. No disorder can be diagnosed in detail simply by feeling pulses. All scientific medical men know that treating symptoms, without finding and tackling the cause of the disorder, is bad medicine.

Hock Chin knew that he was going to die because he had been born in a metal year, so any serious lung problem would probably be fatal. Double lobar pneumonia seldom develops fully nowadays in Western societies because it is treated effectively in the early stages. But both of Hock Chin's lungs had now progressed to a stage of almost complete solidity, his lips and the surrounding skin had an ominous blue tinge and very little oxygen was getting through to his blood. Cooling drugs for his fever, acupuncture and moxibustion were all tried, but failed. The air sacs of his lungs were full of cells and fluid and, although his chest muscles laboured painfully to try to compensate, eventually they gave up. His condition rapidly deteriorated and he died.

Chinese astrology has it that a person's fate is determined by the year of birth. Each decade has five phases. Years ending in 1 or 0 are metal years; those ending in 2 or 3 are water years; those ending in 4 or 5 are wood years; those in 6 or 7 are fire years; and those in 8 or 9 are earth years. Each phase is associated with a particular organ or symptom. Thus, fire years are associated with the heart and people born in fire years are more likely to die of heart disease. Earth years are associated with lumps, so people born in these years are more susceptible to cancer. Metal years are associated with the lungs; water years with the kidneys and wood years with the liver. In each case a person born in these phases is said to be more likely to suffer and die from disease of the corresponding organ.

A careful study carried out of nearly 30,000 American Chinese, described in a report in the *Lancet*, showed that these associations actually hold good. When compared with equal numbers of non-Chinese people born in the same years, Chinese people who develop a disease related to their birth year phase die one to five years earlier than comparable non-Chinese people. Chinese people who develop diseases not associated with their birth years have the same life expectancy as the non-Chinese controls.

Does this mean that the Chinese astrological beliefs are true? They may be, but there are other explanations. The studies show that the more strongly the belief in the traditional system is held, the more years of life are lost. Women with birth-phase diseases almost always lose more years of life than men. But Chinese American women are much less exposed to Western ideas and beliefs than men, so many more of them hang on to traditional beliefs. People who know that they are suffering from a disease associated with their birth year, and whose belief in astrology is strong, will take a fatalistic view and will believe that nothing they can do will alter the fated outcome. Thus, for instance, they may refuse to stop smoking or to give up other unhealthy habits. The statistical analysis of the trial, however, eliminates behavioural changes of this kind as a cause of the earlier deaths. It also eliminates other possible causes of bias, such as a tendency for Chinese doctors, faced with a patient with several diseases, to register as the main cause of death, the disease associated with the birth phase.

Chinese astrology does not hold for non-Chinese or for people who have never been exposed to Chinese traditional beliefs. We also know that Western cancer patients who adopt an attitude of hopelessness die earlier than those who fight. Those undergoing psychological group therapy live for eighteen months longer, on average, than those not having such treatment. Other relevant facts are that death is often postponed until after symbolically meaningful occasions, such as the Jewish Passover or the Chinese Harvest Moon Festival. Mortality rates drop before these commemorations and peak afterwards.

There may be a general lesson to be learned from all this. The Chinese experience shows that strongly held beliefs have a major influence on the effect of a much wider range of diseases than previous Western experience had suggested. Is the Western system of beliefs adequate or even appropriate?

Could it be that our mechanistic biomedical paradigm needs to be amended?

On the other hand, it is possible that this study is statistically flawed. It is only fair to say that its publication in the *Lancet* was followed by a number of critical letters suggesting that the analysis of the authors' data might have been biased and even subject to alternative explanations. These critics did not dispute the conclusion that the state of a person's mind can affect longevity, but simply questioned whether this study proved that it did.

Makes you think, doesn't it?

Miracle at Lourdes

Over 6000 people claim to have been cured of disease after making the pilgrimage to Bernadette's grotto at Lourdes. As a result, the number of sick people attending Lourdes is increasing steadily. In 1992 five and a half million people visited the shrine. This is one and a half million more than in 1982.

The little fortified town of Lourdes lies on the Gave du Pau river in the foothills of the Pyrenees in south-west France. In medieval times it was a military stronghold. In 1858, the fourteen-year-old Bernadette Soubirous had eighteen visions of the Virgin Mary in a shallow cave near the town. These visions were declared genuine by Pope Pius IX in 1862. In 1876 a basilica was built on the site of the grotto and in 1958 an underground church was completed.

Bernadette was born on 7 January 1844. In her visions, the Virgin told her that she was the Immaculate Conception. Four years prior to this, Pope Pius IX, in the Papal Bull *Ineffabilis*

Deus had defined the immaculate conception as a dogma binding on all Catholics. It asserts that Mary, the mother of Jesus, was preserved from original sin from the moment of her conception.

Bernadette's revelations resulted in much unpleasant publicity and eventually she retired to a convent where she remained until her death on 16 April 1879. She was canonized in 1933.

A spring of water near the site of the apparitions soon became identified as having miraculous healing properties. Of the many patients who claim to have been healed at Lourdes, some 2000 have been carefully reviewed. For this purpose, a medical bureau consisting of both Catholic and non-Catholic doctors was set up in 1882. The bureau studies the previous medical records and examines the patient. Only if two-thirds of the doctors agree that there has been a cure is the person referred to a medical commission in his or her own diocese. From there, patients deemed to be cured are referred to an international medical committee consisting of doctors of mixed religious and non-religious affiliations from sixteen counties. If this committee agree that there has been a permanent and unexplained cure, the matter is then forwarded to the church authorities for a decision as to whether there has been a miracle.

Out of the thousands claimed, only sixty-five cases have been deemed miraculous. The last two were both normally fatal cancers that resolved completely after a visit to Lourdes. One of these was a pelvic tumour in a twenty-three year-old man who was carried to the spring in 1963. After his first bath, the recovery began and by 1972, by which time there had been no recurrence, the cure was declared miraculous. The other was a twelve-year-old Italian girl with a highly malignant tumour of bone known as a Ewing's sarcoma. She made a pilgrimage in 1976 and recovered completely. This was declared a miraculous cure in 1989.

In 1993 doctors were investigating the case of a fifty-eight-year-old man called Jean Salaun from Chartres. Salaun had been a multiple sclerosis patient at the Salpetrière hospital in Paris since 1977 and he was quite unable to walk or to lead an independent existence. After he had made a pilgrimage to Lourdes all the symptoms of the disease disappeared and he now regularly rides a bicycle.

A cure for AIDS

Everyone in Malawi knows all about AIDS, and about one in three of the urban population is now HIV-positive. Many people have also heard of Billy Chisupe whose ancestral spirits spoke to him in a dream and told him that there was a certain magical tree whose bark could be used to make a concoction, called *mchape*, that can cure AIDS. This requires three cupfuls taken on consecutive days. If matters have not gone too far, a single cupful of the concoction can make HIV-positive people sero-negative. Only Billy can see this tree so he is, of course, the only source of the medicine. Billy doesn't charge for his *mchape* but will not refuse donations. People have flocked from far and near to partake of this miraculous cure. It has even become popular, privately, with employees of the Ministry of Health whose official attitude is that there is, of course, nothing in it.

Billy's cure has claimed an even more remarkable property. Not only is it alleged to make the recipient immune to the

HIV, but those who have taken it can pass on this immunity to other people by having sex with them. This is, perhaps, the most serious aspect of the whole tragic affair. Drs R. Voysey and J. Gray, district health officers in Malawi, who have recorded the matter with enviable restraint in the *British Medical Journal*, reported that the bar girls, who used to ask, 'Do you have a condom?' are now asking, 'Have you had *mchape*?' Scientific doctors like these continue to struggle to maintain an AIDS control program against the forces of superstition and ignorance.

A pea for incontinence

At a routine check, Harry's GP had found that he had a bit of high blood pressure. Nothing alarming, but enough to justify treatment. So Harry was prescribed a diuretic, a drug that acts on the kidneys so as to allow more water than usual to pass in the urine. Doctors used to believe that diuretics reduced blood pressure by reducing the volume of the blood. This sounded like common sense until someone pointed out that the blood volume quickly returns to normal but the blood pressure remains reduced. We now know that diuretics have a secondary effect in that they relax the smooth muscle in the walls of arteries allowing the arteries to widen. This is what brings the blood pressure down.

Harry was pleased with the result of the diuretic drug, so far as his blood pressure was concerned, but he was not too pleased with the amount of urine he was producing. This was a great nuisance and he was having to get up several times each night. Even worse was an occasional tendency to leakage.

His doctor, however, was adamant that he should continue the treatment.

A friend of Harry's then came up with a solution. 'Tell you what, why don't you put a cork in it? That's what I would do.'

Harry thought this a ridiculous suggestion.

'Well, of course, I don't literally mean a cork,' said the friend. 'What you need is something the right size and shape that's hard and clean.' He thought for a moment, then added, 'Why don't you try a dried pea?'

Harry looked thoughtful.

'Just push it in the end. No problem. You should be able to milk it out.'

A few days later Harry decided that he had had enough of dribbling, so he bought a pound of dried peas. He had to admit that there was something in his friend's suggestion. The peas were of several sizes and he was sure that he could find one to fit. They were certainly hard enough. So he decided to have a go.

The pea was a great success. Harry was now dry and, surprisingly, could manage to urinate quite well when he felt he had to. After a couple of days he thought it might be a good idea to replace the pea, so he tried to milk it out. To his surprise the pea would not budge. He then got a fine pair of eyebrow tweezers. This was a mistake. Trying to get a hold of the pea caused a lot of pain and he succeeded only in pushing it further in. He decided to wait.

A week later things had reached crisis point. Harry's penis had become alarmingly swollen and urination had become almost impossible. There was nothing for it. Embarrassment became a secondary consideration. Harry had to see a doctor.

Harry's GP was frankly incredulous. When he examined Harry's swollen member and felt the hard lump, he decided that there might be something in Harry's story after all. He arranged for an emergency consultation with a urologist.

The real problem was that Harry's pea had begun to sprout. The combination of warmth, moisture and partial darkness had, no doubt, persuaded it that spring had finally come. The surgeon had quite a tussle with Harry's pea and it required a general anaesthetic, a cystoscope and a special pair of long-handled forceps finally to retrieve the offending object. Harry was then given a course of antibiotics and was soon none the worse for his experiment in self-treatment. The pea was kind to Harry and produced none of the expected local damage to the lining of the urethra that might well have led to a permanent narrowing.

On the advice of the specialist, Harry's diuretic drug was stopped and he was given another form of treatment for his high blood pressure. This proved equally effective. What was even more gratifying was that, on terminating the diuretic treatment Harry's incontinence cleared up completely, and he never looked back.

The miraculous water of Tlacote

A young man with muscular dystrophy heard of the miraculous properties of water known as agua de Tlacote that was taken from a spring in Querétaro, Mexico. The waters of the spring became celebrated in 1987 when a dying dog was reported to have recovered after drinking the water. The news spread rapidly and the magic was quickly commercialized. The name

Tlacote was patented and people queued up daily in their hundreds to partake of the miracle.

The dystrophy patient regularly had shipments of the water sent to him of which he drank three cupfuls every day. After he had been drinking the water for some time he developed bloody diarrhoea and abdominal cramps. Medical investigation showed that he was suffering from amoebic dysentery. This was proved by demonstrating the causal agent *Entamoeba histolytica* in the stools. He was given routine treatment with metronidazole and paromomycin and soon recovered fully.

After considering all the possible sources of the infection the doctors concluded that the most likely source of the *Entamoeba* was the supposedly miraculous water. The disease was common in the area from which the water was taken and faecal contamination might have occurred as a result of heavy local rainfall and flooding in the prior three months.

All in the Mind

Folie à deux

Julie was a person of strong, dominant character but reclusive habits, whose strange appearance on the rare occasions when she was seen in public had aroused considerable curiosity in the village. She lived with a quiet younger companion, Jennifer, who was often out and about, but never uttered an unnecessary word to anyone. She would turn away, or even retreat, rather than meet someone who might try to engage her in conversation.

The anonymous poison pen letters had been arriving for months before anyone thought to suspect the pair. These letters, accusing well-known local men of adultery, fornication and incest, caused an enormous amount of distress and trouble. In the end, a police investigation revealed that Jennifer was writing and posting the letters. When she was being questioned it became apparent that her responses were far from normal and after she was charged the magistrate remanded her for a psychiatric opinion. Medical investigation revealed an extraordinary state of affairs.

Jennifer was basically sane and had no desire to harm anyone.

The real root of the trouble lay with the dominant Julie who had become obsessed with the paranoid delusion that the local men were engaged in a sexual conspiracy, the aim of which was to extend their activities to involve all the women in the village. Jennifer was financially and emotionally dependent on the stronger Julie and did not know what she would do if left to fend for herself.

As a result of this situation, Jennifer had wholeheartedly accepted the premises of Julie's delusion and became convinced that it was true. Under Julie's direction, she had written the accusatory letters, incorporating all Julie's mad ideas and adding a few of her own. Everything she did was calculated to please Julie. The psychiatrist advised that Jennifer was in no way responsible for her actions and that this was a case of *folie à deux*.

Folie à deux is a rare delusional psychotic disorder which has developed as a result of a close relationship between an normal and a psychotic person. Sometimes called 'shared paranoid disorder', *folie à deux* affects women more often than men and occurs in couples relatively isolated from the rest of the community who derive mutual gain from the situation. The dominant person is the one with the original delusional psychosis and the submissive person gains the acceptance of the other by adopting the delusions. At the same time, the dominant person retains some link with the real world through the medium of the partner. There is often a deep emotional rapport and sometimes suicide pacts occur. The delusions concerned are usually nearer to reality than in other psychoses and are often persecutory or hypochondriacal.

Normally, the most effective treatment is to separate the pair, after which the induced disorder will, with suitable supportive management, gradually disappear. The dominant partner, however, needs more intensive conventional treatment. When it was suggested that Julie should be admitted to hospital for treatment, Jennifer made an ineffectual attempt at suicide and she, too, was admitted. Julie was treated with phenothizine drugs and, although she remained eccentric and unhappy, her delusions disappeared. The two maintained a close relationship and after a few months returned to their cottage.

It is interesting to note that the shared paranoid disorder sometimes involves more than two people, and the literature contains many cases of *folie à trois*, *à quatre*, *à cinq*, and so on. There is a recorded case of a whole family, in which twelve people were affected. Some of the more extreme religious cults that flourish under a charismatic leader are essentially of this nature.

Munchausen's syndrome

Most doctors have a Munchausen anecdote, generally derived at second hand. These stories refer variously to people who swallow a range of objects such as dinner forks and require surgery for their removal; people who simulate serious neurological conditions and end up having brain operations; people who collapse outside hospitals simulating heart attacks and have to be admitted to intensive care facilities; those who feign severe vomiting of blood by various tricks; even those who complain so persistently of testicular pain that they persuade doctors to remove both testicles. Here is a short account of a typical case of this extraordinary disorder.

Brian Chambers was a slim, ascetic-looking, neatly dressed

man with a scholarly manner and a cultivated accent. It was his practice to present himself to the accident and emergency departments of various hospitals in different parts of the country, usually late in the evening when most of the senior staff were off duty and when he would be attended to by a junior doctor. His manner was so impressive that many young doctors found that the control of the consultation was slipping out of their hands.

Chambers' complaints – usually of a condition normally treated by surgery – were so plausible and circumstantial that, to begin with, few doubted his bona fides. His knowledge of medical conditions was remarkable, but the catalogue of his symptoms was produced in such a diffident manner and with an air of such regret at causing so much trouble, that this was seldom recognized. In most instances, the young doctors were pleased to have such an intelligent and cooperative patient and gratified to be presented with such classical examples of well-recognized surgical conditions.

It was only when the history-taking was over and the examination began that doubt would creep in. There was, for a start, a clear discrepancy between the patient's statements relating to his previous admissions to hospital and the truly remarkable number of healed surgical incisions on his abdomen, chest and back. In addition, the indications were that he had had surgery for an implausibly large number and range of conditions. A few people are unlucky enough to suffer from three or four entirely different surgical disorders; in Brian's case, the scars of incisions appropriate for access to almost every organ in the body strained credulity beyond the limit.

Eventually, details of Brian's remarkable career became widely known and his activities succumbed to the law of diminishing returns. Now aged fifty-five, he had a record of admissions to over 300 hospitals. These admissions had resulted in more than twenty major operations, in none of which had any actual disease ever been found. In spite of that, he had had his appendix and part of his stomach removed (partial gastrectomy); his left kidney had gone (nephrectomy); his spleen and his gall bladder had been removed (splenectomy and cholecystectomy); he had undergone an operation to cut through part of two spinal vertebrae (laminectomy) and expose a normal spinal cord; his chest had been opened (thoracotomy) and a lung inspected; on several occasions a bronchoscope had been passed down into one or other lung for internal examination (bronchoscopy); he had had numerous endoscopic inspections of the inside of his urinary bladder (cystoscopy), always with a normal result; and his rectum and lower colon had repeatedly been examined by different forms of endoscopy (sigmoidoscopy). None of these procedures and operations had been necessary or were of any value and, in spite of this history of surgery, he remained in remarkably good health.

The Munchausen syndrome is a sustained course of deliberate and calculated deception of the medical profession. The underlying reasons are varied and not always clear. There is commonly a very strong masochistic element, and some affected people will go to the most extraordinary lengths to persuade surgeons to undertake major surgery. Some even engage in self-mutilation; some appear content with minor surgery. Sometimes the syndrome appears to have been adopted simply for the purpose of obtaining attention, personal status and free accommodation and food.

People with this condition make a career of simulating disease. They read medical text books with admirably close attention and then report to a doctor complaining of the symptoms of a specific disease, preferably a serious one. Such people are usually very plausible and sometimes subtle, and if previously unknown to the doctor or hospital concerned, are likely to carry conviction and succeed in their desire to be admitted for investigation and treatment. They often establish a close rapport with surgeons, but tend to be deeply suspicious of psychiatrists. Many of them have criminal records.

Sufferers of Munchausen's syndrome are usually pathological liars. They often seem incapable of distinguishing truth from untruth, and many of them appear to believe their own fabrications. On being detected, however, as they invariably are in the end, they immediately discharge themselves from hospital.

There is an even more sinister variant of the condition, known as the Munchausen syndrome by proxy. In this form a person in charge of another person, usually a child, produces symptoms or clinical signs in the person in order to attract medical attention. Cases have been reported in which a child has been injected with insulin to cause coma from low blood sugar (hypoglycaemia), a child's blood has been drained to cause surgical shock, or a child has been partially suffocated. The carer then seeks medical advice and appears to cooperate closely with the doctors in the management of the condition. The abuse may continue while the victim is in hospital, and this has been shown by the covert use of video cameras in suspected cases.

The Munchausen syndrome was aptly named in an article in the *Lancet* in 1951 by the distinguished medical commentator and writer Richard Asher. Baron Munchausen was the fictitious character of the novelist Rudolf Eric Raspe, based on the tall tales of the Freiherr Karl Friedrich Hieronymus von Münchhausen (Monkhouse) of Hanover (1720–87) and published in English in Oxford in 1785. Münchhausen was noted for his outrageously implausible pseudo-autobiographical tales. The Baron, however, never underwent any surgical operations.

Compulsive coprolalia

Gawain's mother was in the habit of remarking that he had always been an annoyingly twitchy child. At first it was just a repeated tendency to wrinkle his nose, then an odd twitch involving a circular movement of his upper lip. As he got older, the tendency got gradually worse and spread to involve most of his face and then his shoulders. Even more annoying was his habit of emitting repeated grunting noises, at first fairly quiet, but as time went on, loud enough to have his two sisters repeatedly asking him to shut up.

One Saturday afternoon, when Gawain was twelve and was sitting on a cushion on the floor in front of the TV his mother distinctly heard him utter 'Oh fuck!' This was not a word that had ever been allowed in the household, and Gawain's reward was a smart clip on the side of his head. At this, he looked so desolate, and his cry of 'I can't help it' was so heartfelt that his mother regretted her impetuosity and gave him a reassuring hug.

Unfortunately, this was just the beginning of a painfully embarrassing sequence of events. Gawain's twitches and grunts became steadily worse and, from time to time, the pressure seemed to build up in him to shout out various obscenities.

He had never been given to bad language and this was quite uncharacteristic. It seemed that the need to swear in this way occurred most strongly just when it was most inopportune. He even succumbed once in church and during a silent moment shouted 'Shit and bugger it!'

Gawain's father, convinced that his son was acting out of deliberate wickedness, decided that a good thrashing was called for. Regrettably, this had the opposite of the desired effect and to Gawain's twitching were added frequent blinking, head-nodding, sniffing and stuttering. Uncontrollable grunting, squealing and barking developed and his compulsive tendency to swearing got worse than ever. In addition, he developed a curious tendency to repeat words or sentences that had just been spoken to him. At first, his father took this for perverse impertinence and was inclined to punish him, but it soon became apparent that Gawain genuinely could not control the tendency.

By the time he was fourteen his teachers were complaining that he was disrupting classes and he was so disturbed himself that he began to play truant regularly. Medical attention was sought and Gawain was referred to a psychiatrist. This doctor did not take long to reach a diagnosis of Gilles de la Tourette's syndrome.

Because of Gawain's distress, growing social isolation and psychological danger it was decided to start him on treatment with the drug haloperidol. After a good deal of experimentation with dosage it became possible to control the twitching, the involuntary noises and the swearing. Gawain returned to a fairly normal life, but after a few years began to develop constant shaky movements of his legs. Although the condition usually lasts for life, about one case in twenty clears up spontaneously after adolescence. Gawain is waiting hopefully to see whether, one day, he can safely leave off the drug.

Gilles de la Tourette's syndrome is an extraordinary disorder of which the most distressing feature is the compulsive need to make scatological or obscene utterances. This feature, known as coprolalia, occurs in about half the cases and in these the condition becomes a severe social disability. The cause remains obscure and the earlier ideas that it was the result of unresolved sexual or other conflicts have now been abandoned. Most experts believe that it is due to minor damage to parts of the brain known as the basal ganglia. The basis for this belief is that a similar pattern of symptoms occurs in the disease encephalitis lethargica which affects this part of the brain in a specific fashion. In addition it is known that drugs such as haloperidol act on the basal ganglia.

Healthy hallucinations

Hallucination – hearing, seeing, smelling, tasting or feeling things that aren't actually there – are generally regarded as symptoms of schizophrenia or of some other mental disorder such as delirium tremens. But this is not necessarily so. There is one circumstance, sadly, in which hallucinations are quite common and normal, and that is after a bereavement.

The study of the experience of a large number of bereaved people has shown that almost half of them have had, and often continue to have, some kind of hallucinatory experience of the dead person – feeling their presence, hearing their voice, even catching brief glimpses of them.

But those who have these experiences are unlikely to talk

about them, even to close friends, probably because of fear that such experience is abnormal and possibly even an indication of mental instability. These hallucinations often last for many years, but are commonest in the first ten years. They are most likely in older people, after a long marriage and especially if the marriage has been a happy one, and if there have been children. The most frequent, experienced by about 40 per cent, is a strong sense of the presence of the dead person. About 14 per cent have a hallucination of seeing the deceased and about the same proportion hear the deceased's voice. About 10 per cent actually find themselves talking normally to the deceased and a very small number, about 3 per cent, feel themselves touched by the dead person.

Bereavement hallucinations are, of course, the result of an unconscious desire for the presence of the deceased, which leads either to the misinterpretation of other sensations, or even to the stimulation of the perceptive parts of the brain so as to produce the effects wished for. The illusion of the presence of the dead person is often comforting, and some bereaved people welcome this and deliberately try to foster it. Most, indeed, find it helpful.

Communication

The door of Dr Munro's consulting room was open and he could hear the nurse outside talking to the patient as one might talk to a small child. When he was wheeled in his face was working and he was trying to speak.

'A-ab ... a-ab, yes, a-ab ...' was all he could manage. Munro did not know what was in his mind but he knew that the Vice-Admiral was a cultivated and educated man, that his intelligence was unimpaired, his memory barely affected and his interest in scientific and artistic matters keen.

The nurse was a kindly, sensible girl who would normally have been entirely respectful. Yet, talking in a slow, loud voice, as if the patient were deaf, and using language appropriate to someone with a mental age of about four, she had been going on about what a naughty boy he was to let his right hand fall into the spokes of the wheelchair. Munro wondered if he were choking with rage inside, or whether he had now learned to accept this kind of thing philosophically ... To get the message across to the nurse indirectly he started to talk to the Vice-Admiral about the disaster of the space shuttle explosion. The Admiral listened intently, his eyes fixed on Munro's face, and nodded appropriately. It was clear that he was grateful.

Why do we treat stroke patients in this way? The nurse's attitude was obviously determined by the extent to which the patient could communicate with her. Although people's appearances influence us a good deal, it is essentially the quality of their minds which cause us to react to them in a particular way. But if their minds have no ready access to us, we are apt to treat them as if they were mindless. The Vice-Admiral, deprived of his habitual channels of communication – speech and facial expression – existed for the nurse only as a rather clumsy and helpless individual, who could not even thank her for what she was doing for him. He could write, but being paralysed in his right side he had to depend on his left hand and writing was very awkward.

The nurse was well aware that many stroke patients have suffered much more serious functional damage than just one-sided paralysis and loss of the ability to speak. She knew that many also have a severe defect of understanding and that some of them, although able to talk freely and fluently, don't make any sense. She was aware that many stroke patients are irritable and bad-tempered, many are withdrawn and uncommunicative, even if they are able to speak, and that many are so wrapped up in their own distress and resentment that they can't concern themselves with anything else. What she had not perceived was that this kind of behaviour is precisely the sort of response one would expect from someone who is being treated in an inappropriate manner and who is incapable of pointing this out. Perhaps it was because she had so often had to deal with patients with whom no sort of communication was possible that she tended to treat them all in this way.

About one stroke patient in three suffers some damage to the function of communication, particularly if the right side of the body is paralysed. The right side of the body is controlled by the left side of the brain and it is in the left half of the brain that the power of speech, and all the other faculties concerned with communication, are usually situated. So cerebral ischaemia or haemorrhage involving the right half of the brain produces a weakness of the left side of the body but would not normally affect speech. In a very small number of left-handed people, the right half of the brain is dominant and if such a person had damage to the right half of the brain, speech would probably be affected.

The Vice-Admiral's case was a little unusual in that the damage to the speech area in the left side of his brain was confined to a comparatively small segment concerned only with the mechanical aspects of speech. He knew exactly what he wanted to say, and the precise words with which he wished to express his thoughts; his ideas were fluid and appropriate and sometimes they were bursting to get out. But when he tried to speak, the only sounds he could make were meaningless noises. He was a quick-minded man who had been capable of clear and effective expression and suffered great frustration in trying to converse by such means as playing 'Twenty questions'. Munro had watched him practising left-handed typing on a laptop computer with a word-processor program, to improve his communication.

The Vice-Admiral had actually suffered more subtle damage than simply one-sided paralysis and loss of the power of speech. Munro's examination had showed that if, having covered his eyes, one of his fingers or toes was moved passively into a new position, he would be completely unable to say in which direction it had been moved. Likewise, if a small object, such as a coin, were put into his hand and he was encouraged to try to identify it by feel, he would be unable to do so. Happily, with the passage of time, and by dint of sheer, stubborn determination, the Vice-Admiral mastered his word-processor (although he always had to look at his fingers when typing) and, within a few weeks, was writing a book on naval intelligence in World War II.

Personality change

One of the most distressing aspects of stroke disability is the change in personality that is so often a feature of the condition.

David McLeod was a British naval architect and had spent most of his working life in Admiralty dockyards and his wife

Constance had borne with patience and good humour the many moves from Rosyth to Malta and from Gibraltar to Hong Kong. At last, David retired on pension and they bought a house in Tayport – rather larger than Constance would have chosen, but they could afford it and David had always been inclined to ostentation. David was building a patio extension and one day Constance went out with a cup of coffee to find him lying on a heap of wet cement, breathing noisily and with his face all lop-sided and twisted.

The consultant at Dundee Royal Infirmary spoke to her gravely. 'Aye, well, it's a pretty massive stroke, I'm afraid. He's had a big cerebral haemorrhage, and you must prepare yourself for the worst.'

'You think he's going to die, then?' asked Constance, desperately trying to control herself.

'Yes I do. I'm afraid there's very little hope for him.' But the consultant was wrong and David did not die. After two or three days on the critical list, he recovered consciousness and, although he was unable to speak, Constance was overjoyed to discover that he could recognize her and could communicate in writing, using his left hand. At first, David's progress was rapid and, within a week he had recovered, not only the power of speech, but also nearly normal strength on his right side. His character, however, seemed to have changed and, from being a positive-minded, dominant man, he had become weakly and apparently wholly lacking in motivation. A month after his admission, David was discharged from hospital. Constance was fit and healthy but she was a small woman and David's sixteen stones of passive weight presented problems. Had he been his usual self, he would have relished the problem and probably come up with a bright idea for some sort of hoist.

But Constance was not getting any cooperation and he just lay there looking at her resentfully as if the whole thing were her fault. It was a difficult effort even to turn him over in bed, but this had to be done frequently because, apart from the question of bed-sores, David was doubly incontinent and soiled the bedlinen several times a day.

Although he could speak, his remarks were confined to self-pitying complaints. Soon after returning home he established the habit of crying out for Constance in a high-pitched voice whenever he had the slightest inclination. Often there seemed to be no reason for this but Constance could not bring herself to ignore him and always went to him. He was especially prone to call her during the night – Constance had had to retire to the guest bedroom because of his incontinence and his restlessness – and she soon reached near-exhaustion from lack of sleep. Constance was a person of great strength of character and was determined to do her duty. She was an optimist and expected every day that some improvement would occur so that she might see some possibility of an end to her perpetual and thankless task.

The weeks passed and, in spite of her every effort and the regular exhortations of the district nurse, David could never be persuaded to cooperate in anything and refused even to allow her to try to get him out of bed. Constance knew that such behaviour was quite out of character and generously attributed it, not to his selfish stubbornness, but to the effects of the brain damage. Even so, it was very difficult for her not to respond as if he were fully responsible and she constantly had to repress an impulse to angry protest.

'There's no actual physical reason why he should not get out of bed,' the district nurse told her, 'He has full muscle power on both sides and could walk fine if he wanted. This lying in bed is dangerous and it would be very good for him if he would get up.'

'Good for me, too,' thought Constance a little bitterly.

For several weeks Constance conscientiously carried out her task of keeping David clean, seeing that he moved his limbs frequently, and turning him many times a day. Then the visits of the district nurse became less regular and finally stopped and Constance felt that she had been abandoned.

Gradually, Constance's anger grew. Finally, one day, when, within half an hour of stripping his bed and putting everything in the wash, she went in to find that David had again soiled voluminously, Constance's restraint broke.

'You're doing it on purpose,' she stormed out at the grinning man in the bed, 'I don't believe you're half as bad as you pretend to be. You can just damn well lie in it!' Half an hour later, she relented and went back, washed him and changed his bed linen, but by now she had come to a decision. 'The doctor says you are able to get up and should get up.'

'Can't,' said David.

Constance went to the far side of the bed and with a strength she did not know she possessed, heaved up the edge of the mattress so that David half rolled, half slid across to the edge. At that point she hardly cared whether he fell out of bed or not.

'What're you doing?' he asked querulously.

Constance compressed her lips, took hold of his ankles and swung his legs over the side of the bed.'

'You'll do me an injury,' protested David weakly.

'Nonsense!' With a supreme effort, Constance forced him into a sitting position and stood back, leaving him to balance or fall over as he chose. David chose to balance and sat, precariously, with his hands on the edge of the bed. 'Now get up on your feet!'

'I'll never stand up again. You don't seem to understand that I've had a stroke!'

'From which you've made an almost complete recovery,' said Constance.

David tried to fall back on the bed, but Constance grabbed his hands and pulled so that he fell forward on to his knees. Something inspired Constance to stand back and leave him. 'You couldn't stay like that if you were paralysed,' she said firmly. 'You'd better get up on your feet.' She went over to the window and turned her back on him.

'What's got into you?' asked David, 'Don't you love me any more?'

'No I don't!' said Constance, 'You're not the man you were. And I'm fed up with your selfishness. You'd better start fending for yourself because I'm not going to be your skivvy any more.'

David began to crawl towards her on his knees and when she heard the sound she turned, went across to him and, with a feeling close to desperation, put her arms round his waist and dragged him up on to his feet. When she let go of him, he stood swaying for a moment. Constance looked at his face and watched the slowly dawning expression of surprise mixed with shame. It was the first time for months that she had had evidence that he was capable of any concern beyond the purely selfish and it was, for her, a moment of deep joy.

David's real recovery dated from that critical moment, and within a few weeks he was back working on the patio and giving a hand with the housework.

* * *

This story is not meant to imply that all stroke patients are malingering. But many of them are likely, if not pushed quite hard, to do much less for themselves than they are capable of. There are many reasons for this, some psychological and related to a sense of resentment, and some the result of organic brain damage affecting the will to action.

Sad songs for Erika

Erika was a strikingly attractive nineteen-year-old student at the Hammarland School of Music. She was one of the most promising young singers the school had had for years. One day, she insisted on seeing the school principal, and told her she was giving up her studies.

Her mother was mildly surprised to see her come home in the middle of the afternoon. She had a paint brush in each hand and one in her mouth. 'Hello, tub!' she said, 'What brings you home?'

Erika muttered something and hurried upstairs. Her mother shrugged.

Erika went into her room and locked the door. She started to write a note, then scrunched it up and threw it on the floor. Then she filled a glass with water and sat on the side of her bed swallowing one tablet after another.

The next day she woke up in hospital. On her admission Erika had been found to be seriously underweight, almost emaciated, and very weak. The indications were that she had had almost nothing to eat for several weeks. Full investigation showed no sign of organic disease. The diagnosis of anorexia nervosa was obvious. Discussions with a psychiatrist eventually led to the root of the problem. Erika's statements were in eerie contrast to her emaciation.

'It's hard for me to say this,' she said, 'but the fact is that I'm so fat that I'm repulsive to Mum ... I've had to slim and slim and it's made me so weak that I just couldn't continue with the heavy schedule at the school. Of course I was hungry. I'm hungry all the time. It's an endless battle and horribly depressing. I want to eat but if I do Mum will find me even more repulsive because I won't be slim enough . . .'

'Oh yes, several boys at the school have seemed to fancy me. But that's because I'm, you know, doing well. They admire success. They actually like me in spite of my appearance. I don't want any of them on those terms, so I just give them the brush-off. And, of course, unless I can become slim there's no way I can go on the professional stage. It's a horrible situation. I feel I'm the victim of a power outside my control. I'm so unhappy . . .'

The psychiatrist found time to talk to Erika every day. His knowledge of music and his interest were so great that soon Erika began to enjoy their conversations. Then he began to apply a little pressure. They could talk, but only on condition that she ate a snack while they were talking. At first Erika tried to avoid swallowing the food and even made one or two attempts to hold it in her mouth and then spit it out into a tissue. But the doctor was wise to such tricks and was very firm with her.

Gradually, over the weeks, Erika became accustomed to eating and her strength improved. One day, the doctor even persuaded her to sing some Schubert to him. He was astonished by the quality of her voice and her control.

After talking about music for a time he decided to take a chance. 'I suppose by now,' he said, 'you are probably aware that your idea that you are too fat is an illusion.'

'Oh really?' she said sceptically.

'Really. It's all part of the disease. Our task, together, is to get you to think about gaining weight in a relaxed way and without panic. The other thing we have to do is to free you of your preoccupation with your mother's idea of you. Frankly, that's an illusion too. There's no possible way she could perceive you as too fat. No way. Now that you have finally managed to put on some weight you are deliciously slim. But you also have to come to terms with the fact that although your mother loves you, she doesn't adore you the way you adore her. She's just not made the way you are. She doesn't have your passion. You're the artist in the family. So it's up to you. You have to come to see the possibility of a different life-style from the one in which you are currently trapped.'

It was a long and uphill task and there were many relapses, but Erika completed her training and, after a short spell in the chorus of a provincial opera company, got her first solo spot. In her mid-twenties she was beginning to be recognized as a most promising coloratura soprano when she fell in love with a young tenor. The affair was tempestuous but, unfortunately, short-lived, and after a few months the man took up with another woman.

Erika became convinced, once again, that she had been rejected because she was too fat. So she climbed to the high catwalk over the backdrops of the stage, tied the end of a loose scenery rope tightly round her neck and stepped off.

*   *   *

Anorexia nervosa is a serious disorder of perception causing the sufferer, almost always a young woman, to believe that she is too fat, when, in fact, she may be very thin. It is common in models, actresses, dancers and others who are much concerned with the appearance of their bodies. In a minority of cases it is a symptom of a serious underlying psychiatric disorder such as severe depression or schizophrenia.

The cause of anorexia is still a matter of debate. Many anorexics come from close-knit families, and have a particularly intimate relationship with one parent. They are often obsessional in their habits. They are conformists and usually anxious to please. Some seem unwilling to grow up and appear to be trying to retain their childhood shape. Others seem to have a genuine fatness phobia. Social factors are probably contributory, especially the arbitrary identification of slimness with sexual attractiveness. Such influences may be powerful on girls who are deeply concerned with the effect they have on others.

Medically, the effects of anorexia nervosa are obvious. If calorie input is less than the energy and structural replacement needs, first the fat stores are used up and then the muscles are used for fuel. In anorexia there is extreme thinness with loss of a third or more of the body weight. There is, inevitably, great tiredness and weakness, and often the effects of vitamin deficiency. The skin becomes dry and the hair falls out. Early in the process there is, in almost all cases, absence of menstruation. Death from starvation, or suicide, is by no means uncommon.

Anorexia nervosa demands skilled treatment in hospital under the care of those experienced in the condition. Personality problems, and the persistence of the disorder, can make treatment difficult. Management depends on psychotherapy and imposed re-feeding but patients will usually make every effort to circumvent treatment, holding food in their mouths until it can be disposed of. Strict control is essential. Unless a watch is kept, food will be hidden or secretly thrown away. Often a system of rewards may be effective, in which privileges, such as visits or relative freedom, are awarded for weight gained.

Even after normal weight has been regained, patients who have had anorexia nervosa may need to remain under psychiatric care for months or years. Relapses are common and, tragically, up to ten per cent later commit suicide or die from starvation.

Crime and punishment

Many psychiatrists hold that the study of crime is within the province of medicine; others take the view that medicine is involved only when disease of body or mind might provide a defence to a criminal charge. It is not particularly surprising that there should be such difference of opinion. A widely accepted definition of crime is that it is behaviour that contravenes the current legal or moral codes of a culture. Apparently, the word cannot be defined more specifically than that. Few would argue, however, that crime falls within the scope of psychology. It seems that human beings have no inherent or 'built in' standards by which they can judge whether or not their conduct is criminal. They can do this only by reference to the laws and principles obtaining at the time.

In spite of the increasing prosperity of the Western world, the incidence of crime continues to increase, and the causes have long exercised the minds of thinkers. Many suggestions have been made, and solutions proposed, but none have been entirely satisfactory. One problem is that the rules and beliefs of societies change with time and differ in different cultures. No single act, not even the killing of another human being, can be said, invariably and universally, to be criminal. Many acts, once thought criminal or deviant, are not now so regarded. In the West we no longer hang hungry children for stealing stale bread or put women to death for committing adultery. Even breaking the law is not always now regarded as criminal by the majority. This may be because in an increasingly materialistic and industrialized society greater pressures are applied to people to disregard certain laws – such as parking regulations, or those against the use of certain addictive drugs. Some of these infractions, although they may incur penalties, are no longer generally regarded as seriously criminal.

Much human wrong-doing has, in the past, been considered both criminal and immoral, but today an increasing part of it is seen to be either one or the other. In the UK and elsewhere, the law now takes no cognizance of many acts which many people still regard as immoral and which were once also regarded as criminal – acts such as homosexual intercourse between consenting adults in private. Again, such views are a product of the culture of the place and time. In contrast, acts such as, for instance, failing to wear a car seat belt, are acknowledged to be criminal but are not considered immoral. Essentially, morality is concerned with individually held personal standards of behaviour, while criminality is concerned with universally applied external principles.

Sociologists and philosophers have given much thought to the causes of crime. In the nineteenth century it was widely believed that criminality was hereditary. In his *Inquiries into Human*

Faculty (1883), the then highly respected English scientist Sir Francis Galton (1822–1911) writes: 'The perpetuation of the criminal class by heredity is a question difficult to grapple with on many accounts. Their vagrant habits, their illegitimate unions, and extreme untruthfulness, are among the difficulties of the investigation. It is, however, easy to show that the criminal nature tends to be inherited.' Galton recounts in detail the 'infamous Jukes family in America . . . which includes no less than 540 individuals of Jukes blood, of whom a frightful number degraded into criminality, pauperism, or disease.' Galton described how the whole Jukes family had descended from a single individual – a 'half savage whose descendants went to the bad, and such hereditary moral weaknesses as they may have had, rose to the surface and worked their mischief without check producing a prevalent criminal type.' In Galton's time many other human activities and attitudes were attributed, on equally slender grounds, to heredity.

No modern thinker would now agree with Galton. There is, of course, no gene or genes for criminality and today most people, aware of the enormous effect of environmental influences on the young developing mind, recognize the fallacies in this kind of reasoning. Criminal families certainly exist but the cause is at least as likely to be nurture as nature. It is known that, in a small proportion of cases, organic brain disorder, chromosomal abnormalities and psychiatric disorder may be associated with crime. True kleptomania is a cause of petty theft and schizophrenia sometimes leads to violent crime. These cases, however, are in a tiny minority and such factors provide no general explanation of the causes of crime.

The difficulty may lie in our tendency to categorize criminality as if it were a specific disorder like tuberculosis rather than being an effect of external stimuli overcoming inadequate prior social training. In deciding the cause of crime, each individual case must be considered on its own and the causal factors identified. Clearly, early childhood experience is important and we know that the influences operating then have a deeper and more lasting effect than later influences. A child brought up to believe that successful theft is a matter for congratulation and that violence is an acceptable response to frustration is more likely to resort to crime than a child conditioned from the beginning to obey rules, conform to discipline and respect the rights of others. Absence of authority is often an important precipitating factor for crime. Unhappy or broken families feature strongly in the background of people habitually engaged in crime, as do low intelligence, poor health and low income. Even so, although some families foster crime, many members of such families do not become criminals.

The family is not, of course, the only conditioning influence. At quite an early age the child is exposed to a wider social environment from which other, and possibly conflicting, influences are derived. Social deprivation is often cited as a cause of crime and this is certainly one of the many motivating factors. Envy of the perceived advantages of others may provide the trigger for criminal activity. There is also a general correlation between educational level and the tendency to criminality. This relates to the fact that a high proportion of criminals were unhappy at school and have a record of frequent truancy. Delinquent tendencies commonly appear in school. High educational achievement is not, of course, incompatible with crime, but the educated criminals – the embezzlers, insider traders, misappliers of funds, monopolists and bribers and blackmailers – form a small minority of criminals.

Gender is another important factor. Most crimes are committed by men. Of reported crime in Western countries, only one burglary in 30 is committed by a woman, one robbery in 20, one assault in 7 and one murder in 6. At least 75 per cent of reported serious crime is committed by men under 25. Murder is an exception; 60 per cent of murders are committed by men over 25. Half of the people arrested for criminal acts are between the ages of 11 and 17.

Abuse of drugs and alcohol is also frequently related to crime. Much crime is committed by drug addicts to get the money to support this habit, but there is no convincing evidence that the immediate physical effect of the drugs is to promote crime. Indeed, drugs like heroin and marijuana have a sedating effect likely to reduce a tendency to criminal activity especially violent crime. The main association in the case of alcohol is with driving offences, which are often serious.

A society's response to crime depends on the prevailing views as to how criminals should be treated. Many will claim that the purpose of punishment is to deter the offender from further crime and will continue to express this view in spite of ample evidence to the contrary. Often the real underlying feeling is that punishment is justified as retribution by society. Even very thoughtful and well-informed individuals will sometimes, in response to what seems to be a particularly savage or horrifying crime, feel that punishment such as flogging or execution is appropriate and justified. Others maintain that capital punishment is never morally justifiable and involves the practical risk that an innocent person may be condemned. The commonest form of punishment – imprisonment – is also often justified, explicitly or otherwise, on the grounds that it protects society against people who are deemed to be its enemies.

These views have been almost universally held from the earliest times, often in an extreme form. As a result penal systems have often been barbarously cruel. Long sentences of incarceration in dungeons and manacles, flogging to the limits of endurance, branding, blinding, amputation and torture of all kinds have been commonplace. The practice of execution by decapitation, strangulation, burning, hanging or crucifixion was widespread. English justice was capable of brutal savagery in the medieval period, when the sentence for treason was public hanging, drawing and quartering. The explicit justification for such punishments – that they would be deterrent – was based on the assumption that potential offenders would act rationally to avoid pain and would contemplate the consequences of their actions. History has shown that these assumptions are seldom justified. The fear of severe punishment does not necessarily deter.

An enlightened and humane early writer on the subject of punishment was the Italian jurist Cesare Bonesana Marchesi di Beccaria (1738–94). In his book *An Essay on Crimes and Punishments* published in 1764 Beccaria argued that a state should legislate for a scale of crimes ranging from those most harmful to the state to those causing the least harm to the individual. The state should also legislate for an appropriate scale of punishments whose function was not retributive but was purely to deter. Punishment should therefore have the greatest deterrent effect consistent with the least harm to the offender. It should be certain, quick and consistent. Punishments found not to deter should be abandoned and others tried. The laws should be clear and known to all.

Beccaria's book was one of the most widely read and influential works of the time both in Europe and in Britain and prompted much thought and argument on penal reform. Voltaire gave it his support and attempts were made to incorporate its ideas into the French penal code of 1791. The English philosopher Jeremy Bentham (1748–1832) took Beccaria's ideas further and pointed out, among other things, that excessively severe punishment defeated its own object because the offender could argue that he or she may as well commit a more serious crime since the punishment would be the same.

In modern society, for most first offenders, imprisonment is an effective deterrent. About three-quarters of those who are imprisoned for the first time do not offend again. But of those who do, and who are again imprisoned, the rate of habitual relapse into crime (recidivism) rises steadily. Overcrowded long-stay prisons often simply promote further crime by reinforcing criminal tendencies through contact with other criminals. Prisons act as schools for criminals. Attempts, such as that of the Borstal system in UK, abandoned in 1982, to apply modern penological theories involving strict discipline, vocational training and close supervision, did not seem particularly successful. Disappointingly, there is little evidence that such systems can reliably achieve rehabilitation. The *therapeutic community* is a small-scale trial in the rehabilitation of criminals. Small groups of offenders are kept under tight discipline but undergo regular counselling and discussion sessions in which they are enlightened as to the effects of crime on others and are encouraged to gain insight into their criminal motivation by narrating their own experience and writing accounts of it. The results show promise.

Accident prone

Is there such a thing as accident proneness? Some doctors certainly think so. A public health specialist and Fellow of the Faculty of Occupational Medicine Dr H. O. Engel, writing in the *Journal of the Royal Society of Medicine* in March 1991, suggests that the syndrome is very real and that people who are accident prone are also illness prone. Dr Engel points out that between 13 and 15 per cent of people create 50 per cent of the work for doctors. He found, from his own long experience in industrial medicine and as a factory doctor, that the employees who were most off work from accidents were also those who were most off work from illness.

What makes people liable to these misfortunes? Dr Engel suggests that this problem stems from childhood or earlier. Parents often recognize that some children are naturally clumsy and much more liable to injury during play than others. Accident-prone children are often hyperactive or aggressive and may come from broken families. While most learn from bitter experience to avoid accidents, people with the accident syndrome do not. When they grow up they may become what are known in the medical profession as 'heart-sink' patients – the ones who make the doctor's heart sink when he or she sees them in the waiting room. They become well known to insurance companies and suffer loading of premiums.

Dr Engel's paper prompted a great deal of critical correspondence. Among his critics was one who suggested that he was indulging in the reprehensible practice of blaming the patient for the disease and that the idea of accident proneness had long been discredited. Another hit even harder and suggested that a far commoner cause of industrial accidents was the side effects of medication prescribed to the workers – especially sedatives, tranquillizers, antidepressant drugs and antipsychotic drugs. It is not entirely clear whether this correspondent was implying that Dr Engel was the real cause of his own statistics. One would certainly hope not. Presumably the editor of the journal hastily terminated the correspondence before someone was prompted to suggest that Dr Engel was himself accident prone.

What is an emotion?

Few people appreciate how intimately the emotions are linked with bodily changes. It is hard to define emotions without reference to the physiological changes that accompany them. Some people have suggested that the bodily changes *are* the emotions, but there are difficulties with this view. It is not unreasonable to suggest that for many, perhaps for all of us, the evocation of certain emotions (such as happiness) is the principal aim in life.

We tend to think of ourselves as rational beings, essentially different from other animals. But there is one element in our nature that is divorced from reason and that is shared with many other species – our emotional life. Emotional reactions, similar, if not identical to, those we experience, occur in animals incapable of mental activity as we know it.

In his book *The Expression of the Emotions in Man and Animals*, Charles Darwin (1809–82) showed how we can recognize emotions in animals and equate them to human emotions. The similarity between the bodily reactions of animals and those of humans in parallel situations is often very close. A comparison with other species shows that the same emotion-producing stimulus produces contraction of the analogous facial muscles. Dogs and humans can snarl, sneer and smile in common and do so in comparable circumstances. Darwin also showed that these expressions of emotions were not learned behaviour but were innate. They occur in different races and in children born blind.

The facial expressions that accompany the various emotions, such as joy, sadness, surprise, anger, fear or disgust, are common across all cultures and are consistent even in remote human groups which have had no contact with the outside world.

When we sample the blood of humans and other animals during times of rage or fear we find that there is a substantial rise in the level of adrenaline. This causes the heart to beat faster, the rate of breathing to increase, the blood pressure to rise, the pupils to dilate, the skin to turn pale, the hair to stand on end, and the muscle ring at the outlet of the stomach to contract tightly, causing a characteristic 'butterfly' sensation in the upper abdomen. Alpha and beta blocker drugs, which prevent adrenaline from causing these actions on the heart and respiration and on the smooth (non-voluntary) muscle of the body, largely eliminate the emotional effect of high blood adrenaline levels and are very calming. The effects of adrenaline are so reminiscent of the features of high emotion that it is not perhaps surprising that this knowledge led some people to equate such bodily changes with the emotion.

This idea seemed self-evident to the great nineteenth-century psychologist William James (1842–1910), brother of the novelist

Henry James. In an article in the psychological journal *Mind* in 1884, James suggested that these bodily reactions were not the result of a prior emotion, but that the mental states we characterize as emotions were the psychological concomitants of the physical changes. These, in conjunction with the perception of the events that had caused the visceral reactions, *were* the emotion.

According to this theory, we feel fear because we are shaking, our heart bounding and our mouth dry; we feel happy because the facial muscles that elevate the corners of our mouths have contracted; and we feel sad because we are crying. There is some evidence that the deliberate assumption of certain facial expressions can produce the kind of physiological changes associated with the emotions that normally evoke these expressions. To some extent, a cheerful countenance deliberately assumed can induce the physiological concomitants of happiness. Similarly, a chronically miserable expression will induce unhappiness.

Nevertheless, emotion is *not* simply the awareness of the bodily reactions to the hormones. The great English physiologist Charles Sherrington (1857–1952) demonstrated that emotions were experienced even when all sensory connections to the parts of the body concerned were cut. Physically paralysed humans still experience all the emotions, although to a reduced degree. It is also clear that the bodily responses are by no means specific to the kind of emotion experienced, and we now know that the emotion precedes the visceral response by one or two seconds. Recent physiological research has taught us a great deal more about the origins of the emotions.

In the middle of the underside of the brain, immediately above the pituitary gland, is an area known as the hypothalamus. Above and around this, is a great vertical ring of grey matter (nerve cell bodies), a primitive part of the brain called the limbic system. The limbic system is the seat of the emotions and it operates in much the same way in both human beings and other animals. We humans have a highly developed cerebral cortex – the outer layer of the brain – which allows us to associate the emotions with complex thought. Other animals cannot do this and operate largely on an emotional level. Electrical stimulation of parts of the limbic system in animals produces a range of emotional behaviour such as fear, rage, contentment, sexual arousal, and so on. These occur with no involvement of the cerebral cortex. Stimulation of the limbic system in humans, in the course of brain surgery, produces a similar range of emotions.

The hypothalamus is the link between brain functions and the endocrine system, and all emotional activity is associated with the production of the hormones adrenaline and cortisol from the adrenal glands, and with the effects that these hormones have on the body. The stronger the emotion the higher the hormonal levels. A rise in the production of adrenaline and cortisol occurs in states of excitement whether these are associated with fear, anger or even pleasurable anticipation. Although an injection of adrenaline causes an emotional response, the nature of this emotion – whether pleasant or unpleasant – is known to be determined by the associated circumstances.

It is now generally accepted that every human emotional experience is a synthesis of bodily (visceral) hormonal arousal and conscious intellectual evaluation of the current situation. Emotion is no longer regarded as an atavistic characteristic. Emotions are aroused when an incongruity or discrepancy occurs between our expectations and the reality. This, for instance, is the basis of most humour and of much literary appreciation. The discrepancy is more readily recognized when the emotions aroused are the powerful and fundamental ones of fear, anger, joy and sadness. The recognition of such an inconsistency between expectation and eventuality produces the hormonally-induced visceral events that bring the matter forcibly to our notice and help us to remember it. Viewed in this way, the emotions can be seen to have high survival value. Recognition and recollection of past dangers, for instance, are greatly enhanced by the powerful memory of the bodily events we experienced at the time. The emotions also induce action, usually of a self-preserving kind. We may retreat hastily from a source of danger, or we may attack it. The physiological changes that accompany emotion might have been calculated to improve our performance in times of stress and danger.

Although there are at least 200 words in English describing different emotions, most psychologists agree that the number of basic, or primary, emotions is much smaller and is probably limited to a list such as fear, anger, joy, sorrow, surprise, acquiescence and disgust. Emotions as experienced, however, are rarely pure, and are usually mixtures of the primary emotions. These may be called secondary emotions. The habitual experience of secondary emotions often characterizes personality. A person who is commonly sad and fearful will have an anxious personality; one who experiences sadness and disgust will be a depressive; one who manifests surprise and joy will be an optimistic extrovert; one who manifests anger and disgust might be said to have a sarcastic personality; and a person who is habitually joyfully acquiescent will be deemed to be sociable.

Axillary attractions

Professor Michael Stoddart, a Tasmanian zoologist and amateur art connoisseur, claims that the frequency with which the armpit – the axilla – is revealed in art is no accident. Early in human evolution, he says, armpit odour was important in attracting a mate. This fact is built into our psyche, so the sight of an upraised naked arm, he claims, prompts erotic feelings and a positive attitude towards the work of art.

Altering the image

Male genital self-mutilation takes various forms. In about 10 per cent of cases it involves the complete amputation of the genitals. In nearly 30 per cent both testicles are removed, leaving the penis. One testicle is removed in 9 per cent. Other mutilations involve various degrees of damage such as partial amputation or partial severance of the penis, or various injuries to the skin or contents of the scrotum, many of which heal very well.

It is commonly assumed that people who do this kind of thing to themselves must be, almost by definition, psychotic, but this is not so. Transsexualism is a very real phenomenon, commonly affecting people who are perfectly sane. It is a lifelong conviction that one is the wrong anatomical sex and is associated with a permanent longing to be changed to the anatomical sex corresponding to the internal mental image. This is a matter of gender identity and it can become the central preoccupation in life. It is not a delusion. Genuine male transsexuals feel and think like women and, internally, *are* women. To them, their male genitals are as grotesque and unnatural as female breasts would be to a normal man. They are constantly trying to persuade doctors to do sex change surgery.

It should not therefore come as a surprise to learn that a fair proportion of men who perform genital self-mutilation are desperate transsexuals. Even so, the act must be regarded as abnormal and studies have shown that the great majority of men who do mutilate themselves in this way are psychologically abnormal. Apart from the 15 per cent or so who wish to appear female, other reasons given for performing self-mutilation include guilt about heterosexual urges including incest; guilt about homosexual urges; revenge against women; obeying the commands of hallucinatory voices; delusions of being female; ritual purification; and to assist in resisting sexual temptation. Extreme religiosity is a feature of about 7 per cent of cases.

Drinking the brain away

The brain is made of nerve cells stuck together with nerve glue (neuroglial tissue). Nerve cells have bodies and long processes known as axons or nerve fibres. Information from the cell body passes out along the axon; information from outside the cell passes in by way of much shorter processes called dendrites. Nerve cells don't divide or reproduce. We have to make do with the number we have at the age of about ten when the development of the structure of the brain is complete.

It is not too easy to estimate the number of brain cells we have, but it is large – somewhere between 15,000 and 30,000 million. Very large numbers are lost every day of our lives, especially as we grow older and the blood supply to the brain is reduced by arterial narrowing. Nerve cells are very sensitive to an inadequate oxygen and fuel (glucose) supply, but if we live reasonably healthy lives and manage to avoid Alzheimer's disease there is no need to worry that we will run out of brain cells. The loss of a million a year over a very long life would be a drop in the ocean.

There is another way, however, to accelerate the rate of loss of brain cells and that is to drink them away. Really serious attention to hitting the bottle, sustained over a long period of time, can be relied on to do the trick. Dedicated drinking can lead to the Korsakoff psychosis – a brain disorder affecting long-term alcoholics who rely solely, or mainly, on alcohol for their nutrition. The main change is in mental function and this may, at first, be subtle. There is considerable loss of functional brain cells and, with it, a severe memory defeat with almost total loss of the capacity to store new information. Research suggests that the part of the brain responsible for storing information, the hippocampus, is especially liable to nerve cell loss.

One danger facing people who manage to rationalize away this warning is that memory loss is concealed, at first even from the victim, by the process of confabulation, in which the affected person makes up stories to fill in the gaps in the memory. People with Korsakoff's psychosis may talk convincingly to strangers, but those who know them soon become familiar with the constantly replayed 'tape recording'. Unfortunately, this condition is usually irreversible and proceeds to profound dementia and the need for constant supervision.

Of sound mind

In his memoirs, Sir George Turner FRCS recounts how, on a visit to Dr Tuke's private asylum at Chiswick House, he was so impressed by the beauty of the house and grounds that he confesses to Tuke 'Verily thou hast almost persuaded me to be a lunatic.'

Tuke, a most humane practitioner, used often to arrange amusements and dances for his patients. Turner and others would often be invited to participate. On one occasion he seems to have been rather taken with a lady patient with whom he often danced. Their conversation led him to conclude that the lady was entirely sane. Convinced that she should be released, Turner put this suggestion to her.

The lady laughed. 'Oh, I am perfectly aware that there is nothing wrong with me,' she said, 'My husband had me certified.'

'Good heavens!'

'But that's not the end of the story. After I had been here a year, I inherited rather a lot of money.'

'And?'

'And then, of course, he wanted me out. But by then I was contented to go on living in this lovely place with so many nice people, that – '

'That you – '

'Decided to stay. Yes. Between my husband and me, you can now imagine who is the more mad.'

Conscience

An eminent historian, interested in the origins of conscience, decided to experiment on his young daughters. He taught them that it was necessary to stroke their noses twice a day. No explanation was given. Later, he found that if, for any reason, the girls had failed to conform to this small ritual they were much troubled by their consciences.

The discrediting of Freud

Sigmund Freud was born in Freiberg, Moravia (now in the Czech Republic) in 1856 but spent most of his life in Vienna. He was a child prodigy who read Shakespeare and Goethe at the age of eight and was versed in the Greek, Latin, French and German classics. In spite of a taste for philosophy, he studied medicine and qualified in 1881. After some excellent early work on aphasia, infant cerebral palsy and neurological connections in the nervous system, he worked for some time in Paris with the French neurologist Jean-Martin Charcot (1825–93). Fascinated by Charcot's work on hysteria, Freud turned his attention to the psychological basis of mental disorder, and at first used hypnotism to elicit painful memories that seemed to be at the root of many psychological problems.

This work led him to the idea of repressed memories and impulses and to a profound consideration of the nature of the unconscious mind. Later he abandoned hypnotism and adopted the method of free association. His interest in the significance of dreams as a source of insight into the unconscious mind led to the publication in 1900 of *The Interpretation of Dreams*. The book was almost ignored. In 1903 he published *Three Essays on the Theory of Sexuality*. At first this caused a storm of abuse, but gradually his ideas gained acceptance.

The psychoanalytic theories of Freud had an immense and pervasive cultural influence, mainly because of their emphasis on sex, and the licence they provided for the general discussion of the subject in an age when such talk had been largely taboo. In addition, although Freud did not 'discover' the unconscious mind, as is sometimes asserted, the light he cast upon it changed the whole aspect of human thought. Throughout, Freud claimed that his theories were scientific.

Freud derived his ideas from the data obtained by encouraging patients to indulge in 'free association'. This 'talking cure' appeared to relieve symptoms such as hysteria. He discovered that his female patients tended to fall in love with him and to become emotionally dependent on him. This phenomenon he called transference and, after some time, he concluded that transference was essential for the success of the method. Throughout his life he continued to develop, revise and amend his ideas and he attracted many devoted followers and disciples.

The primary assertions of psychoanalytic theory were that psychosexual development passes, from birth to sexual maturity, through various stages in each of which pleasure is centred on a part of the body. These were the oral, anal, phallic and genital stages. 'Fixation' could occur at any of the earlier stages, thereby determining various defects in the personality. Little boys of age three to five were sexually jealous of their fathers, whom they wished to kill, and were in love with their mothers, with whom they wanted to have sexual intercourse. This was the Oedipus complex. With little girls the situation was reversed – the Electra complex. The psychological health of the adult was said to be determined mainly by the success or otherwise with which the child coped with these sexual and aggressive impulses.

Freud claimed that everything of importance in the mental life took place in the unconscious mind and that much of this was concerned with sex and aggression. Our inability to live with these unconscious sexual and aggressive impulses caused us to develop neurotic illness, and the only cure was to bring these impulses to light by psychoanalysis. Freud also claimed that every verbal slip or lapse of memory had a cause – usually a concealed expression of sex or aggression. This phenomenon came to be known as the Freudian slip. The expert psychoanalyst could analyse these errors and infer from them the state of the unconscious mind.

Dreams were said to be full of highly significant symbolism, much of it of a sexual nature. The interpretation of this symbolism by the expert provided insight into the unconscious mind. Every elongated object was said to symbolize the penis and every receptacle the vagina. Flying implied sexual arousal because the erect penis could maintain its elevation only by the magic of flying.

There were three layers to the mind – the superego, the ego and the id – respectively the censorious, the mainly conscious, and the wholly unconscious repository of fantasies, repressed ideas, sex and aggression. Narcissism, or self-love, was healthy in the early stages of development, unhealthy later. Thanatos, the death instinct, was a drive leading to self-destruction.

These ideas came largely from Freud's literary background rather than from any observed or scientific sources. They were also very much the product of a sexually repressive era when explicit reference to normal sexual urges was considered obscene. Both he and his followers believed in these theories because they seemed to explain so much. It was this that caused Freud to believe that they were scientific. In fact, the theory was much closer to a religion than to a science. The time came when, as with other prophets of various religions, Freud and his followers came to believe in his pronouncements for no better reason than that he asserted them. Psychoanalytic theory, in the manner of most religions, soon developed its own strict dogmas, prohibitions, sanctions, saints and prophets. It was capable of accepting much that was patently absurd and, like many religions, was to be rent by schisms and distressed by heresies. Two of the most important heretics were Jung and Adler.

With the German invasion of Austria in 1938 the risk to Freud of Nazi persecution became critical and, with great difficulty, he was smuggled out of the country and brought to London. There he died in 1939 from cancer of the upper jaw, from which he had suffered stoically for over sixteen years. His daughter Anna became, in her own right, a leading figure in the psychoanalytic movement.

With the growth of scientific rigour and the recognition, in the early 1960s, by philosophers of science such as Karl Popper, that psychoanalysis was a pseudoscience, the discrediting of Freud began. Psychoanalysis was not supported by scientific proof but by its ability to provide its own verifications. Whatever happened always confirmed it. It could explain everything, even the views of its most bitter critics. People who did not believe in it were suffering from just the kind of mental problems that psychoanalysis could cure. They were crying out for analysis.

Most destructive of all was the fact that psychoanalysis could not be disproved and it soon became clear that this was one of the central features of a pseudoscience. As Popper put it, the criterion of the scientific status of a theory is its falsifiability or refutability. Psychoanalysis could neither be falsified or refuted and therein lay its downfall. Today, although thousands of people are still undergoing lengthy psychoanalytic treatment, and many are deriving benefit from it, it is now generally acknowledged in scientific circles that the theoretical basis of psychoanalysis is entirely imaginary, and has no scientific merit nor any value as a therapeutic tool. This is not to suggest that psychoanalysis may not benefit the patient, but the benefit is likely to result from the effects of the wisdom, maturity, experience and sympathy of the analyst rather than from the application of any of Freud's theoretical ideas.

The ESP phenomenon

The American botanist J. B. Rhine (1895–1980) came to believe in the existence of psychic phenomena after hearing a lecture by Sir Arthur Conan Doyle (1869–1930), a convinced spiritualist. In 1930 Rhine and the psychologist William McDougall (1871–1938) set up a parapsychology laboratory at Duke University, North Carolina. In 1934 Rhine published the book *Extra-Sensory Perception*, which was an account of his experiments into telepathy. In 1937 he published a popular work entitled *New Frontiers of the Mind*. This caused a sensation and became a bestseller, bringing to the attention of the world Rhine's claims to have scientifically proved thought transference.

Rhine's attitude was undeniably scientific and this carried a great deal of weight and conviction with the public. He believed that the supposed paranormal mental powers were an extension of normal psychological activities and were susceptible to statistical analysis. Using packs of twenty-five 'Zener' cards, each card bearing one of five symbols – square, circle, cross, star and wavy lines – Rhine was able to quantify the results of a test in which one person turned over and looked at the cards, one at a time, while another, who could not see the cards, wrote down his or her impression of which symbol was being observed. In a sufficiently large number of trials, pure chance would dictate that correct answers occur, on average, five times for each run of the pack. Rhine claimed that he obtained correct results at a significantly higher rate, and immediately insisted that he had proved the existence of extra-sensory perception. Sometimes he claimed that he obtained significantly *lower* rates – which were equally significant.

As a result of criticisms of his methods, Rhine repeated his trials with the people concerned in different buildings and with wholly independent verification and statistical analysis of the findings. Above-average scores occurred less often, but still occurred. Millions who read his work accepted Rhine's conclusion, and for a time it seemed that ESP was an established scientific fact. Later, Rhine claimed to have proved the existence of psychokinesis – the ability to move objects by the power of the mind without physical intervention. This work was conducted along similar lines to the ESP trials, and it was claimed that randomly thrown dice could be influenced to produce better than average scores. This proved too much for many to swallow.

Science does not accept new data without independent verification, so several other psychologists repeated Rhine's tests under similarly rigorous conditions. Strangely, none of them were able to find any evidence of above-average results. The response of Rhine's supporters to this was that the demonstration of ESP might depend on the attitude of the experimenter. Those who were sceptical might have a negative influence and only those who believed could demonstrate it. Such an argument cut little ice with the scientists. It seemed more likely that, in some way not yet apparent, the powerful desire of the experimenter to prove the hypothesis was leading to unconscious bias or even cheating. Regrettably, events showed this to be so. After Rhine had retired, his successor, Walter J. Levy, was discovered, in 1974, to be fraudulently increasing the scores in an experiment so as to support ESP.

Today, amazingly, formal parapsychological investigation continues. A Chair of Parapsychology has actually been endowed at a Scottish University where much use is made of electronics and automation. Attempts are being made to study the effects of attitude, beliefs, mood and altered states of consciousness on claimed ESP scores. It is said that people with a positive attitude to ESP, and who are relaxed and emotionally healthy, are most likely to produce good scores.

One difficulty about all this is that many people desperately want to believe in this kind of magic and in survival after death. Unfortunately for them the great bulk of claims of paranormal phenomena – of materializations at seances, communications with the dead, levitation, spoon-bending and so on – can be dismissed on the grounds of fraud. Few of them can be sustained after investigation by trained observers. Claims by those who use normal scientific methods are not so easily dismissed, but their case has been weakened by the few notorious examples of cheating.

In fairness to those who believe in parapsychology, it must be said that they do not, and cannot, claim that paranormal phenomena can be repeated at will. If they could, such phenomena would not be paranormal. So it proves nothing to conduct experiments that give negative results. Such paranormal phenomena that have been claimed have been rare; the prevalence of outright fraud among parapsychology workers is also rare, but it is possible that there is a connection. It is possible, even probable, that unconscious self-deception and fraud can account for all the claimed positive findings.

A good deal of support for belief in the paranormal arises from a well-recognized quirk of human nature. If we want to believe something and a highly unlikely coincidence occurs that supports the belief, we will never forget it. We will not, however, remember any of the numerous occasions on which such coincidences do *not* occur. If someone dreams that a friend has died and reads his obituary the next day, he will be deeply impressed and may be persuaded that precognition is a fact. This impression will not be outweighed by the many occasions on which he has dreamed of an event that has *not* occurred soon after.

The public appears to have an insatiable appetite for the wonderful, and will read avidly any account of claimed paranormal phenomena, especially if presented in a seemingly scientific manner. By contrast, there is little interest in accounts that disprove the paranormal. Hundreds of popular books claiming miracles are published every year, but debunking authors have a hard time getting their books published. This means that, in the minds of the uncritical, the 'evidence' for the paranormal enormously exceeds the evidence against it. Perhaps the most impressive finding of all is the strength of our unquenchable longing for proof that we are more than mere machines.

The eminent Scottish philosopher and historian David Hume (1711–76) had some very cogent things to say on the subject of miracles, and his ideas on the subject have been widely influential. Here is a short extract from his book *An Enquiry concerning Human Understanding*:

No testimony is sufficient to establish a miracle, unless the testimony be of such a kind that its falsehood would be even more miraculous than the fact which it endeavours to establish. When anyone tells me that he saw a dead man restored to life, I immediately consider with myself whether it be more probable that this person should either deceive or be deceived, or that the fact which he relates should really have happened. I weigh the one miracle against the other; and according to the superiority which I discover, I pronounce my decision, and always reject the greater miracle.

Kleptomania

This is much less common than is generally supposed. Kleptomania is a rare condition featuring recurrent theft, usually from a shop, of things not needed or even particularly wanted. It is thought to be more common among women than men but this has not been fully established. The purpose behind the theft is not to acquire objects, and the things stolen are often thrown away, carefully hidden or sometime surreptitiously replaced. Most kleptomaniacs can easily afford to pay for the things they steal and the motive is not the same as that of the common thief. The disorder occurs as often among the rich as among those less well off.

The act is not usually pre-planned and the object of the activity is the theft itself. The stealing is not usually reckless, and reasonable precautions are taken to avoid discovery, but sometimes kleptomaniacs seem to give no thought to the probable consequences of their actions and some of them appear outraged when arrested. In the course of the act there is a rising sense of tension focused on the theft; afterwards, if the act is successfully accomplished there is relief of tension and a sense of elation. This may, however, be followed by strong guilt feelings and intense fear of discovery.

Kleptomania is often put forward as a defence against a charge of theft, but this defence is seldom successful. Less than 5 per cent of people arrested for shop-lifting are found, on questioning, to respond in a manner consistent with the diagnosis. The condition is often associated with stress, such as bereavement or separation, and kleptomaniacs also tend to suffer from persistent depression and anorexia nervosa. It has also been associated with arson. Medical investigation of the condition has, of course, been conducted largely on people who have recently been arrested, so this might colour the medical view of the features of the condition.

The cause remains obscure, but many kleptomaniacs feel that they have been wronged, and are unwanted or neglected, and are thus entitled to steal. Many possible explanations have been advanced to explain the phenomenon, some of the most remarkable by psychoanalysts. These include the suggestion by Anna Freud that all stealing is rooted in the essential oneness between mother and child. Others have suggested that, in women, it represents a search for a penis; that the disorder is a means of seeking punishment; and that the excitement engendered is enjoyed as a substitute for sexual intercourse.

Kleptomania tends to be persistent and may, indeed, be a lifelong disorder. Often it starts in childhood. In many cases it is compatible with an otherwise apparently normal life and few affected people receive treatment unless this has been ordered by a court after arrest. Treatment involves a course of psychotherapy designed to provide the affected person with a clear insight into the nature of the condition. Behaviour therapy has also been successful.

Pseudodementia

Of all the old people deemed by the medical profession to be demented, between 10 and 20 per cent are not. The term pseudodementia has been coined to cover this category of people and the phenomenon should be better known.

Dementia literally means 'loss of mind' and its principal feature is severe, progressive and permanent loss of memory and intellectual power due to continuing degenerative disease of the brain. There is loss of intelligence, personality and skills. Most cases of true dementia are due to Alzheimer's disease; about 10 per cent are due to small repeated strokes; 5 to 10 per cent are due to alcohol; about 5 per cent are caused by brain tumours and another 5 per cent by 'water on the brain' (hydrocephalus). The remainder are caused by various conditions such as long-term drug intoxication, Huntington's chorea, liver failure, pernicious anaemia, syphilis, thyroid disease, multiple sclerosis, Creutzfeldt-Jakob disease, epilepsy or Parkinson's disease.

Pseudodementia refers to those cases of disorders that mimic dementia. Many of them do this so closely that the truth is never suspected and no treatment is given. The conditions that can simulate dementia include depression, hysteria, thyroid gland underaction and schizophrenia. There are some clues that can help to distinguish pseudodementia. The onset tends to be uncharacteristically sudden. There is often a family history of depression. People with pseudodementia often complain of poor memory whereas those with true dementia are unaware that they have lost memory and attempt to fill in the gaps by making up stories (confabulation). In pseudodementia the person concerned is often able to give a clear account of the past life and of the illness, if invited in very general terms to do so. They will seem intellectually inadequate only in response to direct and specific questioning.

Most of the causes of pseudodementia can be cured by the correct treatment.

Unconscious thought

A fascinating article in the *Lancet* of 24 December 1994 suggests that unconscious thought is impossible. The authors, Drs A. H. Chapman and M. Chapman-Santana from Bahia, Brazil, point out that the idea that one can have an unconscious thought is a contradiction in terms. Having a thought is a conscious experience. By no possible means can it be proved that any person has had an unconscious thought, and no evidence can be adduced to indicate that an unconscious thought has existed.

This, of course, is in direct contradiction to a number of psychological systems that purport to explain all kinds of mental pathology on the basis of unconscious thought. Freudian, Jungian, Adlerian and Rankian psychoanalysis are all based on the very questionable premise that unconscious thought exists.

We are, of course, capable of failing to perceive all kinds of things in our environments. Indeed it is necessary that this should be so to avoid overburdening the mind. We are also readily capable of failing to perceive the reasons for our emotional states. The authors of this paper cite, as an example of this, the imaginary case of a surgeon operating on a patient with a gangrenous gallbladder. The surgeon is very bad-tempered, irritable with his assistant and snaps at the instrument nurse if there is the slightest delay in handing him what he needs. The surgeon knows that four days earlier he had decided that the patient had mild indigestion and did not need treatment. He knows that three hours ago the patient had been brought in desperately ill and that, as a result of the delay, the operation was now much more difficult and dangerous.

But as he works, the surgeon is unaware that his irritability is the direct consequence of his feeling of guilt and inadequacy. This is not an unconscious thought; it is a current failure of perception. A colleague present in the theatre says, 'Relax, Tom. You're upset because you missed this diagnosis four days ago. But I agreed with you at the time and we all make mistakes.' At once, the surgeon begins to take it easy and is more effective. What his colleague has done is to move important emotion-producing material from non-perception to perception.

All kinds of unperceived causes of emotion, mostly damaging, can exist and can have adverse effects. But perception and non-perception of the emotional effects of past events are not unconscious thoughts; they are simply qualities or attributes of these effects. The ease with which emotions and their causes may pass from non-perception to perception varies considerably from person to person and from one type of life experience to another.

Makes you think (consciously), doesn't it?

The emotional sex

It is widely believed that women are more emotional than men. This is a rather loose comment that usually means that women, on the whole, are more prone to express emotion than men. How freely we express our emotions, however, is very much a cultural matter and varies a good deal from society to society. In contemporary western societies research has shown that women do, on average, display the facial expression of emotion more readily and more fully than do men. This was shown in trials conducted in 1972. Both men and women were covertly watched by observers over closed-circuit television, while being shown projected pictures chosen to prompt emotional responses. The observers could not see the pictures but were asked to identify the type of picture from the facial expression of the subjects. They scored significantly higher when watching women's reactions than when watching men.

But does this really mean that women are more emotional? Can one judge true emotional response by facial expression alone? It seems not. The right way is to measure the response by the physiologically changes induced in the body. Among many other physiological responses, emotion produces slight to profuse sweating and this is sensitively reflected in the electrical resistance of the skin. When this and other physiological parameters were used to measure emotional response to various scenes, women were found to respond less markedly than men.

So it seems possible that men are actually more emotionally responsive than women but that women show their emotions more. Culturally, of course, western men tend simply to behave in accordance with the standard stereotype of the stoical male because they have learned from an early age to repress the expression of emotion.

Apocryphal

Stoical Ludendorff

General Eric von Ludendorff (1865–1937) was Chief of Staff to the German Army from 1914 until after the end of the war. In 1918 he planned the offensive on the Western front that nearly won the war for Germany. From 1924 to 1928 he was a Nazi member of the Reichstag.

In November 1926 Ludendorff called in the famous surgeon Professor Ernst Sauerbruch. When Sauerbruch appeared he found the General pacing up and down his office, tearing a handkerchief to pieces and plainly anxious, agitated and nervous. Sauerbruch noticed that the collar of Ludendorff's tunic was, uncharacteristically, open and that his thyroid gland was enlarged. He immediately inferred that the General was suffering from hyperthyroidism – a condition that would of course, account for his disturbed state.

As he asked the General about his symptoms and examined the swelling of the gland, Ludendorff's agitation increased. 'This trifling lump cannot be important,' he said, 'it is just a local swelling.'

Sauerbruch's searching questions soon revealed, however, that the problem dated back to as early as 1914. As his worst fears were brought out into the open, Ludendorff turned pale. He was now forced openly to face the fact, which he had been repressing for years, that his judgement, on which the fate of all Germany had depended, had been affected by his illness. Under his own harsh personal code of honour, his previous failure to face up to this, and either seek treatment or resign, was wilful neglect of his duty.

There was just one slender hope. 'Would this thyroid disorder necessarily affect my competence?' he asked.

Sauerbruch hesitated. 'It would,' he said slowly, 'make it harder for you to remain calm, especially in emergency, or when you had to make important decisions.'

Ludendorff sighed. 'Yes,' he said, 'that is what I thought.' He steeled himself, knowing that the moment for atonement had finally come.

'Sauerbruch,' he said, 'you are to operate. And you are to do so without anaesthetic.'

Sauerbruch was horrified. 'But General,' he said, 'you could never tolerate the pain. And you would make my work much more difficult. This is a highly dangerous area, with large arteries and important nerves. Any movement could be fatal.'

'There will be no movement.' said the General. 'And as to the operation, may I remind you that you are a mere Brigadier in the Medical Services. I am ordering you to do it.'

Sauerbruch stiffened. 'Yes, sir,' he said.

The next day Sauerbruch operated on a fully conscious and unanaesthetized patient, opening his neck and removing the greater part of the thyroid gland. Ludendorff lay as still as a corpse and no sound passed his lips. When Sauerbruch had finished, Ludendorff, pale as death, said, 'Sauerbruch, if you had done this in 1914 Germany would have won the war.'

The General made an uncomplicated recovery. Some weeks later he appeared in Sauerbruch's office in full military uniform and wearing his medals. 'I require your word of honour, as an officer and gentleman, that you will remain silent on this matter until after I am dead. I also require that you hand over to me all medical records concerning it.' Sauerbruch removed the clinical notes from the file and gave them to him, assuring him that he was already bound by the Hippocratic oath to maintain secrecy. The General nodded briefly and left.

This story is so extraordinary that you may be wondering why it is not better known. Sauerbruch did indeed perform a routine operation on Ludendorff for goitre, but in his later years (see 'The Demented surgeon is operating'), Sauerbruch's magnificent career was marred by a brain disorder which deprived him, intermittently, of full insight into his behaviour. One result was a tendency to make things up, and in fact Sauerbruch made up this entire story.

Sexism

Prudence Mitford, one of the first female medical students, was a woman of character and courage. She had to be, because of the sexist prejudices of the virtually all-male studentship. Some of the men were amused at the idea of a female doctor, some outraged, nearly all were disapproving. This prejudice, which was based largely on a repressive attitude to sex, was shared by the teaching staff.

One professor in particular missed no opportunity of making a joke against women. His favourite declaration, repeated annually to each new batch of students was: 'Woman is an animal who urinates once a day, defecates once a week, menstruates once a month and copulates whenever she gets the chance.' This sally was always eagerly awaited by the students and invariably greeted with cheers.

The presence of Prudence, as the sole female in his anatomy class, did not deter him although the professor may have been disappointed at her lack of reaction, for soon afterwards he asked her to come out and to make a blackboard drawing of the male external genitalia.

Prudence got up, picked up the chalk, and with a bold flourish produced a large and strikingly impressive representation of a scrotum and a fully erect penis. There was deathly silence in the lecture theatre as she returned to her place. Up to this point she had shown admirable composure. But now a faint blush mantled her cheeks. She glanced at the professor and saw that he was torn between anger and a powerful impulse to laugh. At last, the struggle to maintain his professorial gravitas was lost.

'Tell me,' he said, his mouth twitching, 'why did you draw it like that?'

'Because,' she said, with as much courage as she could muster, 'I had the distinct impression from your lectures that this was its most habitual state.'

The professor walked up to where she was sitting, picked up her hand, and, with unpractised gallantry, kissed it. His apology was drowned in a storm of applause.

* * *

This apocryphal story is a reminder of the extraordinary prejudice of the time against women in medicine. Until the middle of the nineteenth century, women were, in general, barred absolutely from becoming doctors. A number of upper-class and well-to-do women insisted on studying medicine at university but were not allowed to take their degrees. Two exceptionally talented German women, a mother and daughter who had qualified as midwives, managed to obtain degrees in obstetrics from the University of Giessen in 1815 and 1817. The daughter, Charlotte von Siebold, became an internationally known expert and was asked to attend the deliveries of the future Queen Victoria of England. But these were isolated cases. After German unification in 1871, the Reichstag maintained its refusal to admit women to university education until 1908.

The first woman from an English-speaking country to become a doctor was the American Elizabeth Blackwell (1821–1910). During her studies at Geneva Medical College in New York State, she was ostracized and ignored and excluded from all university social functions. After graduating, she worked in France and in St Bartholomew's Hospital, London. In 1853, against the strong opposition of politicians and the male public, she founded the New York Dispensary for Poor Women and Children. Later, during the American Civil War, she trained nurses in the management of war casualties. Throughout her career in America and England, she met with various forms of opposition, even including threats of mob violence. Elizabeth continued to crusade tirelessly for women's rights in medicine until her death in 1911.

A curious tale

Here is a story found in the Annual Register (a year book of historical, political and literary events) for the year 1766.

On the 20 of February 1765 Richard Barton and three others met at a private house in Chalford in order to play cards. They played at Loo until about eleven, when they changed their game for whist. After a few deals a dispute arose about the game. Barton asserted, with oaths, that he was right, which the others denied.

At this Barton said: 'I wish that the flesh might rot upon my bones if I am wrong.' This wish was several times repeated, both then and afterwards.

Presently they adjourned to another house and there began a fresh game, when Barton and his partner had great success. Then they played at Loo again till four in the morning. During this second playing Barton complained to one Rolles, his partner, of a bad pain in his leg, which from that time increased. There was an appearance of a swelling, and afterwards colour changing to that of a mortified state.

On the following Sunday he rode to Michin Hampton to get the advice of Mr Pegler, the surgeon in that town, who attended him from the Thursday after February 27. Notwithstanding all the applications that were made, the mortification increased, and shewed itself in different parts of his body. On Monday March 3, at the request of some of his female relations, the clergyman of Bisley attended him and administered the sacraments. Barton appeared to be extremely ignorant of religion, having been accustomed to swear, to drink, to game, and to profane the Sabbath, although he was only in his 19th year.

After this he was in great agony, chiefly delirious, and seemed as if his imagination was engaged at cards. He started, had distracted looks and gestures, and in a dreadful fit of shaking and trembling, died on Tuesday morning the 4th of March. His eyes were open when he died, and could not be closed by the common methods; so that they remained open when he was put in the coffin. When the body came to be laid out, it appeared all over discoloured or spotted; and it might, in the most literal sense, be said, that his flesh rotted on his bones before he died.

Mr Dallaway, having desired Mr Pegler, the surgeon, to send him his thoughts of Parson's case, received from him the following account:

Sir, you desire me to acquaint you, in writing, with what I know relating to the melancholy case of the late Richard Barton; a request I readily comply with, hoping that his sad catastrophe will serve to admonish all those who profane the sacred name of God.

February 27 last, I visited Richard Barton, who I found had an inflamed leg, stretching from the foot almost to the knee, tending to a gangrene. The tenseness and redness of the skin was almost gone off, and became of a duskish and livid colour, and felt very lax and flabby. Symptoms being so dangerous, some incisions were made down to the quick, some spirituous fomentations made use of, and the whole limb dressed up with such applications as are most approved in such desperate circumstances, joined with proper internal medicines. The next day he seemed much the same; but on March 1 he was worse, the incisions discharging a sharp foetid ichor (which is generally of the worst consequence).

On the next day, which was Sunday, the symptoms seemed to be a little more favourable; but, to my great surprise, the very next day I found his leg not only mortified up to the knee, but the same began anew in four different parts, viz. under each eye, on the top of his shoulder, and on one hand; and in about twelve hours after he died.

I shall not presume to say there was anything supernatural in the case; but, however, it must be confessed, that such cases are uncommon in subjects so young and of so good an habit as he had always been, previous to this illness.

Waking the dead

Delusions of being dead are very rare but have occasionally been reported. Here are two amusing accounts of effective methods of treating delusional disorders of this kind. The first comes from the book *A History of Angels*, by the English dramatist and poet Thomas Heywood (1574–1641).

A young man, troubled with a hypochondriacal disorder, had a strong delusion that he was dead, and not only abstained from food, but importuned his parents that he might be carried to his grave and buried before his body was putrefied.

By the advice of his physicians, he was accordingly laid upon a bier, and carried upon men's shoulders towards the church, but upon the way they were met by two or three merry fellows, hired for that purpose, who enquired aloud whose corpse they were going to inter, and being informed by the bearers, 'Well,' says one of them, 'the world is happily rid of him, for he was a man of a wicked life, and his friends have cause to rejoice that he did not make his exit at the gallows.'

The young man hearing this, raised himself upon the bier, and told them he had never deserved the character they gave him, and that if he were alive, as he was not, he would teach them to speak better of the dead. But the fellows continuing to treat him with opprobrious language, being not able to bear it any longer, he leaped from the bier, fell upon them with great fury, and beat them till he was quite weary.

This violent agitation gave such a different turn to the humours of his body, that he awakened, as one out of a sleep or trance, and being carried home, and taken proper care of, in a few days he recovered his former health and understanding.

The second is from a work entitled *de Complex* by the German humanist and poet Simon Lemnius (1505–50).

A person of rank verily believed he had departed this life; and when his friends entreated him to eat, or threatened to make him, he absolutely refused it, telling them that food could be of no service to a dead person. Having continued in this condition seven days, and his friends fearing that his obstinacy would really prove the occasion of his death, they bethought themselves of the following stratagem.

They sent into his bed-chamber, which they had purposely made as dark as possible, some fellows wrapped in shrouds, who carried with them victuals and drink, and who sat down at the table and began to eat heartily. The disordered man, seeing this, asked who they were, and what they were about. They replied they were dead persons.

'What then,' said the patient, 'do the dead eat?'

'Yes, yes,' say they, 'and if you will sit down with us, you may eat likewise.'

Upon this, he jumps out of bed, and falls to with the rest; and having made a hearty meal, and drank a composing draught which they provided for him, he went to bed again, fell into a fine sleep, and in a short time recovered his health and senses.

Koro

Inche Mat bin Kutching looked down at his penis and shuddered. There was now no doubt. It was getting smaller. And Inche Mat knew beyond a shadow of a doubt that if his penis shrank away to nothing he would die. Everyone knew that ghosts had no genitals.

So Inche Mat dressed quickly and went to see his friend Abu bin Mohammed. 'Oh Abu,' he cried, 'I need your help. Look at this.' He pulled down his fashionable baggy slacks and his Y-fronts.

'What's up?' asked Abu, 'Got the clap?'

'No. Much worse than that . . .' He looked down. 'My God,' he said, 'It's getting bigger!'

'Nothing to boast about,' said Abu.

A couple of days later there was a spell of unusually cold weather and the Out-patient Department of Singapore General Hospital was crowded with men. Most of them had one hand in a trouser pocket; some had a hand under their dhotis; some, unashamedly, had strings visibly tied to their penises and some of these had rocks tied to the string. Others used adhesive tape. In all cases the object was to prevent the penis from disappearing inside. One and all were convinced that a penis that did so could never come out again and that the unfortunate victim would turn into a ghost. All the men were terrified. And if there is any emotion calculated to reduce the size of the penis, it is terror. The resulting shrinkage, of course, simply added to the fear.

Mat was more enterprising than most. He had managed to push a large safety-pin through the glans of his penis. To this he had tied a length of string and to the string he had tied a half kati weight (about ten ounces) borrowed from his mother's kitchen. Mat's penis was horribly bruised and looked very sorry for itself. Eventually, after a long wait, he was called in to see a weary and harassed doctor.

Dr Kassim took one look, rolled his eyes despairingly upwards, and deftly unfastened and removed the safety-pin.

'Don't do that!' cried Mat, grabbing his penis.

The doctor poured iodine solution over the safety-pin punctures. Mat danced around the surgery in agony, still holding his penis. The doctor grabbed him and pushed him down into a chair.

'You look reasonably intelligent,' said Dr Kassim, 'so I'm going to waste some time on you. Maybe I'll get through. Now shut up and listen. Penis is fixed to bone of pelvis by strands of fibrous tissue. There is no way – NO WAY – it can disappear into body. It is impossible. Penis contains three columns of spongy tissue into which blood can flow. When you have a hard-on blood under high pressure. Other times you can have nearly no blood in it so penis is small. OK? When weather cold, or if you swim in cold water, nearly all blood runs back out of penis into your veins and penis can be very small. You can squeeze a sponge small, right?'

Inche Mat nodded.

'OK,' said Dr Kassim, 'What kind of weather we have recently?'

'Very cold weather,' said Mat.

'Good boy,' said the doctor. 'Very cold weather – very small penis. Get it?'

'But,' said Mat, 'everybody knows that ghosts don't – '

'Everybody doesn't. Only superstitious and ignorant fools like you and all these idiots outside. All bloody nonsense.'

'OK,' said Mat, still holding on to his penis, 'Just one thing. 'How come my grandfather's willie was so small just before he died?'

'Get out!' shouted the doctor.

This extraordinary delusional disorder is known as *koro* and is of fairly common occurrence in south-east Asia. This particular epidemic in Singapore in the autumn of 1967 was the result of a spell of very cold weather, but sporadic cases occur from time to time. In this instance, rumour had it that the outbreak of *koro* was caused by eating pork from pigs that had been vaccinated against swine fever. There was so much panic, waste of working time and absenteeism that the government was seriously concerned and enlisted the aid of the Singapore Medical Association. Fortunately, the epidemic was short-lived. After about a week, the weather – and penile dimensions – returned to normal and everyone relaxed.

A poisonous woman

The French scholar, teacher and physician Laurent Joubert (1529–82) refers to the written legend that an Indian Rajah sent a remarkable gift to Alexander the Great. This was an exquisitely beautiful woman who, from childhood, had been systematically fed poison so that she had become venomous. Anyone who made love to her invariably died of poisoning. Happily, Alexander's tutor, Aristotle, with remarkable perception, aware of the poisonous propensities of the Indian monarchs, was able to deduce the facts of the case from the wild, staring and serpent-like appearance of the woman's eyes.

Alexander was most anxious to enjoy the woman but Aristotle outlined his suspicions and talked him out of it. His point was amply proved when, shortly afterwards, several of Alexander's courtiers who had enjoyed her favours died in agony with all the symptoms of poisoning.

Joubert, however, is highly sceptical of the truth of this story. While acknowledging that, as Galen had recorded, a person can become accustomed to a poison by taking gradually increasing quantities, such a person would not be venomous to others. The virulent poisons of vipers, he points out, harms only if the snake's saliva comes in contact with broken skin.

He then considers whether a woman could poison a man by inserting poisonous material into her vagina. If she put the poison deeply inside, he says, she would be in much greater danger than the man. Any strong poison placed there would pervade her whole body in the manner of garlic which, placed in these parts, can be smelled, he says, on the woman's breath. Moreover, since she could never be sure when the man would want to make love to her, she would be exposed to the poison for much longer than he was.

Joubert does concede, however, that a woman might poison a man if she were to put into the vagina some kind of poisoned tube or gut, lodged in such a way that the man would put his member into it. A woman of large dimensions, he suggests, might succeed. But who, he asks, would be so stupid and unobservant as to fail to notice the difference?

Bibliography

This bibliography lists the original sources for many of the anecdotes in book. In most cases the titles of papers are given here in non-technical terms.

BMJ   British Medical Journal
BJHM   British Journal of Hospital Medicine
JRSM   Journal of the Royal Society of Medicine
NEJM   New England Journal of Medicine
JAMA   Journal of the American Medical Association
Eye   Journal of the Royal College of Ophthalmologists
Sci Amer   Scientific American
New Sci   New Scientist

Academics claimed mental disorder, *Lancet*, 1 Jun 1991
Accidental nitroglycerine patch, *JAMA*, 6 Jan 1993, p. 47
Acres of antibodies plants farming, *Lancet*, 14 Apr 1994
Air indoor risks of, *Lancet*, 21 Jun 1986, pp. 1191, 1419
Air bag heart rupture, *NEJM*, 4 Feb 1993, p. 358
Airport trolley injuries, *BMJ*, 23/30 Dec 1989, p. 1567
Alcoholism loss of neurons, *Lancet*, 13 Nov 1993, p. 1201
Amok, *Lancet*, 16 Jan 1988, p. 124

Amputation in Saudi Arabia, *Lancet*, 14 Apr 1990, p. 904

Anabolic steroid psychosis, *Lancet*, 11 Apr 1987, p. 863

Anal incontinence plug, *Lancet*, 3 Aug 1991, p. 295

Anophthalmia clusters, *BMJ*, 7 Aug 1993, p. 340

Another inhaler story, *BJHM*, 15 Jun 1994, p. 53

Antenatal sucking blisters, *BMJ*, 11 Sep 1993, p. 692

Appendicectomy risk pig occupations, *BMJ*, 10 Aug 1991, p. 345

Argentine patients killed for organs, *BMJ*, 25 Apr 1992, p. 1073

Astrology kills alternative, *Lancet*, 6 Nov 1993, pp. 1126, 1142

Athlete's running nose, *BMJ*, 10 Sep 1988, p. 660

Autotransfusion, *Lancet*, 17 Aug 1991, pp. 418, 1435

Babies find nipple by smell, *Lancet*, 8 Oct 1994, p. 989

Baboon to human liver transplant, *Lancet*, 9 Jan 1993, p. 65

Bacon therapy for myiasis, *JAMA*, 3 Nov 1993, p. 2087

Bacon for myiasis, *Lancet*, 4 Dec 1993, p. 1377

Baldness and Minoxidil, *Lancet*, 2 May 1987, p. 1019

Baldness and heart attacks, *JAMA*, 24 Feb 1993, pp. 998, 1035

Bean in urethra for incontinence, *BMJ*, 22/29 Dec 1990

Beauty parlour stroke syndrome, *JAMA*, 28 Apr 1993, p. 2085

Benzodiazepines and sexual fantasies, *Lancet*, 2 Feb 1993

Biblical leprosy, *JRSM*, Feb 1990, p. 127

Bilateral hip replacement & heart transplant, *JRSM*, Oct 1993, p. 599

Birth weight fallacy, *BMJ*, 19 Dec 1992, p. 1576

Black 'tumour' in baby, *BMJ*, 23 Apr 1994, p. 1112

Blindness epidemic in Cuba, *BMJ*, 29 May 1993, p. 1434

Body packers drug abuse smuggling, *BMJ*, 28 Oct 1989, p. 1082

Bogus professor, *BMJ*, 5 Jun 1993, p. 1499

Boy grows fetus, *BMJ*, 25 Jun 1994, p. 1726

Boy girl ratio changes, *BMJ*, 24 Dec 1988, p. 1627

Boy survives 16.4 degrees temperature, *NEJM*, 20 Jan 1994, p. 219

Breast cancer fraud, *BMJ*, 26 Mar 1994, p. 809

Broken abuse needles abscess risk, *NEJM*, 13 May 1993, p. 1426

Buerger's 4 limb amputation smoker, *BMJ*, 14 Dec 1991, p. 1538

Bungee jumping, *BMJ*, 19 Dec 1992, p. 1520

Cannibalism in Brazil, *Lancet*, 30 Apr 1994, p. 1090

Cardiac arrest psychological consequences, *JAMA*, 13 Jan 1993

Case of hypothermia, *JRSM*, May 1994, p. 293

Catalytic converter prevents suicide, *Lancet*, 20 Nov 1993, p. 1295

Caterpillar hairs in eye, *Eye*, Vol 8 Part 5, 1994, p. 596

Child abuse or not? *BMJ*, 16 Feb 1991, p. 371

Child killed by jellyfish, *JAMA*, 11 Sep 1991, p. 1404

Cholesterol and violence, *BJHM*, 6 Apr 1994, p. 329

Christmas convulsions, *BMJ*, 19 Dec 1992, p. 1580

Circumcision in USA and UK, *BMJ*, 30 Oct 1993, p. 1154

Cocaine binds to sperms, *JAMA*, Oct 1991, p. 1956

Colonic crunch, *BJHM*, 18 Aug 1993, p. 194

Conjoined twins of 1680, *JRSM*, Feb 1993, p. 106

Contraception in elephants, *Lancet*, 5 Sep 1992, p. 583

Copy cat suicides Final Exit, *NEJM*, 11 Nov 1993, p. 1508

Coronary disease in heart transplants, *Lancet*, 19 Dec 1992, p. 1500

Coronary with normal coronaries, *BMJ*, 13 Nov 1993, p. 1255

Courtroom science evidence, *NEJM*, 7 Apr 1994, p. 1018

Covert video in Munchausen's, *BMJ*, 4 Sep 1993, p. 611

Dangerous spiritual intervention, *BMJ*, 19 Dec 1992, p. 1578

Dangers of MRI, *BMJ*, 7 May 1994, p. 1181

Death determines a career, *BMJ*, 22 May 1993, p. 1402

Deaths in drug trial, *Lancet*, 11 Jun 1994, p. 1494

Deep sleep treatment, *BMJ*, 5 Jun 1993, p. 1501

DES daughter claim $4 million, *Lancet*, 2 Nov 1991

Diabetic child denied treatment dies, *BMJ*, 13 Nov 1993, p. 1232

Doctor kills a king, *BMJ*, 28 May 1994, p. 1445

Doctor charged after hysterectomy, *BMJ*, 1 Oct 1994, p. 828

Doctor resigns after wrong diagnoses, *BMJ*, 13 Aug 1994, p. 430

Doctors kill most in August?, *BMJ*, 24 Dec 1994, p. 1690

Doctors and sexual misconduct, *BMJ*, 7 May 1994, p. 1186

Doctors sued for uninterest, *BMJ*, 3 Dec 1994, p. 1461

Doctors and sexual harassment, *NEJM*, 12 May 1994, p. 1388

Doctors and litigation, *BMJ*, 11 Jun 1994, p. 1580

Doctor's duty to report colleague, *BMJ*, 26 Mar 1994, p. 809

Dog gets cancer from passive smoking, *BMJ*, 8 Oct 1994, p. 960

Double chin cure, *BMJ*, 6 Nov 1993, p. 1222

Drink industry sleaze, *BMJ*, 14 Dec 1994, p. 1597

Drug advertisements, *BMJ*, 24 Dec 1994, p. 1734

Drug promotion wars, *NEJM*, 17 Nov 1994, p. 1350

Dutch euthanasia on TV, *BMJ*, 29 Oct 1994, p. 1107

Ear lobe creases and atheroma, *BJHM*, 16 Sep 1992, p. 339

Embarrassing porter, *BMJ*, 22 May 1993, p. 1397

Enforced hysterectomy, *BMJ*, 30 Apr 1994, p. 1163

Enforced hysterectomy, *BMJ*, 11 Jun 1994, p. 1574

Epidemic scalp black spots, *Lancet*, 1 May 1993, p. 1127

Erlenmyer flask-shaped bones, *BJHM*, Sep 1991, p. 175

Errors in blood transfusion, *BMJ*, 7 May 1994, pp. 1180, 1205

Experiments on pregnant women, *BMJ*, 29 Jan 1994, p. 291

Fat female fecundity, *BMJ*, 20 Feb 1993, p. 484

Female priapism, *New Sci*, 3 Jul 1993, p. 5

Fingerprints fetal development BP, *BMJ*, 14 Aug 1993, p. 405

Fish odour syndrome, *BMJ*, 11 Sep 1993, pp. 639, 655

Fraternity hazing, *JAMA*, 28 Apr 1993, p. 2113

Fraud in breast cancer trial, *Lancet*, 26 Mar 1994, p. 784

French buy corneas for transplants, *BMJ*, 11 Jun 1994, p. 1528

French mothers encouraged bottle-feed, *New Sci*, 7 May 1994, p. 7

Garlic affects leeches, *BMJ*, 24 Dec 1994, p. 1689

Genetic researchers solve own puzzle, *JAMA*, 17 Nov 1993, p. 2374

Ghosts and hallucinations, *BMJ*, 19 Dec 1992, p. 1517

Giant ovarian tumour, *BJHM*, May 1991, p. 315

Gifts from pharmaceutical firms, *NEJM*, 13 May 1993, p. 1426

Goya's living skeleton, *BMJ*, 21–28 Dec 1991, p. 1594

Growth hormone and Creutzfeldt-Jakob disease, *BMJ*, 31 Jul 1993, p. 281

Gynaecomastia, *NEJM*, 18 Feb 1993, p. 490

Handedness and longevity, *BMJ*, 24 Dec 1994, p. 1681

Hepatectomy for brain oedema, *Lancet*, 9 Oct 1993, p. 898

Heterotopic ossification, *BJHM*, 17 Feb 1993, p. 229

Honey for wounds, *Lancet*, 9 Jan 1993, p. 90

How to insert a suppository, *Lancet*, 28 Sep 1991, p. 798

Hypothermia, *BMJ*, 4 Jan 1991, p. 3

Hysterectomy for infertility, *BMJ*, 25 Sep 1993, p. 754

India outlaws organs trade, *BMJ*, 25 Jun 1994, p. 1657

Induced psychosis *folie à deux*, *BJHM*, 16 Mar 1994, p. 304

Inhaled shot bullet, *BMJ*, 29 May 1993, p. 1488

Iraq doctors do punishment amputations, *BMJ*, 3 Dec 1994, p. 1516

Iraqi doctors ordered to amputate, *BMJ*, 24 Sep 1994, p. 760

Japanese drug kills shingles sufferers, *BMJ*, 10 Sep 1994, p. 627

Kevorkian and assisted suicide, *Lancet*, 7 May 1994, p. 1153

Knee replacement and swimming, *BMJ*, 19 Dec 1992, p. 1579

Laser in the brain, *NEJM*, 15 Jul 1993, p. 207

Lead poisoning from Mexican pottery, *Lancet*, 15 Oct 1994, p. 1064

Left-handed people die younger, *New Sci*, 12 Mar 1994, p. 16

Left-handedness and short life, *BMJ*, 18 Dec 1993, p. 1577

Legalizing prostitution, *BMJ*, 27 Nov 1993, p. 1370

Lethal injection, *BMJ*, 11 Jun 1994, p. 1575

Lightning nakedness, *JRSM*, Sep 1993, p. 556

Liver resection reimplantation, *Lancet*, 14 Aug 1993, p. 386

Liver failure external pig's liver, *NEJM*, 28 Jul 1994, pp. 234, 268

Malaria transmitted heart transplant, *BMJ*, 14 Dec 1991

Male breast cancer, *BJHM*, 20 Jan 1993, p. 104

McBride fraud Debendox thalidomide, *BMJ*, 27 Feb 1993, p. 541

Medical manslaughter New Zealand, *Lancet*, 30 Apr 1994, p. 1091

Medical waste on beaches, *BMJ*, 17 Apr 1993, p. 1042

Medicinal toads, *Lancet*, 13 Nov 1993, p. 1229

Medicine in the Gulag, *BMJ*, 24 Dec 1994, p. 1726

Memorable brain-dead patient, *BMJ*, 22 May 1993, p. 1390

Miracle at Lourdes, *BMJ*, 6 Nov 1993, p. 1165

Missed intraocular foreign body, *BMJ*, 17 Apr 1993, p. 1060

Modela and menstruation, *BMJ*, 19 Dec 1992, p. 1575

Moscow abortion clinic sells fetal tissue, *BMJ*, 29 May 1993, p. 1433

Mouse produces human antibodies, *New Sci*, 26 Mar 1994, p. 4

Mouth and foot painting artists, *JRSM*, Aug 1994, p. 457

Mud wrestling dermatitis, *JAMA*, 27 Jan 1993, p. 502

Mummy had TB, *BMJ*, 26 Mar 1994, p. 808

Nail in the brain, *NEJM*, 4 Mar 1993, p. 620

Near death in twins, *JAMA*, 14 Oct 1992, p. 1860

Non-epidemic necrotizing fasciitis, *BMJ*, 11 Jun 1994, p. 1576

Nurse guilty of multiple murder, *BMJ*, 29 May 1993, p. 1431

Nutmeg psychosis, *JRSM*, Mar 1993, p. 179, Sep 1993, p. 556

Nutmeg psychosis, *JRSM*, May 1994, p. 308

Obstetrician suspended research fraud?, *BMJ*, 3 Dec 1994, p. 1459

Ocular injuries from exploding bottles, *BMJ*, 20 July 1991

Organs from animals, *BMJ*, 11 Sep, 1993, p. 637

Paediatrician guilty of misconduct, *BMJ*, 10 Dec 1994, p. 1533

Patients remembering surgery, *BMJ*, 15 Oct 1994, p. 967

Penis always points to side of lesion, *BJHM*, Dec 1988, p. 459

People who refuse blood transfusion, *BMJ*, 28 May 1994, p. 1423

Pepper and pain, *Lancet*, 6 Nov 1993, p. 1130

Physicians capital punishment, *NEJM*, 28 Oct 1993, p. 1346

Physicians kill kings? Hadrian, *BMJ*, 29 Jan 1994, p. 346

Pimlico poisoning, *BMJ*, 24 Dec 1994, p. 1720

Plastic bag suicides, *NEJM*, 11 Nov 1993, p. 1508

Pneumothorax from needle biopsy, *BMJ*, 14 Sep 1991, p. 627

Pre-eclampsia and sexual intercourse, *Lancet*, 8 Oct 1994, p. 969, 973

Pregnancy after 50, *Lancet*, 6 Feb 1993, pp. 321, 344

Prescribing in four countries, *Lancet*, 13 Nov 1993, p. 1191

Pulmonary embolus keep-fit fan, *BJHM*, 15 Sep 1993, p. 342

Radium in medicines, *Sci Amer*, Aug 1993, p. 78

Religious objection, *Lancet*, 13 Nov 1993, p. 1189

Resuscitation hours after 'death', *Lancet*, 16 June 1993

Reuse of transplanted organs, *JAMA*, 24 Nov 1993, p. 2469

Reuse of a transplanted heart, *NEJM*, 4 Feb 1993, p. 319

Sartorial eloquence, *BMJ*, 24 Dec 1994, p. 1710

Scrotum stuck in bathchair, *BMJ*, 23 Jan 1993, p. 282

Self-stigmatization dermatitis artefacta, *BJHM*, 23 Jan 1993

Semen collection in paralysed men, *Lancet* 30 April 1994, p. 1072

Separation of Siamese twins, *JRSM*, Feb 1994, p. 108

Sex and headache, *BMJ*, 17 July 1991 p. 202

Silicone implant litigation, *BMJ*, 4 Sep 1993, p. 582

Smallpox virus destroyed, *BMJ*, 16 Feb 1991, p. 373

Snake appears on coughing, *BMJ*, 8 Oct 1994, p. 966

Static electricity cure, *JAMA*, 26 Feb 1992, p. 1068

Steel pole though chest, *BJHM*, May 1991, p. 264

Stomach in the scrotum, *BJHM*, 5 Oct 1994, p. 360

Stretcher's scrotum, *NEJM*, 5 Aug 1993, p. 436

Stuck in the bath, *BMJ*, 19 Mar 1994, p. 762

Stump growth juvenile amputees, *Lancet*, 17 Aug 1991.

Sudden death in young athletes, *NEJM*, 1 Jul 1993, pp. 50, 55

Surgeon accused of manslaughter, *BMJ*, 7 May 1994, p. 1187

Surgeon jailed for infecting patient, *BMJ*, 8 Oct 1994, p. 896

Swallowed coins, *BMJ*, 1 June 1991, p. 1321

Swallowed barium cup, *BMJ*, 30 April 1994, p. 1178

Swallowing live fish, *BMJ*, 19 Dec 1992, p. 1578

Swallowing the tongue, *BMJ*, 29 May 1993, p. 1467

Swedish men have double sperm counts, *BMJ*, 12 Jun 1993, p. 1579

Sydney surgeon HIV transfer, *BMJ*, 14 Dec 1994, p. 1603

Telling whisky from brandy, *BMJ*, 24 Dec 1994, p. 1686

Thalidomide doctor struck off, *BMJ*, 14 Aug 1993, p. 404

Thalidomide given pregnant women, *BMJ*, 23 April 1994, p. 1061

Tobacco death brand, *Lancet*, 7 May 1994, p. 1109

Tourettes syndrome creativity, *BMJ*, 19 Dec 1992, p. 1515

Transplants of pig organs, *Lancet*, 3 Jul 1993, p. 45

Trends in twinning, *Lancet*, 7 May 1994, p. 1151

Tretinoin unlabelled indication, *NEJM*, 17 Nov 1994, p. 1348

Trombonist's neck *NEJM*, 19 Nov 1992, p. 1533

Umbilical cord ligation in utero, *NEJM*, 17 Feb 1994, p. 469

Unnecessary caesarian section USA, *Lancet*, 28 May 1994, p. 1351

US Surgeon General resigns, *BMJ*, 14 Dec 1994, p. 1604
Using the recent dead to teach resuscitation, *NEJM*, 15 Dec 1994, p. 1652
Uvulectomy in Cameroon, *Lancet*, 25 Jun 1994, p. 1644
Vancouver doctor shot by antiabortionists, *BMJ*, 19 Nov 1994, p. 1322
Vasectomy man sires child, *BMJ*, 31 Jul 1993, p. 299
Vasectomy failure, *Lancet*, 2 Jul 1994, p. 30
Video game epilepsy, *Lancet*, 22 Oct 1994, p. 1102
Walnuts heart disease blood pressure, *NEJM*, 4 Mar 1993, p. 593
Wart cure lady of Kansas, *JRSM*, May 1992, p. 307
Warts on butchers, *Lancet*, 7 May 1994, p. 1114